D0995031

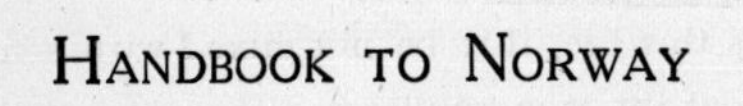

Handbook to Norway

"What is this life, if it be not mixed with some delight? And what delight is more pleasing than to see the fashions and manners of unknown places?"

A NEW HANDBOOK TO NORWAY

With Map of Norway; Street Plans of Oslo, Bergen, Stavanger and Trondhjem, and Six District Maps.

SIXTY ILLUSTRATIONS.

LONDON:
WARD, LOCK AND CO., LIMITED
WARWICK HOUSE, SALISBURY SQUARE, E.C.4
AND AT MELBOURNE

Printed in Great Britain by Butler & Tanner Ltd., Frome and London

CONTENTS

ILLUSTRATIONS

MAPS AND PLANS

TOURS IN NORWAY.

The Charm of Norway—When to Go—Routes to Norway—Plan of Tour—Yachting Cruises—Overland Tours—Motoring and Cycling—Walking Tours.

WITHIN the memory of many who now visit Norway, the tourist who talked of spending his holiday in that country was looked upon as something of a pioneer. He expected to rough it, to live on rough fare and to meet with roughness from the people. Modern touring has dispelled the last notion as completely erroneous and has reformed the other two almost out of existence; and the tourist who visits Norway to-day goes to a country prepared to welcome him and to do its utmost for his comfort.

A Hospitable Country.

In a sense Norway is still a new country for tourists. The great stream of visitors that flows through its main arteries of travel is only a tithe of the number that will visit the country as years go on, for it is in an early stage of its development. Norway stands in a peculiar position in this respect, that it has no traditions, and it is therefore developing along the soundest and most modern lines. The main routes of travel offer, owing to the spirit of progress that animates the Norwegians, more than adequate comfort to the most exacting traveller; and the native inclination to do the best for the visitors is involved in that fervid patriotism and pride of country which is the dominant characteristic of the Norwegian people.

For the English-speaking races Norway has an especially warm welcome. There is much in common between the Norman, as the native calls himself, and the Englishman, who has the blood of the old Norsemen in his veins, and shares many customs and traditions with their direct descendants.

The Charm of Norway.

Nature has fashioned Norway on a grand scale, and has endowed the land with a charm that cannot fail to appeal to those in search of a real holiday—a sense of restfulness. The coast is rugged and wild; the coastline is indented with innumerable fjords; and the sea, broken to stillness by a breakwater of a hundred thousand islands, runs by deep channels into the heart of countless towering mountains. There, indeed, is loneliness and peace amid the silence of mountains and sea.

Towns are rare in Norway, big towns can almost be numbered on the fingers; for Norway is a land of snow-capped mountains and wonderful glaciers, of many waterfalls and lakes and fragrant pine forests, a land of trim little farms with brightly-painted wooden homesteads, perched high on the mountain-sides or nestling on the shores of the fjords. Thus Norway has the refreshing charm that only great contrasts and surprising variations can afford. In the course of a single day one can traverse smiling valleys, lofty mountains, plateaux and snow-clad wilds, and sail on deep blue fjords. And no other part of the civilized world can rival Norway in the glories of the long summer evenings and the nights without darkness. In summer the Midnight Sun reigns supreme over a great part of the land, and in winter the star-gemmed sky is illumined by the marvellous Northern Lights—the Aurora Borealis.

Norway, in short, is an ideal summer land, in addition to which the eastern half and some parts of the western are fully as ideal winter lands. The charms of a holiday in any part are unending, and the experience of them but a whetting of the appetite for more.

Holidays in Norway.

If change is the essence of a holiday, Norway must appeal to us in quite a special degree, more particularly if the normal scene of our daily life is laid in the rush and bustle of a town. The ways of spending a holiday in the country are as various as its scenery. One may settle in some comfortable seaside hotel on the water's edge, far in one of the fjords, with the majesty of mountains on all sides, and with access by land or water to a fresh excursion for every day. Or one may elect to stay at some high-lying resort, with a choice between climbing mountains or resting content with contemplating them. Or one may go from place to place, spending one, two or more nights at each. Or one may join a yachting cruise in one of the big liners, that have so justly earned the name of floating palaces, and proceed lazily up each fjord, penetrating into remote waterways where the simple fisherfolk and herdsmen, before tourists had found their country, rarely saw a face they did not know. One may go for the winter sports—the ski-ing, skating, tobogganing, sleighing—concerning which notes will be found on pages 36–8. Or one may go for the angling, which in Norway is exceptionally attractive (*see* p. 32); for shooting (p. 33); or for mountaineering (p. 34).

One may go as a member of a touring party or as an independent traveller, either provided by an agency with all the necessary travelling tickets and hotel coupons, or buying tickets and meeting other expenses as occasion arises. For those who dislike constant movement and haste, and who do not seek anything beyond pure air, rest, good living and superb scenery—with a very sporting chance of perfect weather—there are everywhere what the Norwegians call *sanatoria,* which word in their use does not invariably mean a place for invalids, but very often a country residential hotel, similar to our hydros, usually on the shores of some fjord, or high in the mountains. Many of these have been built in spots ideally suited for a restful holiday.

When to go.

This will depend upon the purpose of the visit.

The season for travelling in Norway is from June to September. If the mountain passes are to be crossed on foot or by car, July, August and September must be recommended, for it may happen that the snow hinders motor traffic over the mountains until the end of June. The mountain crossings to be avoided during spring and early summer are the Valdres route between Fagernes and Lærdal, the route between Otta and Nordfjord, and the Telemarken route between Odda and Dalen.

June combines the fresh tints of spring with the long days and bright nights of early summer. September is generally as warm as if it belonged to the summer, while mountain and valley are resplendent with the richest hues of autumn.

For the winter sports the best time is from January to

April. In April and May the sports are still pursued on the upper slopes of the mountains, where the snow is still lying deep, but the sun has already the warmth of summer.

Those who go for the purpose of seeing the Midnight Sun, must be guided by the dates given on p. 194.

Those who go for mountain climbing must remember that the extreme length of the day in June and July keeps the snow soft, thus making the higher ascents more fatiguing. For anglers and those who go for shooting, the time of a visit is, of course, regulated by the dates between which their sport is permissible (*see* pp. 32–3).

The Journey to Norway.

The methods of reaching Norway from England are primarily four :—

(I) By sea to Oslo, Bergen or Stavanger.

(II) By sea to Denmark, thence to Oslo.

(III) By one of the shorter sea-routes, thence overland *viâ* Hamburg, Denmark and Gothenburg to Oslo.

(IV) By air and rail. For current arrangements, apply to Imperial Airways, Ltd., or K.L.M. (Royal Dutch Air Lines) at Croydon Aerodrome.

I. ALL-SEA ROUTES.*

1. Hull to Oslo viâ Kristiansand by Ellerman's Wilson Line.

During the summer season (June, July and August) a steamer with excellent accommodation for first, second and third-class passengers leaves the Riverside Quay, Hull, every Saturday at 3.30 p.m. The 10.10 a.m. train from King's Cross, London, always connects with this steamer.

Passengers are disembarked at Kristiansand early Monday morning and at Oslo Monday afternoon.

Fares, which include victualling : 1st class, £7 single, £13 return ; 2nd class, £5 10*s*. single, £10 return ; 3rd class, £4 single.

In the spring, autumn and winter months the service is maintained by cargo steamers with limited accommodation for passengers, leaving Hull every Friday p.m. tide from the Albert Dock.

* Wherever times or fares and names of vessels are mentioned throughout this book they should be verified by current programmes and time-tables, in case of alteration.

For full particulars, apply to *Ellerman's Wilson Line, Limited,* Passenger Department, Hull; to the *United Shipping Co., Ltd.,* 108 Fenchurch Street, London, E.C.3, or any tourist agency.

2. Newcastle to Bergen.

This is the favourite route for those who intend to explore the Fjords, to join local yachting cruises to the North Cape, or to work eastward down to Oslo. During the summer the *Bergenske-Nordenfjeldske Line* (Norwegian Royal Mail S.S.) —the *B. & N. Line*—steamers (*Jupiter* and *Leda*) leave Newcastle for Bergen on Tuesday, Thursday and Saturday afternoons (the rest of the year Tuesday and Saturday), arriving the following evening (open sea passage, 22 hours). On the return journey, the steamers leave Bergen at 11.30 a.m. on Tuesdays, Thursdays and Saturdays, Newcastle being reached in the afternoon of the following day. In connection with the outward sailing on Saturdays during the height of the season, a train leaves King's Cross Station, London, at* 9.30 a.m., calls at Grantham and York and arrives at Newcastle at 3.19 p.m. On Sundays, beginning with the last two in July and ending with the first two in September, a restaurant train leaves Newcastle at 4.55 p.m. (or on later arrival of the boat from Bergen), and is due at King's Cross, London, at 10.30 p.m. Single fare, Newcastle to Bergen (including food): 1st class, £7 2*s.* 6*d.*

For full particulars and programmes, apply to *B. & N. Line* Office, Central Station, Newcastle-on-Tyne; or to *B. & N. Line,* Royal Mail, Ltd., 21 Charing Cross, London, S.W.1, and to the latter for reservation of berths.

3. Newcastle to Stavanger and Bergen.

By the *Venus* of the *Bergenske-Nordenfjeldske* (*B. & N.*) *Line* every Thursday afternoon, arriving at Stavanger late on Friday evening and Bergen on Saturday morning. Fares to either Stavanger or Bergen, 1st, single, £6 2*s.* 6*d.* (including food on board).

For full particulars and reservation of berths, apply as above.

4. Newcastle to Oslo.

By the *Fred. Olsen Line* every Saturday afternoon, by the steamers *Bessheim* and *Blenheim.* Due in Oslo on Monday

* See footnote, p. 12.

morning (40 hours). The return boat leaves Oslo on Saturday at noon and arrives at Newcastle early Monday morning. Agents in London: Norwegian State Railways, 21 Cockspur Street, London, S.W.1; in Newcastle: Messrs. P. H. Matthiesen & Co.

II. OVERLAND ROUTES.

1. London to Oslo viâ Harwich, Esbjerg and Frederikshavn.

One of the most direct routes. Every weekday by boat train from Liverpool Street. Sea-passage, Harwich to Esbjerg, about 22 hours; train, Esbjerg to Frederikshavn, about 9 hours; crossing to Oslo, 15 hours; to Kristiansand S. (daily), 11 hours. (Note: The service from Frederikshavn onward is less frequent than that from England to that point, and intending travellers should make certain of through connections before leaving London.) The fares, which are subject to alteration, compare favourably with those from London *viâ* Hull or Newcastle. Apply United Shipping Co., 108 Fenchurch Street, London, E.C.3.

2. London or Newcastle to Oslo viâ Gothenburg.

A Swedish Lloyd boat leaves Tilbury every Saturday about noon (boat train from Fenchurch Street) for Gothenburg, which is reached on Monday morning. Thence to Oslo by rail. A boat also leaves Newcastle for Gothenburg on Friday at noon. Apply The British and Northern Shipping Agency, Ltd., 5 Lloyds Avenue, London, E.C.3.

III. SHORT SEA ROUTES.

1. London (L.N.E.R., Liverpool Street) to Oslo *viâ* Harwich, Flushing, Osnabrück, Hamburg, Sassnitz (or Warnemünde) and Gothenburg.

2. London (L.N.E.R., Liverpool Street) to Oslo, *viâ* Harwich, the Hook, Osnabrück, Hamburg, and as 1.

3. London to Oslo *viâ* Boulogne or Calais, Brussels, Hamburg or Berlin, thence *viâ* Warnemunde, Copenhagen, Helsingborg, Gothenburg.

4. London to Oslo *viâ* Boulogne or Calais, Cologne, Hamburg or Berlin, and as above.

5. London to Oslo *viâ* Ostend, Brussels, Hamburg or Berlin, and as above.

For fares and full details of above routes see *Continental*

Handbook (free), obtainable on application to Continental Department, London & North-Eastern Railway, Liverpool Street Station, London, E.C.2, or Continental Enquiry Office, Southern Railway, Victoria Station, London, S.W.1.

Pleasure Cruises.

The Steamship Companies undertaking cruises to Norway's Fjords and to the North Cape, etc., include :—

1. *Bergenske-Nordenfjeldske Line* (*Norwegian Royal Mail SS.*), Bergen. Chief office in England, 21 Charing Cross, Whitehall, S.W.1. In addition to the regular services between Newcastle and Norway, noted on p. 13, this line arranges cruises to the Western Fjords and Trondhjem, to the North Cape, Spitzbergen and the Polar Pack Ice: 10 to 21 days.

The Company's *Stella Polaris* was built exclusively for pleasure cruises, and its *Prince Olav* was the British Royal Yacht *Alexandra*. The royal apartments on the main deck remain unaltered. The popular cruising S.Y. *Meteor* belongs to the same company,

2. *Royal Mail Steam Packet Co.*, Atlantic House, Moorgate, London, E.C.2, and 32 Cockspur Street, S.W.1. Cruises *de luxe* in R.M.S.P. *Arcadian* (12,500 tons) from 13 to 17 days to the Western Fjords, Midnight Sun, North Cape, Spitzbergen and Baltic ports.

Popular 12-day cruises from London (Tilbury) and Leith by R.M.S.P. *Araguaya* (10,196 tons) to Southern Fjords of Norway.

3. *Orient Line*, 14 Cockspur Street, London, S.W. Cruises of varying duration to the Western Fjords as far as Trondhjem.

4. *Peninsular and Oriental Line*, 14 Cockspur Street, London, S.W.1. Cruises of varying duration to the Western Fjords, June–August.

5. *Cunard Steamship Co.*, Pier Head, Liverpool; 26–7 Cockspur Street, S.W., and 51 Bishopsgate, E.C., London. Cruises in the 20,000-ton liner *Carinthia* and other luxuriously fitted vessels of the company,

On all the larger liners there is a tourist bureau in charge of an experienced official, who renders assistance to tourists and organizes a series of launch excursions, which are a notable feature of the pleasure cruises.

Plan of the Journey or Tour.

In Norway, more than in any country visited by tourists, it is necessary to proceed on the lines of a definitely thought-out plan, especially on the occasion of a first visit. Few travellers realize till they have visited the country how enormous are the distances, how leisurely the means of communication, how remote and how scattered the towns and villages. We have to bear in mind that Norway, from north to south, is twice the distance from Land's End to John o' Groats; that it is nearly twice the area of England and Scotland; and that it contains only about half as many people as Lancashire. The need for some preparation in a country so vast and scattered is at once apparent.

Yachting Cruises.

Of the several ways of visiting Norway the simplest is the yachting cruise. The traveller goes on board his yacht (often a giant liner) at some English port, crosses the North Sea to Bergen or Stavanger, and then in the smooth water behind the Skjærgård, the chain of islands which screens the mainland, potters leisurely up and down the coast. He need not leave the ship and its comforts for a single night. The yachts make their way up the deep fjords into the inland country, stopping here and there for the passengers to go ashore for land excursions. Many find this an altogether delightful way of seeing Norway.

Overland Tours

are not quite so leisurely a proceeding as the yachting cruise. They generally combine travel by rail, by road, and by water, and to a greater extent than a yachting cruise, enable the visitor to make acquaintance with the people, their mode of life and the characteristics of their land.

As regards material and comfort, the railways are on a level with the best in Europe. Through express trains with sleepers, restaurant cars and observation cars connect the west, east and south of Norway, and also the north as far as Trondhjem.

A 1st-class sleeping compartment contains one berth, a 2nd-class compartment two berths, and a 3rd-class compartment three berths. Berths may be booked in advance.

During the day there are usually only 2nd and 3rd class cars.

The Observation Cars are provided with large plate-glass windows and the corridor runs between two seats on one side and one seat on the other. For these seats there is a

Wilse,] *[Oslo.*

THE BRIDAL VEIL, GEIRANGER FJORD.

Wilse,] *[Oslo.*

THE NÆRÖ FJORD.

slight extra charge (2nd class, 2 kr.; 3rd, 1 kr.). When starting from a terminus, the ticket should be taken there. *En route* it can be obtained of the guard, if there is a vacancy.

Steamers are largely used on the fjords, large lakes and along the open coast. On the larger boats good meals are served at a reasonable price, and there is a limited amount of sleeping accommodation.

Services of **motor-cars,** usually called " Bils," working in connection with the railways and the steamer services, have very greatly diminished the use of horse-drawn vehicles, by which road journeys were formerly made. The cars are mostly of the type of private vehicles holding five to seven persons. They are driven by experienced and careful men.

The *Time-tables* of the trains, the steamers and the motor-car services are all given in the *Rutebok for Norge,* price 60 öre. An edition is published weekly.

The principal road vehicles other than motor-cars are the **Stolkjerre** (approximate pronunciation *stoll-cherry*), and the **Caleche.** The former is a two-wheeled cart, drawn by one horse. The seat (sometimes padded and sometimes not) is on springs, with a small rail at the back. Behind the seat is a smaller " dickey " for the driver. There is space under the seat for a moderate supply of luggage.

The **Caleche** is a four-wheeled carriage with a hood and a seat in front for the driver. It is drawn by two horses and will hold four persons. Luggage is generally carried on the box.

The **Cariol,** a single-seated cart on two wheels, innocent of springs, and drawn by a single horse or pony, is now seldom seen on the more regular routes.

Owing to the extension of the railways and still more to the establishment of the motor-car services, there is now little necessity for *posting,* and the strictly regulated system of former days has become disorganized (*see also* p. 22).

Motoring and Cycling.

Some of Norway's visitors take with them their car or bicycle. From either of the great automobile clubs a member can obtain a customs permit enabling him to take his car into and out of Norway free of duty. The Cyclists' Touring Club can confer a similar privilege on its members. Without such permits cars are subject to a duty of 40 per cent. of their value, and for a cycle one must deposit about Kr. 30, refunded when the machine is taken out of the country.

Norway possesses an admirable network of highways, some of which have been constructed solely to meet the needs of the tourist. The condition of the roads varies very much in the different districts, and also according to the time of year. In normally fine weather the surfaces are very good; after much wet they loosen, and in periods of drought are apt to become insufferably dusty. Cyclists who tour must be prepared for a good deal of collar work; unrideable hills and impossible descents are fairly frequent. But by way of compensation one may often free-wheel for miles after a short but steep ascent.

The **Rule of the Road.**—When meeting another vehicle, drive to the *right*. When overtaking drive to the *left*, but it is not courteous to pass without asking leave. It should be remembered that Norwegian horses are extremely shy.

Walking Tours.

The most suitable districts for mountain tours are Jotunheim and Trollheim, the latter best reached *viâ* Lökken. Among the many other districts popular with pedestrians are the valleys, where one can always find suitable small hotels with reasonable prices. These hotels are not equipped with the latest comfort, but most of them are absolutely clean and have good cooking. In the mountainous districts the quarters are generally at farmhouses with very simple accommodation, or at huts provided by *Den norske Turistforening* (the Norwegian Tourist Association, p. 20) or by local touring clubs. For the accommodation available members have preference over non-members, and for them also the charges are reduced. Members of *Den norske Turistforening* receive a reduction of Kr. 2.50 a day at the huts of that association and also a reduction at the huts of the other touring clubs.

The modern Norwegian knapsack generally gives most satisfaction, as it is made on scientific lines. The knapsack should contain a change of underclothing, spare pair of shoes, a raincoat, food for one meal, tincture of iodine and a cream for the feet, a cup, compass and a map. (For the Jotunheim the best map is the *Kart over Jotunheim*, by Finn Kross.)

The exhilarating air should not tempt the beginner to overtax his powers. For the first two days one should not walk for more than 4 or 5 hours a day. The time can then be gradually increased and may go up to 9 or 10 hours a day.

NOTES FOR TOURISTS.

Agencies.—Tickets for the various routes to Norway and for certain specified tours, or for tours according to the requirements of the traveller, can be obtained from the following offices :—

Norwegian State Railways Travel Bureau, Norway House, 21–4 Cockspur Street, London, S.W.1. The official enquiry office, in Britain, for all matters relating to travel in Norway. Here tickets are issued and information is freely given on such matters as routes to Norway, hotels in Norway, the various tours organized by the office itself or by the agencies named below, and others, winter sports, fishing, etc. The office is always up-to-date on all questions on travel in Norway and connections abroad. In Norway there are enquiry offices at Oslo East Station, at Bergen Station, and at Trondhjem Station.

Bennett's Travel Bureau (*Messrs. Bennett & Sons*), Chief Office, Karl Johans Gate, Oslo; London, 66 and 68 Haymarket, S.W.1; Paris, 4 rue Scribe; New York, 500 Fifth Avenue, and also at Bergen, Trondhjem, Kristiansand S., Stavanger and Molde. This firm, established by an Englishman many years ago, makes a speciality of tourist traffic in Norway. It is worked on the coupon system, with an exact estimate in advance, and covers every recognized route. A list of the tours is sent gratis on application.

Messrs. Thomas Cook & Son. This firm organizes a number of tours in Norway, varying in time from six days to six months. A list of these tours is issued gratis on application (Head Office, Devonshire House, Berkeley Street, Piccadilly, W.). Other tours not so planned can be arranged for, or parts of different tours combined. This well-known firm has offices at Oslo (20 Karl Johans Gate), Bergen (10 Torvalmenning), and Trondhjem (Nordre Gate).

Other agencies giving information regarding travel in Norway include The *Polytechnic Touring Association*, 309 Regent Street, London, W.; *Messrs. Dean & Dawson*, 84 Piccadilly, W.; *American Express Co.*, 6 Haymarket, S.W.1.

The principal **Steamship Companies** catering for the holiday-maker in Norway are noted on p. 15.

Care should be exercised in selecting an agency, as instances have occurred of visitors landing in Norway looking in vain for the promised accredited representative, and being entirely cast on their own resources.

Quite numerous are the **Tourist Clubs,** of which the *Norwegian Tourist Association* is especially worthy of the support of visitors, particularly of those who climb, motor or cycle. It corresponds in the main to the Swiss and German Alpine Clubs. The subscription is 10 kroner per annum for the first member of a family and 5 kroner for each additional person of the same family. There is no formality about membership; members can be received at any of the tourist agencies in Norway. The Club does excellent work in the making of roads, marking routes, maintaining club huts, issuing maps, etc.

Clothing.—In summer, tourists not going farther north than Trondhjem may dress as they would in England, but should have strong footwear and carry a light raincoat. If the mountains are to be crossed in a motor, it will be wise to have a "pull-over" or some other woollen garment for that occasion. On a yachting cruise along the western fjords and a North Cape trip, a good overcoat and a warm rug should be taken. For the winter season, warm woollen undergarments and stout tweed suits and dresses are necessary. Fur gloves lined with wool are always useful in winter; they can be obtained in Norway. The country makes excellent ski-ing boots, and all other necessaries for winter sports can be obtained there.

Customs Examination.—The luggage of passengers arriving by the steamers from abroad is generally examined before debarkation, and of those arriving by train from Sweden on the platform of the railway station or in the train. If there be nothing subject to duty and the officer be told so, only a slight examination takes place. As a rule articles for personal use are duty-free. Tobacco, playing cards and boxes of provisions are subject to duty. The importation and exportation of arms and ammunition are prohibited.

Hotels.—A large number of really good hotels have been erected both in town and country, and in them the traveller will find all modern comforts and conveniences, electric light, central heating, baths, etc. English, German, and often French are spoken, the fare is good and plentiful and, being quite international in character, generally meets the most varied requirements.

The country inns are, as a rule, clean and comfortable,

and provide good, plain food without, however, much variety.

As to *gratuities,* the 10 per cent. rule works satisfactorily in Norway as elsewhere, and in most places it is customary to add this *pourboire* as "service" to the bill, but it is not shared by the concierge (hall porter) and the "boots," who should be remunerated according to the services they have rendered. The Norwegians, even in the towns, are not rapacious tip-hunters.

Generally speaking the hotel charges are about the same as in England. Definite information is contained in two publications issued by the *Landsforening for Reiselivet i Norge* (Tourist Traffic Association of Norway). *Hotels in Norway* contains particulars of the hotels in tourist districts which can be recommended to British and American visitors. The *Norges Hoteller* (1 kr. 50 öre) contains information of about 2,000 hotels and boarding houses. In Norway these publications can be bought at the railway bookstalls, kiosks, etc., and in England through the Travel Bureau, Norway House, 21–24 Cockspur Street, London, S.W.1.

Luggage.—Those who travel by one of the cruising steamers have an advantage in the matter of luggage, as most of the steamers have accessible baggage rooms. The traveller who intends to tour by road is advised to cut his luggage down to the smallest possible compass. For a trifling fee luggage can be insured at all travel bureaux, at all railway stations in Norway and at some of the steamship offices.

Passports.—Every traveller to Norway must be in possession of a passport. Its visa by a Norwegian Consul has been abolished for British subjects, the subjects of most other European countries, and for American citizens born in Norway, Sweden, Denmark, Finland, or Iceland. Other American citizens must have their passport viséd.

British subjects resident in the British Isles can procure a passport direct from the Passport Offices, 1 Queen Anne's Gate Buildings, Dartmouth Street, London, S.W.1; or the Branch Passport Office, 36 Dale Street, Liverpool; or through a tourist agency for a small charge in addition to the official fee. The first step is to apply to the Passport Office or to an agency for an Application Form.

Porters.—Porters from the hotels generally await the arrival of trains and steamers. If other assistance is needed only an authorized porter should be engaged. Authorized porters have the word *Bybud* (porter) on their caps and bear a number which should be noted (at Oslo there are station porters bearing the words *Faste Bærere*).

" Bybuds " will convey luggage to the hotels. They carry a tariff which they are bound to produce on demand. During the day it varies from 50 to 85 öre per 150 lb. (70 kilogrammes), according to the distance; at night from 60 öre to 1 krone.

Posting.—Previous to the introduction of the motor, conveyance on the high roads depended upon a system of **posting** called skyss (*shyss*). Now the business no longer pays. Many of the station-holders have thrown up their contracts, and the system is only maintained at the discretion of the local Rural or Town Council.

The **Posting Stations** (skyss stations), which are really farmhouses, are usually about nine English miles apart. The farmers at the stations are bound to provide the traveller with food and accommodation, and with a vehicle and horse for the next stage. Allusion has been made on page 17 to the vehicles in common use. A day-book is kept at each station, in which the traveller is obliged to enter the name of the place whence he has come, that to which he is going, and the number of horses engaged, and may enter any complaints. The book is inspected from time to time by an official. The accommodation in the Skyss stations is usually plain but good; on the more frequented routes the station was often the best hotel in the place, it being an advantage to the proprietor to take on the somewhat onerous duties entailed by the provision of horses and vehicles.

A table of distances will be found in the day-book kept at the Skyss stations.

There is also *posting by rowing boat,* for which there are regulations regarding the number of persons and weight of luggage which the various-sized boats may carry. The charges also are fixed.

Time.—Norwegian time is that of Middle Europe, i.e. one hour in advance of Greenwich time, but during the period of " summer time " in England, the time of the two countries is alike, as Norway makes no seasonal change.

PRELIMINARY INFORMATION.

BEFORE proceeding to a detailed description of the attractions of Norway, it may be well to set out, in alphabetical order a number of items of interest and importance relative to the country generally.

Area and Population.—Norway extends from 58 degrees to 71 degrees north latitude, i.e. from the latitude of the North of Scotland to a point only 19 degrees from the North Pole; and it extends through 26 degrees of longitude, the most westerly point being on the same meridian as Amsterdam, the most easterly on the same meridian as Leningrad.

It has a total area of 125,000 square miles, while the population numbers only some 2,800,000, so that Norway is the most thinly-peopled country of Europe.

The largest *towns* are all situated on the coast, and most of the others are there also. The six having the greatest population are Oslo, 256,000; inhabitants, with suburbs, 350,000; Bergen, 100,000; Trondhjem, 57,000; Stavanger, 47,000; Drammen, 26,000; and Kristiansand S., 19,000.

The great bulk of the country consists of mountain ridges, but each of the four sections of the land, North, South, East and West, has its own natural features.

North Norway is rugged and wild. To the tourist who sees the coast in the wonderful summer, and in the glow of the Midnight Sun, the country is somewhat of a fairyland with natural scenery of imposing beauty. *South Norway* is a land of seas between reefs and islands, fertile pastures and delightful mountain landscapes. The scenery is bright and smiling and full of poetic charm. *East Norway* has fertile, broad and open valleys, generally with a foaming river or a dark blue lake at the bottom. Forests and cultivated fields cover the hillsides right up to the mountains, of which the loftiest summits are always clothed with snow, and there are miles upon miles of mountain wastes sparsely covered with vegetation. Of *West Norway* the characteristics are lofty and precipitous mountains, snowfields and glaciers, mountain dales, deep, far-penetrating fjords and a rich vegetation comprising much that a stranger would expect to find only in a more southern land.

The **Army and Navy** are maintained primarily by conscription. Although several times threatened with hostilities, Norway has not taken part in any War since 1814. The existing military system came into being on January 1, 1911. During the Great War and since a number of minor changes have been made, and in 1920 a civilian commission was appointed to inquire into the re-organization of the Army and Navy.

The present organization is a compromise between the voluntary and the conscription systems, the more important posts being held by salaried personnel. The remainder of the officers and privates are conscripted, and are only called up for service during military training and when war threatens. General conscription prevails, without preference of position. Conscripts are enrolled during the year in which they reach the age of twenty and they begin their military service in the following year. During the first twelve years they belong to the *First Levy* (line) ; the next twelve years are spent in the *Second Levy* (reserve).

In addition, in time of War every man able to bear arms (excepting clergymen, pilots, etc.) between the ages of fifteen and fifty-five is liable to be called up as "war reinforcements."

The expenditure on the Army amounts to about 7 per cent. of the State Budget.

Climate.—The climate of Norway varies considerably from east to west, and from north to south, but the whole land has one common feature, a relatively high average temperature, due to the warm currents that flow along the coasts. Oslo, which lies on the same line of latitude as the most southern part of Greenland, is occasionally the hottest city in Europe.

The rainfall on the west coast is in excess of that of England ; but this is largely a matter of local geographical position, the town of Bergen and the island of Florö having the highest rainfall on the coast. The eastern coast enjoys a fine dry climate, bright in summer and winter.

Distances, Weights and Measures.— Distances are

officially calculated by *kilometres* (8 kilometres = 5 miles roughly), both on the railways and in driving. The *kilogramme* is the customary standard of weight, equivalent to about 2 lb. 3¼ oz. avoirdupois. The pound is sometimes used; it now means half a kilo. In all other respects the metric system is employed.

Education in Norway stands on a very high level. Elementary schools are to be found everywhere, and to them must go *all* children from their seventh year to their fifteenth, unless before reaching the latter they have passed through the seven classes. In connection with the elementary schools there are continuation schools, the course in which includes modern languages. There are evening and other schools for young adults, and in both town and country there are secondary schools and grammar schools. Oslo is the seat of a University, and Bergen is to have one. It already has a high school for mathematics and natural science, with several faculties. Trondhjem has a technical high school and a high school for teachers. At the head of the agricultural education is the Agricultural College at Ås, about twenty miles south-east of Oslo. Its students are trained to act as investigators, experts and instructors at the agricultural schools, which have winter courses largely attended by farmers' sons.

Government.—Norway is a kingdom under a constitutional monarch. The royal house consists of King Håkon VII (*see* p. 45), Queen Maud, a sister of King George V of England, and the Crown Prince Olav.

The governing power is shared between the sovereign and the people, represented by the **Storting** (Parliament), for which women as well as men are eligible. Every man and woman over 23 years of age can vote at the election of parliamentary representatives. In addition to the direct member, the electors must choose a vice-member to take the place of the member when he is unavoidably absent. The members are paid for attendance. When a deputy takes the place of a member, it is he who receives the pay.

After an election the Storting resolves itself into the **Lagting,** consisting of one-fourth of the members and forming an upper chamber, and the **Odelsting,** consisting of the remaining three-fourths of the members and forming a lower chamber, to which all Bills are first presented. If the Lagting rejects a measure a second time, it comes before the full

Storting and is then accepted if passed by a two-thirds majority.

The King has power to veto any measure, but if three successive Stortings are against him his veto is automatically removed. It was thus that the law for the abolition of hereditary nobility was passed in 1821.

Local Government is largely administered by town councils and rural district councils.

The **Licensing Laws** relating to the sale of wine and spirits have undergone important changes. An old law permitted wine to be sold by wine merchants, and in Oslo and Trondhjem these also sold spirits, the sale of which elsewhere was confined, under very strict regulations, to companies established for the purpose. Any profit above 5 per cent. was devoted to charitable and philanthropic objects. After many years the extreme temperance party succeeded in suppressing these companies in several towns. Then, during the War, the sale of spirits was entirely prohibited. At the end of 1926 the opinion of the country on the question was ascertained by means of a plebiscite. A decisive vote in favour of the sale was recorded, not, it was said, because the people wished to drink spirits, but on account of the difficulty and expense of preventing smuggling and suppressing private stills. The Storting accordingly amended the law in the sense desired by the country. Generally speaking, the sale is for cash, but only to persons who have attained their twenty-first year, and only between hours locally fixed.

The *Norway Year Book* contains information regarding intellectual, political, economic, commercial and administrative conditions in Norway. It is in English.

Industries.—Contrary to what one might expect from the general character of the surface of Norway and the high latitude of even the southern border, **agriculture** is Norway's principal resource. One-third of the population lives by it. One-thirtieth of the land is devoted to tillage and pasture.

Most of the agriculturists consist of families working their own land, and most of the fishermen have their own boats and equipment. Three-fourths of the farms have an area of less than 13 acres. Large estates are remarkably few, and the policy of the Government is to distribute land and property as widely as possible. By an ancient law a family has a right to redeem at an appraised value landed property that has been sold. The descendants of a landowner have also the right to claim the estate at a low price. By the exercise of these rights, farms which otherwise would be alienated are kept in the family for generations.

One-fifth of the country consists of **forest land.** The trees are mostly Scottish fir, Norway spruce and the birch. There is a large export of timber, wood-pulp, cellulose, paper and cardboard. About 12½ per cent. of the forests are owned by the State, which by annual purchases is pursuing a policy of increasing the public ownership.

Fisheries constitute one of the most important means of livelihood and fish is the most important article of export. The main coastal fisheries are the cod and herring. The profit of the seal and whale industries approaches two million pounds sterling a year. Before the War, Norway's production of whale oil amounted to about three-fourths of the world's supply.

The **minerals** of prime importance are silver, iron and copper. The silver mines at Kongsberg, about fifty miles south-west of Oslo, have been the property of the State since 1623. Around Trondhjem are mines producing iron pyrites and copper. Coal is mined in Spitzbergen. Nickel deposits are scattered throughout the country. The most important are near Oslo, Kristiansand S. and Stavanger.

Of late years **factories** have increased in number and importance. In addition to the canning factories and to factories making use of the timber, there are electro-chemical works, engineering works, spinning mills and boot factories. The driving power mainly comes from the waterfalls. No other land in Europe has so much water-power as Norway. At present only about one-tenth is utilized.

A comprehensive Factory Inspection Act establishes the principle of the eight-hours day. Insurance against sickness and accidents is compulsory. Voluntary insurance against unemployment is State-supported.

The **Shipping** trade is one of Norway's chief sources of income. The Norwegians have always been a seafaring people. In proportion to her population Norway has a much larger mercantile marine than any other land, and what is even more remarkable, she ranks high among the countries of the world for the number of her vessels. When the Great War broke out, only England, Germany and the United States possessed more and larger ships.

In such a mountainous country the construction of **rail-**

ways is exceedingly difficult and expensive, while the sparseness of the population makes the income comparatively small. Thus it has come about that nearly all the railways in Norway have been constructed by the State. Only about 270 miles are privately owned. The first Norwegian railway was built by Robert Stephenson in 1851–1854, between the capital and Eidsvoll. The principal lines are the Bergen-Oslo, the Dovre (Oslo-Trondhjem), the Rauma or Romsdal railway, connecting the west coast near Molde with the Dovre railway, and the South Coast line (Oslo-Kragerö). On the main lines the track ascends from the level of the sea at the coast to the region of perpetual snow and then descends to the sea-level again.

The gauge is that of the continental lines, so that through carriages can be run between Norway and the other countries of Europe. During the Great War, the only open route between east and west ran through Norway. Some years ago electrification of the railways was begun.

Language.—The difficulties of language need not deter the tourist from visiting Norway. English is widely understood in the towns, while in the country places many of the peasants who have been for a sojourn in America to secure a little capital are only too glad of the chance to assist the visitor by a display of their skill as interpreters. At the same time a small phrase-book will be found of great assistance and interest. Norwegian is not a difficult language ; those with some knowledge of German will find it comparatively easy.

During the long union with Denmark (1380–1814) the Norwegian language gradually became superseded in public and literary use by the Danish language, which was closely akin to it. In the course of time it adopted so many Norwegian elements that the language now spoken and written in Norway can no longer be called Danish, but must be regarded as a distinct language. In 1848 a peasant's son, Ivar Åsen, published a grammar of the Norwegian dialects and demonstrated that they were direct descendants of the old Norse tongue. He further showed that they might form the basis of a literary language. The language he thus introduced is known as the **Landsmål**—country speech. In 1889 an Act of Parliament provided for the teaching of the Landsmål in the institutions training primary school teachers. The local governing boards of the elementary schools are entitled to decide in which of the two languages—the Landsmål or the **Riksmål**—the school books shall be written and the lessons given. The pupils in the higher schools are at liberty to choose in which language they will write their compositions, but they must show their competence in the other as well. The Landsmål is of no value whatever in commercial life. In the scheme of business there is no place for those who cannot speak and write the common literary language—the Riksmål.

Owing to the existence of the two languages, often the same thing bears different names in different places ; a variation that travellers cannot fail to notice.

The **Norwegian alphabet** consists of our twenty-six letters and three others—å, æ and ø or ö. Å (å), formerly written aa, is pronounced as *aw* in awe, æ is generally pronounced as *a* in bare and ø or ö as *u* in fur.

J, which seems to come so awkwardly in many words, has the English sound of *y* in " yes," *except* that *kj* has the Scottish sound of *ch* in " loch " ; *skj* the sound of *sh* in " shall " ; and *bj* the initial sound in " beauty."

The final *e* of words forms a syllable. It is lightly pronounced and always short, as in Molde (molder), *but* the personal pronoun *De* is pronounced *dee.*

As this is not a treatise on the language, we will only add that the indefinite article and the definite are alike, *en* for common gender and *et* for neuter (the only two genders), but whilst the indefinite article is placed before the noun, the definite is added to it, which explains why one meets with *et vann* (a lake) and *vannet* (the lake) ; *en vei* (a way) and *veien* (the way) ; *en bakke* (a hill) and *bakken* (the hill).

Money.—Norway's monetary system, adopted in 1875, is in all respects similar to that of Denmark and Sweden. Gold is the standard of value. The unit of reckoning is the *krone* (silver).

At the normal value of the currency at par £1 = Kr. 18·16, so that 1 krone is then worth nearly 1*s.* 1¼*d.*

The coins are :—

Copper,	5	öre, equals rather more than	½*d.*
Silver,	10	,, ,, ,, ,,	1*d.*
or	25	,, ,, ,, ,,	3¼*d.*
Nickel	50	,, ,, ,, ,,	6½*d.*
	1	krone, equals approximately	1*s.* 1¼*d.*
	2	,, ,, ,,	2*s.* 2½*d.*
Gold,	5	,, ,, ,,	5*s.* 6¼*d.*
	10	,, ,, ,,	11*s.* 0½*d.*
	20	,, ,, ,,	22*s.* 1*d.*

But, as in England, the gold coins are not in circulation. National Bank of Norway notes for 5, 10, 50, 100, 500, and 1,000 kroner are in circulation, and are legal tender. English and American bank notes, circular notes and letters of credit are readily exchanged in the towns, but it is not always easy to get them exchanged in remoter parts. Swedish and Danish copper coins pass in Norway, but not the silver money. In Norway it is more advantageous to exchange money at a bank than at an hotel.

Postal Information.—The **Post Offices** in Norway are open from 8 a.m. to 7.30 p.m. There is no Sunday delivery.

The postage of a letter not exceeding 20 grammes in weight, posted and delivered in the same town, is 10 öre, but if sent from one part of Norway to another part, 20 öre. It is the same from Norway to Sweden and Denmark; to all other foreign countries, 30 öre.

For each 20 grammes after the first, the postage is increased by one-half of the minimum sum.

As in England, should the postage not be prepaid, or be paid short of the full amount, the receiver is charged double the deficiency.

Inland post-cards must bear a stamp of 15 öre, as must cards sent to Sweden and Denmark. For all other foreign countries the postage is 20 öre.

Letters from England to Norway must be stamped with 2½*d.* for the first ounce, and 1½*d.* for every additional ounce.

Parcels from England are sent every other day. The size is limited to 3½ feet length, breadth or depth, or 6 feet length and girth combined. The rates are 2 lb., 2*s.*; 7 lb., 3*s.* 6*d.*; 11 lb., 4*s.*; 22 lb., 6*s.* 3*d.* Letters may not be enclosed in parcels. A Customs note must be filled up.

Letters from England to Western Norway should be sent *viâ* Newcastle, and so marked on the envelope. There is an overland mail twice a day *viâ* Holland from London to Oslo and *vice versâ*.

Registering fee for foreign letters 30 öre, except those to Sweden and Denmark, for which the charge is 20 öre, as for inland letters.

Cash remittances can be enclosed in *inland* letters, for which special envelopes with at least two wax seals must be used. The postage for inland money letters containing up to Kr. 250 is 40 öre; Kr. 500, 60 öre; Kr. 750, 70 öre; Kr. 1,000, 80 öre.

Foreign money letters can only be sent as registered letters, the responsibility of the post office being as for a registered letter and not for the actual value.

Telegrams.—The charge for telegrams to any part of Great Britain or Ireland from any part of Norway is 25 öre per word, three words being the minimum number. The cost of telegrams from one part of Norway to another is 50 öre for the first 10 words, and 5 öre for each additional word.

From Norway to Sweden or Denmark, Kr. 1·30 for the first 10 words, and 12 öre more for every additional word. To Canada and the United States the charge ranges from Kr. 1·05 to Kr. 3·25 per word, according to the distance of the telegram's destination beyond New York or Quebec.

To Austria, 28 öre per word; Hungary, 34 öre; France, 30 öre; Germany, 21 öre; Russia, 41 öre; Switzerland, 20 öre.

Telephone.—The Norwegian telephone system is excellent and extensive. Quite remote parts of the country are connected with the trunk system. The telephone can be used to advantage for ordering conveyances, rooms and meals. For calls in the same town or district, from a public call office, the fee is only 10 öre. The charge for other calls for a three-minutes' conversation varies according to the distance between the two stations. A telegram can be telephoned to the nearest telegraph office and then forwarded as a telegram.

Religion.—Norway has an Established Church—Evangelical Lutheran. It is endowed by the State. Its clergy are nominated by the King. All religious bodies, except Jesuits, are tolerated. The Roman Catholic community numbers not more than 3,000. For a note on the *Stave Churches, see* pp. 49–51.

SPORT IN NORWAY.

NORWAY has come to be looked upon by sportsmen as one of the most attractive playgrounds of Europe. Fast steamers have brought the country districts within easy reach of England, the new railways and the motor services have further opened up districts previously inaccessible to the man who did not want to spend a large part of his holiday in getting to and from his playground, and the vast improvement in the hotel accommodation of the more recognized resorts has rendered a holiday in Norway less of a pioneering effort than was formerly the case, without robbing it of the charm of remoteness. The country is so vast and so thinly populated that wild nature can be reached almost by railway, and probably will long remain so.

Angling.

In the sport which it offers to anglers, Norway is ahead of any other country in Europe. There are some 200 salmon rivers. As a rule they are short, a condition favourable to the angler, as the quickly-rising surface of the country leads to the formation of pools and rapids. Many of the best-known salmon rivers have been leased to British and other sportsmen, but there are still plenty of rivers affording good sport. Even on those that are leased, there are usually stretches which can be had at some time during the season, and there are hotels which have fishing rights for their guests.

The same applies to sea-trout, though there are a few places where this sport is more easily obtained.

The Norway salmon is, scientifically speaking, the same as the Scottish and the English salmon. But the Norwegian rivers are so fierce and swift, the natural conditions are so difficult, that in Norway the odds are on the hooked fish rather than on the fisherman. It may be only the fierce current of the river, but it seems as if the first instinct of the hooked salmon is to make at once for the sea—and he often gets there.

The season for salmon and trout fishing varies greatly,

Knudsen & Co.,] [*Bergen.*

THE SOGNE FJORD AT BALHOLM.

Photos by] [*Wilse and Mittet & Co.*

(1) ON THE WAY TO CHURCH, HARDANGER. (2 & 3) GIRLS OF THE HARDANGER.

even on neighbouring rivers. Generally speaking, July is the best month, but in the southern and western districts and near Trondhjem the last half of June is also a good time; and in the northern districts the first half of August may be as good as July.

Trout are in almost all the streams and lakes, and in many they afford good sport. In the Mjösen lake trout of 20 to 25 lb. are taken every year, and from many of the other large lakes fish of 12 to 15 lb. are occasionally landed. From the lakes at a high elevation, the fish taken usually weigh from ½ lb. to 2 lb., but these waters frequently yield trout of 4 or 5 lb. and even of greater weight. In the upland waters the trout are very plentiful, and none are pinker, fatter or of better flavour.

Char is abundant in the north. Some of these go down to the sea, where they become silvery and grow quickly. Then they return to the rivers and lakes to spawn. These sea-char afford good sport, and their flesh is excellent.

There is no general law for the protection of fresh-water fish other than salmon and salmon-trout.

Fly-fishing in the rivers begins, as a rule, as soon as the weather generally becomes settled and warm. It is at its best in ordinary rivers from the end of June to the early days of September. In mountain lakes and streams, the best time is July and August. During the fly-fishing period trolling with minnow near the surface affords good sport.

For names of the best angling stations and how to reach them, the flies to use, the dates when fishing begins and ends, and much other necessary information too voluminous to be given here, anglers should obtain *Angling in Norway*, a booklet distributed free of charge through the Tourist Bureaux and through the Norwegian State Railways Travel Bureau, 21–24 Cockspur Street, London, S.W.1.

Shooting.

Foreigners are by law excluded from the game-shooting rights accorded to Norwegians, with the exception that on payment of 200 kroner for a licence and 100 kroner to the Norwegian exchequer they may shoot three reindeer and any beasts or birds of prey (bears, wolves, lynxes, foxes, etc.) met with while hunting. For the destruction of the noxious creatures a small premium is paid.

Other shooting can only be acquired by foreigners by

renting it from landowners, and in all cases 100 kroner must be paid to the State.

Elk may be stalked in the pine forests, and deer hunting may be obtained near the west coast. And as a rule only one of each kind may be killed on a separate estate. In certain of the State forests from two to five elk may be shot on the same estate.

Most of the red deer are shot on the island of Hitteren and in the district of Fosen.

Hares are more or less abundant all over Norway.

Various species of wild duck abound on almost every mountain tarn, in the quieter reaches of every river and in the adjoining swamps and backwaters. These birds and sea-fowl are not protected, with the exception of the broad-billed duck (March 15 to August 15) and the eider duck, which in certain districts is very strictly preserved. There is good woodcock shooting in various parts of the country, but the most popular sport is grouse shooting in the high mountains. Hundreds of thousands of grouse and ptarmigan are shot every year.

All information desired can be obtained by writing to the Tourist Traffic Association of Norway, 2 Stortings Gate, Oslo, or to the State Railways Travel Bureau, Cockspur Street, London.

Mountaineering.

Norway as a climber's playground is most insufficiently appreciated. To some it can never have the charm of Switzerland, partly because of association and partly on grounds of convenience. The climber in Norway, even on some of the better-known peaks, is still something of a pioneer. Those climbers, however, who seek novelty and fresh ground will find in Norway—more especially in the northern part—a most satisfying field. One must be prepared to dispense with some of the recognized comforts of mountaineering in the better-known parts. There is seldom, for instance, a clean-cut path to the point where, ordinarily speaking, one expects the work to begin, there are few huts, and not everywhere are there kindly directions put up by a fatherly Alpine Club, though excellent work is being done by the Norwegian Tourist Club. Often the climber has to find his route for himself, and the unexplored nature of the climb calls forth the best of his intelligence and keenness. Therein lies its chief charm. As a rule, the ascents are no easier than those of Switzerland, though less high. They call for extreme caution, owing to the greater rottenness of the rocks and the continuous dangers of the couloirs. Loose rock is the principal danger; but as a set-off against this there are seldom snow avalanches in summer, and dangerous cornices are rare. Daylight also is, of course, longer—in fact, during the climbing season there is practically no night. These latter facts, coupled with the aforementioned dangers, make Norway a splendid training-ground for the independent climber. One or two things must be borne in mind. The climber should never go alone. He should take a supply of climbing nails with him, and should never allow a single member of the party to accompany him without boots properly nailed. He should never go into a gully where dirty marks indicate that stones fall. Climbers should not clamber over loose rock directly behind one another; a mere touch will often set in motion an appalling quantity of stone.

At well-known centres there are first-class guides. Generally the prices are lower than those demanded in Switzerland by the Guides' tariff. A bargain should be made beforehand.

Two excellent books on mountaineering in Norway are W. Cecil Slingsby's *Norway, the Northern Playground*, and Mrs. Aubrey Le Blond's *Mountaineering in the Land of the Midnight Sun*. The former is the more practical; the latter contains some good tips. The year-books of the Norwegian Tourist Club contain occasional articles in English.

Note.—The word *tolk* is used in Norway to indicate a courier, *förer* indicates a guide for mountaineering.

Sailing.

The western fjords are tempting for sailing in small boats. The entrances are well marked, the coast is well lit and buoyed, and the charts are fairly accurate and up-to-date. For sailing outside the Skjærgård in a larger boat it is desirable that a pilot or local hand or two should be shipped. Inside, the navigation, though intricate, is not very difficult. The greatest danger is from squalls. In the Westland fjords these come with great suddenness, passing from a howling gale to a flat calm in less time than it takes to shift a jib, and without the slightest visible warning, owing to the mountainous steepness of the shores. Power, as an auxiliary at least, is advisable. Paraffin can be obtained everywhere, petrol at the principal coast towns and ports. Stores can be procured more cheaply in Norway than in England. The *Norway Pilot*, published by Potter, in connection with the Admiralty, is issued in three parts, (i) from Vikna to the North Cape, (ii) Vikna to Lindesnes, and (iii) Lindesnes and the Oslo Fjord. It is minute in detail.

The Royal Norwegian Yacht Club, "Kongelig Norsk Seilklub" (K.N.S.), has 4,000 directly enrolled members, and forms the central authority for other clubs comprising some 5,000 members. The K.N.S. owns the summer restaurant *Dronningen* near Oslo. The building contains the club rooms, and to them foreign yachtsmen have access.

WINTER SPORTS.

Norway is the home of the ski, and ski-ing predominates among the winter sports to a much greater extent than in Switzerland. This is especially the case at the smaller resorts among the mountains. Visitors desiring greater variety of sport might do better at one of the resorts on the outskirts of Oslo; here, too, there is greater facility for evening gaiety. The Norwegian winter is severe and long, but dry and healthy, more especially on the eastern side of the great mountain chain. The principal sports are ski-ing, skating, tobogganing and sleighing. There are also curling rinks, and visitors to the mountain resorts may have the experience of sleighing behind reindeer. The great international ski-ing competition on Holmenkollen Hill, near Oslo, generally takes place at the end of February or the beginning of March. In addition to the many ski-ing competitions there are skating contests, ice-hockey matches, trotting races on the ice, ski-racing, etc.

Ski-ing

is really the national sport of Norway. In the great forest districts the snow lies deep and firm from the middle of December until well into April, and during this period practically the whole of the rural population goes about on ski.

Ski-ing is not difficult to learn. For beginners the slopes round Oslo will be found an excellent training-ground; but the sport is over earlier than in some of the more northerly districts. Trondhjem also provides good and convenient grounds for beginners. There are, however, many high mountain resorts where the sport can be carried on

[E.N.A.

REINDEER HERDERS ON SKIS.

[E.N.A.

REINDEER FORDING THE RY STRÖM, NEAR TROMSÖ.

Wilse,] *[Oslo.*

A SKI-JUMP.

Wilse,] *[Oslo.*

SKIKJÖRING.

under ideal conditions. The higher stations on the Bergen Railway (about 4,000 feet above sea-level) generally retain deep snow till the end of May; near these stations modern hotels have been erected, and are open during certain winter months. *Finse* especially deserves mention in this connection; two hours' distant is the *Hardanger Glacier*, where ski may be used all the year round. Other centres are: *Geilo, Haugastöl, Ustaoset* on the Bergen Railway, *Hösbjör* (near *Hamar*), *Lillehammer, Fefor* (Vinstra Station), *Dombås* and *Opdal* on the main line from Oslo to Trondhjem. At all these resorts excellent ski-ing may be had throughout the winter (from December till April): there is also skating at some resorts. At all these places there are good hotels. A favourite district for Norwegian sportsmen is *Nordmarken*, just outside Oslo.

As districts for high mountain ski-ing, the following have great repute: The *Dovrefjell*, of which the principal centres are Röros (2,060 feet, 399 kilometres (250 miles) from Oslo, station on the narrow-gauge railway to Trondhjem), and Dombås, 343 kilometres (about 215 miles) from Oslo, at the junction of the Dovre and Romsdal lines. The *Jotunheim* district, reached also by the same line from Oslo, with some good climbing routes. The *Hemsedal Mountains*, with a few good hotels and satisfactory posting stations. The *Telemark Mountains*; *Rondane* and the south-eastern mountain country; *Filefjell*; *Norefjell* and the *Trondhjem Mountains* are all favourite ski-ing areas where good hotel accommodation is to be had in winter.

As a rule, it is possible to obtain all the gear of the sport in Norway—Norwegian skis are famous—but special windproof ski-ing suits should be obtained in England. An illustrated booklet, *Norway, the Home of Ski Sport*, published by the State Railways, is distributed free of charge by the tourist agents; and in the *Winter Sports Annual* are given several detailed routes. Sportsmen are advised to write from England to the hotel of their choice before proceeding to Norway, in order to ascertain if it remains open for the winter. *Scandinavian Health Resorts*, by Dr. T. N. Kelynack, gives some information on this point.

Skating.

The best time for skating is during November and December, when the ice is smooth and the snow has not fallen. Except in the towns, where rinks are cared for, skating is over with the first snow, although at Finse, where is a covered rink, and certain other outlying resorts it is just possible throughout the winter.

The best rink is that of *Frogner*, on the hills outside Oslo, where figure skating is taken quite seriously. Speed skating and touring on skates are both enthusiastically practised during the early winter. Oslo, Hamar and Trondhjem are the best centres. Trondhjem boys are among the best skaters in the world. Norway generally provides a champion at the world's annual meeting.

Tobogganing.

The long hilly roads of the country districts lend themselves admirably to tobogganing and lugeing. The native sleigh (*kjelke*) is about 5 to 7 feet long, a somewhat primitive form of bobsleigh. But tobogganing is not yet the organized sport in Norway that it is in Switzerland. *Holmenkollen* and *Voxenkollen*, outside Oslo, are good centres, as in these places sleighs can be taken to the summit of the run by the electric railway.

Sleighing

hardly comes into the category of sports in the ordinary sense, but in Norway it is invested with a particular sporting charm because it is in this way that the Norwegians race their trotting ponies. In almost every district and in the neighbourhood of almost every small town a trotting course of this kind will be found.

HISTORICAL SKETCH.

WHEN the inhabitants of Norway begin to emerge from the mists of unrecorded time—which does not happen till the eighth century at the earliest—they do so with a civilization organized to such a degree that some inquiry into their antecedents is profitable. Two outstanding considerations become evident.

The first is that they approached Norway from the south. They are a Teutonic race—a branch of the great Teutonic migration from Asia; this much is evident from their language, their physical peculiarities and their folk-lore.

The second point that obtrudes itself is that this arrival was long antecedent to the first records of their history. They were in Norway in the Bronze Age—possibly, though we do not know for certain, the Stone Age overlapped them—since it has been proved, as any traveller can see for himself in the museums of northern antiquities, that their tradition of ornament descended directly from that epoch When the Norwegians appear in history, their social organization went no further than the family and the folk, with here and there combined allegiance to some petty chief, and perhaps the vague consciousness of some solidarity of race behind the barriers of forest and sea that separated them from Swede, Goth and Dane.

The Vikings.

They were in this state when the era of the Vikings began, farmers who lived as husbandmen in harvest and in seedtime, and who in the times between fared forth as sea-robbers, as pillagers, as raiders and as settlers.

It is probable that the parts of Norway first settled by the race now inhabiting the country were the southern and eastern coasts, and particularly the fertile sections along the shores of the Oslo Fjord, of which the western part was, and is, called Vestfold, the eastern Östfold, and the entire district was in saga-times known as Viken. As this district is known to have been, on account of its fine farming lands, forests and harbours, the seat of a multitude of dreaded fighters, its name may well have been the origin of the name Viking, which came to be the common appellation of all sea-warriors of the North. Viking simply means " one who lives in a vik " (a bay, inlet), and was perhaps originally the name given to " the men of Viken."

The earliest of the Vikings seem to have gone forth on private venture ; at first a man with his own people, later a combination of vessels for a combined but not organized end, and lastly a fleet, owning allegiance to a chief through the allegiance of individual commanders, and for the gaining of some common political end in tribute or territory. Even after the welding of these pieces of social undertaking into a complete nation the habit of setting forth on private enterprise was still strong in the Viking.

" Sweyn had in the spring hard work, and made them lay down very much seed, and looked much after it himself. But when that toil was ended, he fared away every spring on a viking-voyage, and harried about among the southern isles and Ireland, and came home after midsummer. That he called spring-viking. Then he was at home until the corn-fields were reaped down, and the grain seen to be stored. Then he fared away on a viking-voyage, and then he did not come home till the winter was one month off, and that he called his autumn-viking."—*Orkneyinga Saga* (twelfth century).

The Sagas,

recorded in Iceland during the dark centuries when Europe was being thus harried, are our principal sources of information for these times, but much myth is blended with historical accounts in the most bewildering fashion. The tale begins with **Sigurd,** the Volsung hero, descended from Odin, against whom the fate ordained by the gods rolled on with a merciless inflexibility of purpose such as is found in Greek tragedy.

Not until the arrival of **Siegfried,** in A.D. 777, does history emerge from the mist, but from thence onwards events are rapidly clearer. Kingship, however, did not develop till fully a hundred years later ; even then the king divided his possessions among his sons, a proceeding that was fruitful in petty wars.

Harald, the Fair-haired.

Then came Harald Hårfagre, or the Fair-haired, who first consolidated these petty kingdoms into a united nation.

He did it by the sword, and at sea. The saga says that the King wanted to marry Gyda, a lady "of wondrous beauty and of high mood withal." Her message in reply to his ambassadors was that she would marry him only on condition that he put the kingdom under one sway, as had already been done in Sweden and Denmark. Harald thereupon vowed that he would not cut his hair till he had subdued the whole of Norway, "with scat, duties and lordships"—made a feudal country of it in fact. Finally, he did so in a great battle at Hafrsfjord, off Stavanger, in A.D. 872, after twelve years of continuous fighting. The people, however, did not take kindly to the new laws, which fitted ill with their more democratic form of self-government by families; and many of them went across the seas in further Viking raids, or were forced into exile (Rolf the Ganger, the conqueror of Normandy, was one) for some breach of a system of law and order for which they had no sympathy.

Saint Olav.

Of the earliest efforts to introduce Christianity into Norway, late as they were, we know very little, although there is evidence that Irish priests made some attempts in isolated missions. More definite but vain were the endeavours, in the tenth century, of **King Håkon the Good,** who had been brought up in England at the court of King Athelstan. It was left to **King Olav II**—St. Olav, as he became—who ascended the throne in 1015, to give his countrymen choice between the new faith and cold steel. They took the former, but not before they had tried the latter at the Battle of Stikklestad (north of Trondhjem), where they succeeded in killing Olav, 1030. Londoners will recall with interest that St. Olave's, near Fenchurch Street, the "our owne church" of Pepys the diarist, is dedicated to this royal saint, about whom something more must be said in connection with Trondhjem Cathedral.

Early Christianity.

Christianity overlapped with paganism, however, for some century or more, and it is thought that we may perhaps trace the survival of pagan emblems in the decorations of the primitive Norwegian churches. The stories of the sagas were doubtless more familiar to the bulk of the people than the lives of the saints. Moreover, the introduction of Christianity did not bring with it the inculcation of brotherly love in sufficient degree to stop wanton piracy and pillage. The Norsemen fared a-viking as before, and left in the litanies of southern peoples the plaintive line—

"a furore Normanorum libera nos, Domine."

The practice only died down when, with the economic advance of the later middle ages, the Norwegians began to turn their attention to the internal development of their country. The arts had begun to make some progress; religious houses, at that period the chief disseminators of culture, had begun to establish themselves in Norway, and statecraft had commenced to get the upper hand of anarchy.

The Union with Sweden and Denmark.

Håkon IV restored order in the first half of the thirteenth century, and **Magnus the Law-giver,** 1263–80, put civil government on a sound basis for the first time; many of his laws are substantially in use to-day. With the death of Håkon V in 1319 the male line of Harald Hårfagre's descendants became extinct and the crown passed to Magnus, son of a daughter of Håkon married to a Swedish duke. Magnus's son, Håkon VI, married Margaret, daughter of the Danish King, and their son Olav ascended the throne of Denmark. Four years later, 1380, he was also proclaimed King of Norway, and the two kingdoms thus united remained so until 1814.

Sad is Norway's story during that period. Twenty years after the union of the crowns of Norway and Denmark, hereditary succession led to the well-meant but disastrous Convention of Oslo and the Union of Norway, Sweden and Denmark. For Sweden the step was not a serious matter; the Swedes, richer and more powerful, soon broke away. But for Norway it was disastrous. Her markets passed into the hands of the Hanseatic League, established at Bergen during the reign of Magnus the Law-giver. During the reign of the next Magnus, the grandson of Håkon V, the Black Death swept her valleys of two-thirds of their population, and the old Norse nobility, dying of plague and inanition, was replaced by Danish adventurers. Norway sank into apathy; the budding arts died; liberty, except as a sullen memory, ceased to exist, and social life stagnated.

The Reformation in Norway.

An illustration of this apathy is afforded by the introduction of the Reformation. The movement which in most Teutonic states was heralded with enthusiasm, and which fired the noblest spirits of the time to lay down their lives for an idea, aroused no interest whatever in Norway. In 1520 the movement had some early beginning in Bergen, at that time wholly under the influence of a large resident German community, to whom the Reformation was at least an echo of great events that were going forward in their fatherland. Elsewhere in Norway we hear nothing of it till forty years later, when it came as an administrative change—to which the people were no party—in the hands of ill-educated Danish pastors, in a country where no preparation had been made for its reception, and it probably left the Norwegians at first rather worse off than before.

The reign of **Christian IV** (1588–1648) saw the first signs of amelioration in the internal condition of Norway. The King, according to the lights of the period, had some ideas of town-planning, and his solicitude for the welfare of his realms in this connection gave a certain impetus to Norway's cities. Heavy taxation, however, due to the cost of wars from which the country could derive no benefit, retarded the progress that might have been made. Nevertheless, Norway was already in a condition to take advantage of such possibilities of progress as might accrue as the result of the Danish Revolution of 1660.

The Danish Revolution.

On account of the common governmental system that she shared with Denmark at Copenhagen, Norway did not derive all the benefits from this event that had been hoped for; but she ceased to be a subject principality, and now took the status of being equal with and united to Denmark. This really meant that either Norway or Denmark must rule; and Danish influence was dominant both in the chancelleries of Europe and in those at Copenhagen. The result was that Norway produced no statesmen. Perhaps as a consequence of her exclusion from political life, Norway also produced no art worth speaking of, and no literature at all.

The Union of Norway and Sweden.

But the Norwegians, who, throughout their apathetic submission to the rule of Denmark, had never lost their theoretical feeling for independence, profited by the new status, which was but a stage on the journey to which they were tending. In the year 1814, the Powers allied against Napoleon, having defeated and banished him, compelled Denmark to cede Norway to Sweden. Denmark, which had sided with the arch-enemy, was thus punished, and Sweden, which had lost Finland to Russia, was compensated. The Norwegians, however, did not at all fall in with the idea that they should be handed over to Sweden without a word to say in the matter. They claimed that, their allegiance to Denmark being at an end, they were free to settle their own affairs; and they elected Prince Christian Frederik, who had been viceroy under Denmark, as their King. But Sweden was too strong for them; a brief campaign ended with the Norwegians accepting the terms of the Treaty of Moss, in 1814, whereby the Storting was recognized, and Christian Frederik agreed to abdicate. By the terms of this treaty Norway was left free, but was united to Sweden under a common hereditary King and his descendants; the King appointed a viceroy; the nation was to be represented by the Storting, elected triennially; the Storting alone was to have the right to levy taxes; the legislative authority was to be exercised by the King and Storting together; and the King was to have a suspensory veto, limited to three years, except in cases of alteration of the fundamental law, when the veto was to be absolute.

In 1821, the Norwegians abolished the nobility; later they abolished the office of Viceroy, which had with few exceptions been held by a Swede. On each occasion friction arose between the Storting and the King as to his right of veto.

The Separation from Sweden.

In 1880 these conflicts became much more severe. Norway, with a preponderating maritime trade and a much larger fleet than Sweden, found the necessity of separate consular representation abroad, and followed this up by announcing the need of a separate Foreign Office and separate diplomatic representation. It is probable that these requirements

Wilse,] [*Oslo.*

THE SKJEGGEDALSFOSS, HARDANGER.

Wilse,] [*Oslo.*

HITTERDAL STAVE CHURCH.

[E.N.A.

BORGUND STAVE CHURCH.

were but the outward sign of an inward discontent at being dominated by what the Norwegians could only regard as foreign influence. The quarrel with the King dragged on for some fifteen years, and was then settled by a plebiscite taken on the question of severance from Sweden; 368,208 persons voted in favour of it and 184 against. After overtures made to King Oscar on behalf of his family had been declined, the crown was offered in 1905 to Prince Charles, second son of the King of Denmark, the selection having first been carried by popular vote. The Prince, then in his thirty-fourth year, accepted it, and on June 22, 1906, was crowned at Trondhjem as **King Håkon VII.** Ten years previously he had married H.R.H. Princess Maud (born 1869), daughter of King Edward VII, of Great Britain and Ireland. Their only child, Crown Prince Olav, was born in 1903.

Norway To-day.

The Norwegians, by their moderation and their progressive self-government, have to-day justified the step they took. They are now bent on developing the resources of their country; their watchword is "Alt for Norge," meaning "All for Norway," and they are doing as much as they can without the assistance of foreign capital. With unlimited power at their disposal, derived from the waterfalls of their rugged mountain lands; with a mineral wealth that has never been thoroughly investigated; and with a fine climate and an energetic population, they are beginning to take a place among the industrial countries of Europe. Meanwhile the influx of thousands of visitors annually to the country in search of pleasure is adding considerably to the national wealth.

A LITERARY NOTE.

There is no really first-class history of the whole of Norway published in English. That issued in the *Story of the Nations* series is good of its kind. The subject can be studied with greater thoroughness in *The History of Church and State in Norway*, by the Rev. T. B. Wilson (1903), which covers the period from the earliest times to the middle of the sixteenth century; and in *Scandinavia, a Political History*, by R. N. Bain, which carries events from 1513 to 1905, the year in which it was published. As a concise history of the Norwegian kings from Harald Hårfagre to Håkon the Old,

870–1350, readers are reminded of *The Early Kings of Norway*, by Thomas Carlyle.

The literature of Norway had its beginnings in the folk-tales that survived through the ages. Some of these tales the earliest ancestors of the Norwegian people doubtless brought with them from their Eastern home of origin, for among them are found several story-cycles, such as a version of the "Master Thief" and another parallel with Tell and the Apple, and a third similar to Llewelyn and Gelert—folk-tales that in varying forms are found throughout the world. The best collections are *Popular Tales from the Far North*; Sir George Dasent's *Popular Tales from the Norse* and *Tales from the Fjeld*; and H. A. Guerber's *Myths of the Norsemen*. These myths, however, were not reduced into writing until quite modern times, and in their written form hardly belong to the ancient literature of Norway.

The first dawnings of literary expression are found in the poetical *Edda*, the earliest known form of which was produced by the Norwegian settlers in Iceland in the eleventh century—a consolidation of floating fragments. It was written in Icelandic, which was, of course, the language of Old Norway in the days before the Danish domination. Then there followed (also in Iceland) a period of historical—as opposed to merely heroical—record, which took form in the *Sagas*. These, the *Heimskringla Saga*, the *Orkneyinga Saga* and the *Volsunga Saga*, told the lives of the kings of Norway, and are the earliest foundations of recorded history—with a free admixture of myth and miracle. They have been published in English in the *Saga Library*, edited by William Morris and Eirikr Magnússon; the Volsunga Saga has been issued in the Scott Library. May also be mentioned *Asgard and the Gods* by W. M. Macdonall; *Tegner's Frithjof's Saga*, translated by Holcomb; *The Story of Frithjof*, by J. Henderson. For further details of the literature of this period reference may be made to the *Corpus Poeticum Boreale*, of Vigfússon and York Powell.

The long period of domination by Denmark, right through the Middle Ages down to modern times, crushed out of the Norwegians any temperamental genius for literature. The Danish language having been imposed on Norway, what literature was produced counts as Danish; indeed the Norwegians had little enough to do with it. The birth of modern Norwegian literature—one can hardly call it a revival—did not occur till the beginning of the nineteenth century. Holberg, the satirist and comedy writer, was a native of Bergen, where he was born in 1684; but most of his plays were written in Copenhagen (where he was professor) about Denmark and Danish customs, and the Danes lay claim to him. Wergeland, the poet, was the first to come into notice as striking a true Norwegian note of national inspiration, though there had been sporadic outbreaks immediately before him. The movement he began was followed by Welhaven and Andreas Munch (both national, though in opposition to the methods of Wergeland), Asbjörnsen and Moe (who sought inspiration in the folk-tales of their country) and a host of others. Norway was ripe for the florescence of its literature, for within half a century it had produced in **Ibsen** and **Björnson** two men of first-rate genius. The works of Ibsen are of world-wide reputation, and the extent of his influence upon the drama has not yet been measured. His plays are best known in England in the translations of William Archer. Björnson, a native of the wild Dovrefjell, though he also wrote plays, sought rather the medium of the novel to express the genius of his country. Most of his works have now been collected in an English uniform translation; they depict the life of the people of Norway with intimacy and directness. There is no sign that the vigour of the Norwegian outburst is in any way lapsing; a younger school of novelists, poets, essayists, historians and critics is coming on and is doing excellent work for the nation.

The best-known Norwegian author to-day is **Knut Hamsun,** who in 1920 won the Nobel Prize for his novel *Growth of the Soil.* Several of his books have been translated into English, including *Children of the Age, Pan, Mothwise, Wanderers,* and *Victoria.* One of the most remarkable of the younger writers is the novelist **Olav Duun,** author of *The Juvikingerne* and other works. Then there is the dramatist Nordahl Grieg, a relative of Edvard Grieg, who wrote the music to *Peer Gynt.* His first book, *The Ship Goes On,* published in 1926, was within a year translated into nine languages. In 1927 he published a volume of poems and finished two dramas, *Barabbas,* and *The Love of a Young Man,* works which led the critics to acclaim him a worthy successor of Henrik Ibsen.

Among the lighter reading dealing more or less with the Norwegians and their country, readers may recall, in addition to the works of the novelists and dramatists mentioned above, the following translations: *Dry Fish and Wet*, by Elias Kræmmer; *Into the Dark*, by Barbra Ring; *The Garland*, by Sigrid Undset; *Life*, by Johan Bojer.

With few exceptions the English reader must study Norwegian literature either in the original or through the medium of German.

English interest in Norway has chiefly been as a venue for sport and leisurely travel. It would be impossible here to frame a list of the volumes that have been written on these themes. They began with S. Laing's *Journal of a Residence in Norway*, in the eighteenth century, and they are still going on. At the risk of seeming invidious we will mention Kennedy's *Thirty Seasons in Scandinavia*, Munro's *In Viking Land* (Boston, U.S.A.), Goodman's *Best Tour in Norway*, Spender's *Two Winters in Norway*, *The Land of the Midnight Sun*, by Paul du Chaillu; *Three in Norway*, by Two of Them; C. F. Keary's *Norway and the Norwegians*; *Norway at Home*, by Thomas B. Willson; *Peaks and Pines*, by. A. C. Lees; *Norway and Its Glaciers*, by Forbes; *The Cathedrals of Norway, Sweden and Denmark*, by T. F. Bumpus; Robert Medill's *Norwegian Towns and People*; *The Norwegian Fjords*, produced for the Orient Line by the Medici Society; S. C. Hammer's *Things Seen in Norway*. Mrs. Aubrey Le Blond's *Mountaineering in the Land of the Midnight Sun*, and most especially W. C. Slingsby's *Norway, the Northern Playground*, deserve to be enumerated. The best colour book is perhaps that by Nico Jungman.

The long list of books on sports include *Norway* (in the Modern World Series) by G. Gathorne Hardy; A. Chapman's *Wild Norway*; *Flood, Fell and Forest*, by Sir H. Pottinger, Bart.; F. Sandeman's *Angling Tours in Norway*; Lord Walsingham's *Fish* and also his *Hit and Miss*; *A River of Norway*, by C. Thomas-Stanford; and Bradnock Hall's *Norwegian and Other Fish Tales*.

THE STAVE CHURCHES OF NORWAY.

SO much has been written on this subject that it is not proposed here to offer any original contribution to its literature, but merely to note for the benefit of the traveller the principal features and points of interest these churches present. The classic monograph on the subject is that of Professor Dietrichson, of Oslo University; but it is written in Norwegian. Its principal conclusions are summarized in an appendix to T. B. Willson's *History of Church and State in Norway*, to which the author himself adds some valuable remarks. There is a note on the subject in Bumpus's *Cathedral Churches of Norway, Sweden and Denmark*, while in periodical publications several good papers on the subject have appeared, one in the *Architect* of December, 1894, and one, by Mr. Romilly Allen, in an early number of the *Studio*.

The origin of these stave churches (ancient *wooden* churches) is uncertain. There were formerly some three hundred in Norway, but neglect, fire, and other causes have reduced them to about a score. Those now existing are cared for, and are likely to be preserved. They are found chiefly in the interior, hardly ever near the coast, where stone churches were the rule. Doorways and other specimens of the woodwork of various demolished churches survive in the principal museums.

A reference to the index will indicate the principal stave churches that the ordinary tourist is likely to see.

In the strange structure of the stave churches may be seen the direct influence of the old pagan days, for it is commonly supposed that these wooden churches were fashioned after the style of the Viking ships. In a country where shipbuilders were the best carpenters, wooden buildings constructed by them would be likely to be influenced by the traditions of the shipyard. There is external evidence that goes to support this idea; many features, such as the wooden pillars, the use of knees in support of joins, and the method of locking together planks, certainly smack of the methods of the shipbuilder. The general appearance of these churches, seen end on, is suggestive of ships on the stocks. The practice of ornamenting the gables with dragons' heads is also suggested to have been borrowed from the dragon-head beaks of the Viking ships, though the two may have been derived from some common source. Wooden churches somewhat similar in appearance—that is to say, with the same pagoda-like character—are found in Russia, Bohemia, Hungary and Germany. Professor Dietrichson classified them, and came to the conclusion that they had nothing to do with the development of the Norwegian Stave Churches. The only one he discovered that bore any similarity in method to that of the Norwegian churches was that of Greenstead, in Essex, which was built early in the tenth century, if not earlier, under what circumstances is not known. Christianity came late into Norway. The earliest Norwegian church, Urnes, dates only from the year 1090. There may be no connection between the method of construction of the churches at Greenstead and Urnes except perhaps a common workshop tradition; the method is seen once again in the belfry of Brooklands Church in Kent—for what it is worth. It may be that the churches were direct descendants of the Norwegian Hov, or temple, of pagan times, and that the pioneers of Christianity, although they introduced the new faith with fire and sword, did not despise pagan emblems, just as elsewhere they adopted pagan festivals under new names.

The general appearance of these churches is thus briefly described by Mr. Willson :—

" The church generally consisted of a nave, a chancel, and a semicircular apse, and was surrounded by a sort of cloister (svalgang, or omgang), which was generally open except at the east end, though occasionally, as at Hedalen, it was completely closed in. The entrances to this cloister were opposite the doors of the church itself, and were often in the west end, or under one of the many gables of the roof. From the cloister roof there sprang the wall of the south aisle, then came another roof, and then the nave wall, supporting the largest roof, which was crowned by a pointed tower often placed on a sort of cross roof. The chancel was similarly constructed, though the dimensions were smaller, and there was often no tower, while the apse did not generally exceed two storeys, and was semicircular in shape, often finished off in a small round tower."

A belfry, or klokketårn, often stood beside these stave churches, as at Ringebu, Borgund, and Hitterdal. It has been suggested that this idea may have been brought home by the men who returned from Sigurd's Crusade in 1111, as a reproduction of the campanile.

A school of decoration essentially national in character developed in connection with these churches. On the wooden capitals, and especially on the portals of the doorways, wood-carving, showing the wildest imagination, is found. Birds, beasts, centaurs, dragons, trees and figures are laced and interwoven with an unrestrained exuberance of scroll-work, derived in the first place from Byzantine sources, and debased with pagan admixtures. Sometimes stories from the sagas are found mixed in with the scheme, especially noteworthy in this connection being the jamb of the doorways at Hylle-stad, in the Setesdal, and Vegusdal, where the story of Sigurd, King Gunnar, Regin, the dwarf, with the sword "Gram," the roasting of Fafnir's heart, and the tree with the talking birds—all instances from the Volsunga Saga—may be clearly discerned. It is evident that the scheme of decoration was simpler and more restrained in the earlier than in the later stages; compare the portals of Urnes with those, say, of Fantoft, near Bergen, and Gol, now at Bygdöy near Oslo.

BERGEN.

Approaches.—From Newcastle (p. 13), from Stavanger by steamer (p. 180), from Trondhjem by steamer (p. 183), from Oslo by train (pp. 61–74).

Bands and Concerts.—A band plays in the Town Park almost daily from 1 to 2, and in the summer evenings there are often concerts here and in the Nygårds Park.

Banks.—At Bennett's and Cook's offices. There are several Norwegian banks.

Baths.—Hot and cold baths at the *Sykehus*, near the Theatre, and at the Kurbadet Vestre, Torvgate 11. Sea-baths at Nordnes, at the extremity of the peninsula between the two harbours.

Cafés and Restaurants.—*Norge*, Ole Bulls Plass; *Nobel Spisesal* (Dining Room), Nygådsgate; *Hotel Bristol*, *Hotel Rosenkranz*, Rosenkranzgate; *Börskafeen*, on the Strandgate; *Hotel Terminus*; *Bellevue* (on the hill); *Flöien Restaurant* on top of the Flöien mountain. Many smaller cafés.

Churches.—*St. Maria*, in the Övre Gate which runs parallel with Tyskebryggen (the German Quay); *Johannes Church*, on a hill overlooking the central market square; *Roman Catholic Church*, in Christies Gate; *Cathedral*, in Kong Oscars Gate; *Kors Kirke*, Kong Oscars Gate.

English Church Service.—Apply at a Tourist Office.

Consulates.—*British*, Slots Gate (seaward continuation of Tyskebryggen). *U.S.*, Småstrand Gate (centre of town).

Ferries.—Every few minutes between the landing stages on the Vågen harbour, continuously between Holbergs Almenning and Bradbænken, and between Mur Almenning and the German Quays.

There are ferries from Sukkerhusbryggen to Laxevåg; from Möhlenpris to Damsgård; from the Fish Market to Sandviken.

Hotels.—*Grand Hotel Terminus*, opposite railway station; *Norge*, Ole Bulls Plass; *Rosenkranz* (near the harbour); *Victoria* (facing the cathedral); *Bristol* (Torvalmenning); *Hospitset* (Revelsgården Tyskebryggen); *Raadhushotellet* (Småstrandsgate).

Market Days.—Wednesday and Saturday.

Places of Interest.—*Bergen Museum*, at the top of Christies Gate. Collection of northern antiquities and of peasant crafts. June to September, every weekday, 11–2 and 4–6, Sunday 11–2. The zoological collection is open only 11–1. September to June the Museum is open only Sundays, Mondays, Wednesdays and Fridays 11–2.

Vestlandske Kunstindustri Museum (*Museum of Industrial Art*), facing the town park, round the corner of the Hotel Norge. Weekdays, 11–2 and 4–6; Sundays, 11–2.

The *Art Gallery* is in the same building. Daily, 11–2, admission 50 öre.

Hanseatic Museum, Tyskebryggen (the German Quay). Daily, 10–6. Admission 1 kr.

Håkon's Hall, on the Fortress Quay. Open, 11–1. Admission, 50 öre.

Rasmus Meyer's Picture Gallery, near the Lille Lungegårdsvann. Week-days summer, 11–2 and 4–6. Tuesdays, Thursdays, Saturdays, Kr. 1. Other days free.

Theater Museum, in the old wooden theatre.

Population.—About 100,000.

Porters wear the word *Bybud* on their caps. They will convey luggage from the station and steamers to the hotels in the town. The tariff, fixed according to distance and weight, varies for day work from 50 to 85 öre per 70 kilogrammes (about 150 lb.), for night work from 60 öre to 1 kr.

The porters carry a tariff which they are bound to produce on demand.

Post Office.—Corner of Domkirkegate and Allehelgen Gate, connected with the market square by Småstrandgaten. Open from 8 a.m. to 7.30 p.m. on weekdays.

Telegraph Office, opposite the town park, open day and night.

Telephone Office.—For trunk calls, in the Telegraph Office. There are call offices in all the newspaper kiosks.

Quays.—The Newcastle steamers and the tourist steamers arrive at and start from the quays at the entrance to the Vågen—the Mail Steamers' Harbour, on the right bank proceeding from the town to sea. On the left bank, at the foot of Holbergs Almenning, is the quay of the Hardanger Fjord steamers; a little farther on, near Smeby's Hotel, is the quay for steamers to the Sogn, Sunn and Nord fjords; and at the mouth of the Harbour are the quays for the Hull, Hamburg and Rotterdam steamers.

The pleasure yachts and tourist steamers use the outer harbour known as the Puddefjord, on the west side of the town.

The steamers for the island of Åsköy start from the electric ferry landing-quay at the bottom of the Mur Almenning (left bank of the Vågen).

Railway Station.—On the south-eastern side of the town. One minute from it is a tramway stopping place. At the station is an information office.

Taxicabs are to be found at the station, the piers, and at various places in the town.

Theatre.—*New National Theatre*, in the centre of the town.

Tourist Agencies.—*Bennett's*, Ole Bulls Plass; *Cook's*, Torvalmenning; Travel Bureau, Railway Station.

Trams.—Every five minutes from Holbergsalmenning, via the Market Place and through Kalfaret to Nystuen; from Nordnes to the railway station; from Möhlenpris to the Fæstings Pier and from Sandviken to Minde, on the outskirts of the town.

Few scenes are more charming than that which Bergen presents to those approaching it from the sea on a fine summer evening. Slowly it reveals itself as a place where commerce and beauty exist side by side. A great part is situated on a hilly peninsula. The red church of St. John crowns its highest summit, and the town pours down on all sides to the water's edge, spreading its quays round branches of the Byfjord, where the flags and painted funnels of steamers of every size and nationality add colour to the picture. Then on three sides of the town rise, high above the puny hills of the peninsula, seven mountains, rocky, steep and grey; and on the fourth side are islands of the Skjærgård, sheltering the town from the sea. Bergen has this peculiarity among Norwegian towns that the view, which "composes" charmingly from all points, is not distant but close, and the town therefore seems more in proportion to its surroundings.

Bergen is a place of considerable antiquity. It was old, no doubt, when Olav Kyrre (the Quiet, i.e. Peaceful), the son of Harald Hårdråde, raised it to the dignity of a town in the year 1070. It was a place of great importance in the Middle Ages, when it was noted for the number and splendour of its churches. It was a frequent royal residence, and he scene of the coronation of some of Norway's greatest sovereigns. It suffered much from civil wars in the twelfth and thirteenth centuries, and several times during its history it has been wholly or in part destroyed by fire. After a great conflagration in 1855, it was decreed that there should be no more wooden buildings in the heart of the town, and the destroyed portion was rebuilt in brick and stone. In 1916 Bergen was again ravaged by fire. The central portion of the town—one-twentieth of the whole—was completely destroyed, the damage amounting to 50,000,000 kroner. The municipality seized the opportunity to lay out the area on an improved plan, and architects from the whole of Scandinavia were invited to submit designs.

From far back in the Middle Ages Bergen has been the emporium of Norway's exportation of fish and fish products, dried fish roes and fish oil. When, therefore, the Hanse Towns engaged in the fish traffic, it was natural that the German traders should settle in Bergen. This they did in 1445 and secured the whole of the trade. The Hanseatic merchants had their own quarter of the city where they lived under their own laws, and though more than 150 years have elapsed since the last of their premises became Norwegian property, the Hanseatic quarter is still known by its old name—Tyskebryggen, the German Quay. In the seventeenth century the power of the League declined, and the trade gradually passed to a corporation of native merchants established in the town.

Besides the exportation of fish, shipping is the most prominent feature of the commercial life of Bergen. It participates in the international transportation of merchandise on every sea, and although its ships are largely built in foreign yards, the construction of vessels in its own shipyards is conducted on an extensive scale.

The principal imports are grain, a large proportion of the salt required for the fisheries, and coal. Bergen is the second largest seaport in the country.

As Bergen is so much visited by tourists it may be well to say that spring generally comes early to it, with long bright days and mild evenings. In the beginning of May the trees are in full leaf and by the middle of the month the weather is, as a rule, quite summer-like. The summer is not excessively warm. The winter is mild, but often very rainy.

Visitors sometimes find the ground plan of Bergen a little difficult to master; but the town divides naturally into

Wilse,] *[Oslo.*

BERGEN.

Knudsen & Co.,] *[Bergen.*

THE FISHMARKET, BERGEN.

Knudsen & Co.,] *[Bergen.*

THE TYSKEBRYGGE, BERGEN.

four quarters, with the **Market Square** as centre. We may take for our starting-point the *Statue of Ludvig Holberg*, the Norwegian poet-playwright, born at Bergen in 1684. The famous **Fish Market** of Bergen is held on the quay opposite the statue; it is known throughout the world, and has been painted and described over and over again. One sees it at its busiest and best in the morning between 7 and 10, and especially so on Wednesdays and Saturdays, when the fishermen come in with their boatloads of fish.

Facing the fish quay go to the right and there, alongside the harbour, runs the **Tyskebrygge,** or German Quay. The large wooden premises of the Hanseatic League have in great measure disappeared and have been replaced by stone houses. As these have generally been erected in a style corresponding to that of the earlier buildings, the picturesqueness of the spot in former days has been preserved.

A model of the League's settlement as it was may be seen in the Bergen Museum.

The best preserved of the League's buildings stands on the corner of the quay and is now the **Hanseatic Museum,** a municipal institution (*see* p.52 *re* admission).

In this unique museum, which is not at all like the usual museum, one is suddenly, to the smallest detail, transported back to the life of some hundreds of years ago. The building was both residence and warehouse and is more or less in the state in which a Hanse merchant and his staff lived and in which the merchandise was stored. It must be remembered that the employés of the League were not allowed to marry, this in order that the League might retain its control of the trade; the house is therefore constructed with due regard to the celibacy of the occupant. The outer room shows the tools, apparatus, lamps, and so on, arranged for use. Inside is the parlour, with the neatly kept office books of the merchant, next the dining-room, with the bed for use during the winter months, there being an opening in the wall so that it could be made from outside. Upstairs are the summer bed, and the quarters for workmen and apprentices.

Continuing along Tyskebryggen to the end of the block of buildings, we find there a wide space, Drægsalmenningen. At the lower end is the **British Consulate**. At the upper end is the **Maria Kirke** (St. Mary's Church), Bergen's only church now of particular interest.

This was built in 1183, and bears traces of the Norman influence that had been at work in England for the previous century. The church has two towers, which are probably of slightly later date than the nave. The square pillars separating the nave from the aisles can be paralleled in many instances in England. The Renaissance pulpit is noteworthy, though inferior to that at Stavanger. Note the main entrance doorway, with semi-circular head and heavy and curious mouldings. The church came into the hands of the Hanseatic League in the fifteenth century, and was maintained by them for the benefit of their employés, who were, of course, German. The church passed out of the possession of the League in 1766, but the services continued to be held in the German tongue till modern times, and many of the gravestones in the churchyard bear German inscriptions.

Farther along the quay are the offices of the Nordenfjeldske S/S Co., and of the Bergenske S/S Co. (B. & N. Line). A little beyond this fine building is the **Walkendorff Tower,** or Rosenkranz Tower, as it should more properly be called.

A tower stood here, and was part of the defensive scheme of the town, in the middle of the thirteenth century; this tower is built into the present Walkendorff Tower, which largely owes its present appearance to Count Rosenkranz, the Governor who in the early part of the sixteenth century effectively cowed the Hanseatic merchants in the town. It was restored in 1665.

On the wall near the entrance from the quay is a large bronze tablet placed there in 1921. The inscription, in English and also in Norwegian, is as follows :—" To honour the memory of that great company of true Norsemen who, though at peace with all men, dared to defy the perils and horrors of war, and in a rightful service endured fearlessly to the end. This monument is set up by their friends and admirers in Great Britain."

Just beyond the tower is **Håkon's Hall,** the banqueting hall of King Håkon Håkonsŏn, by whom the building was begun in 1247. In 1261 it was used in connection with the marriage festivities of Magnus the Law-mender, and in it public festivals were held for six hundred years. The Hall has been much restored, chiefly under the direction of the painter Dahl, about 1850. The decorations are by Gerhard Munthe. It gives a good idea of the surroundings amid which royalty and nobility feasted. (*Open* 11–1. *Fee,* 50 öre.) By continuing along the shore we should pass

Bontelbo, and the suburb of **Skudeviken,** a settlement of fish warehouses at the water's edge, and reach **Sandviken,** a picturesque fishing village, with its sheds standing right in the waters of the fjord. We could return from Sandviken by tram, or we could climb the steep side of the mountain to the **Fjellvei,** a fine broad promenade on the lower slope, descending to the market-place by the steep footpath or the gentler road, or instead of descending from the Fjellvei, we could ascend from it to **Flöien** (p. 59), or continue along the level road far into the Isdal Valley and to the Svartedeket Lake, where the road ends in wild surroundings.

Crossing to the opposite (western) bank of the commercial harbour, by the ferry opposite Drægsalmenning, we land at the lower end of **Mur Almenning,** in which stands a building called **Muren,** a toll house at the entrance to the town, erected by Count Rosenkranz in 1561 out of the remains of a monastery. It was at this point that the great fire of 1916 broke out. At *Strand Gaten,* one of the principal shopping streets of the town, we turn to the right, and as we proceed we get on the right occasional glimpses through the narrow alleyways of the waterside life that goes busily on below. At the *Holbergs Almenning,* we have on the right the Hardanger steamers' pier, and on the ridge to the left an open space called Klosteret, where stood the monastery of Munkeliv, from which Count Rosenkranz took his materials for Muren. A short distance farther is **Nykirke** (new church). Its " almenning " (open space) leads down to the pier used by the Sogne Fjord and certain other steamers. Continuing, we come to the **Toldbod** (custom house) **Almenning,** and thence we follow Nordnes Gaten to the point of the promontory of **Nordnes,** which has been laid out as a park.

Returning by the *Haugevei* (" high road "), we have a fine view across the outer harbour, where yachts and warships usually moor. At the derelict citadel of Fredriksberg, erected in 1665, almost the whole of the town and its immediate vicinity can be seen. On the other side of Puddefjord is **Laxevåg** with its shipbuilding yards. At the head of the fjord is Johannes Kirke with the Museum beside it. Eastward (across the Vågen) will be recognized the principal buildings noticed early in the walk, while to the right of Tyskebryggen rise Kors Kirke (Holy Cross Church) and Dom Kirke (the Cathedral).

Haugeveien leads us to **Klosteret,** which we cross and

enter **Klostergate.** Continuing its line we pass *Muren* and enter **Store Marke Vei** in which we almost immediately turn to the right to the **Theatre,** a fine modern building, the first stone of which was laid in 1906 by King Håkon. Before it stands a statue of Björnson, in a pleasant open space called **Engen.** Just westward of it, in *Theatergaten*, is the curious old wooden theatre that did duty before the present one was built. In it Ibsen and Björnson made their first appearance as dramatic authors, and of it each, whilst still a young man, was manager. It is now a museum.

The prime mover in the establishment of the theatre was a native of Bergen, Ole Bull, the great violinist and the founder of the national stage. There is a statue of him in Ole Bull's Plass, before Hotel Norge.

In the Town Park, which we reach by the fine thoroughfare bearing Ole Bull's name, is a statue of another of Bergen's famous sons, *Edvard Grieg*, the exponent of the national music, born in Bergen, on June 15, 1843. The band usually plays here daily (except Saturday) between 1 and 2.

Facing the south-west side of the park, near the Hotel Norge, is the **Vestlandske Kunstindustri Museum** (Industrial and Arts Museum) (*see* p. 52).

Alongside this and the south-eastern side of the park runs **Christies Gate,** a wide thoroughfare named in honour of the first president of the Norwegian Storting and containing his statue at its upper end. Leftward the road leads to the vicinity of the market place, rightward to **Bergens Museum** (*see* page 52).

At the back of the Museum is a pleasant garden which contains the botanical collection, and opposite the main block are buildings which are the embryo of the Bergen University. One is now the Antiquarian Museum and also contains a collection of furniture.

A short distance to the right of the Museum is **Johannes Kirke** (St. John's Church) and by going to the left of the Museum by H. Hårfagres Gate one arrives in a minute or two at the **Nygårds Park,** extensive and well laid-out. From the Park we can return by tram to the Market Place or to the station of the funicular railway to Flöien (*see* below).

From the Market Place *Kong Oscar Gate* goes to the right from Tyskebryggen, and runs near **Korskirken** (the Church of the Holy Cross) and to **Domkirken** (the Cathedral). The former is a large cruciform building of the thirteenth century, but has little to indicate its antiquity. In it the

Wilse,] [*Oslo.*

WALKENDORFF TOWER AND HÅKON'S HALL, BERGEN.

[E.N.A.

FANTOFT STAVE CHURCH.

Lutheran doctrine was first preached in Norway. The Cathedral is a restored Franciscan church, and, although of quite modern appearance, has two thirteenth-century aisles.

THE ENVIRONS OF BERGEN.

Many pleasant excursions may be made in the neighbourhood of Bergen.

1. The first, taken by the majority of visitors, is to **Flöien** (the vane) on the summit of **Flöifjellet,** the hill some thousand feet high skirting the eastern end of the town. It is a much-frequented spot, as there is a good restaurant, and from the elevated site is revealed the full loveliness of the panorama of which Bergen is the centre. The ascent is most speedily made by a funicular railway on which one is carried up in about eight minutes. There is a train every half hour, or more frequently if necessary. The lower terminus is at the upper end of Vetrlidsalmenning, a thoroughfare at the junction of Tyskebryggen and Kong Oscar Gate. One can also drive or walk up by an excellent zigzag road. But except for the young and energetic, it is better to walk down than up.

From Flöien a path leads past the little tarn of Blåmandsvann to the summit of the **Blåmand Mountain** (1,853 feet), reached in about an hour and commanding a still more extensive view.

Those who are going to walk down from Flöien by the zigzag road will go to the little shop near the restaurant and there turn to the left. The road ascends for a short distance and then goes down hill. If it is desired to prolong the descent this may be done by going north-westward through the rugged **Skrædderdal** to Sandviken (p. 57) or in the opposite direction by a path leading to **Möllendal,** whence the return can be made by walking to the southern end of the lake and there taking the tram.

2. To **Fjösanger,** for the church of Fantoft. In point of popularity this excursion rivals that to Flöien. It can be made by motor-car, or Fjösanger can be reached by train in about 18 minutes, whence it is an easy and pleasant walk to the church at **Fantoft.** (*Admission* 1 *kr.*)

This is one of the best examples of the ancient wooden Stave Churches of Norway. It was brought here from Fortun, on the Sognefjord. The church at Fantoft has the principal characteristics of these churches—the massive pillars and runic carving—but it lacks the open ambulatory, and is less interesting in all respects than the church at Hitterdal or that at Borgund. It is, however, one of the sights of Norway, and should not be missed.

3. **Round Arne and Fantoft.** A motor run of about 55 km. (35 miles). The route lies through **Sandviken,** which has many old wooden houses, to **Munkebotten,** which gives its name to a zigzag road affording particularly fine views and leading to an elevation where a mountain panorama presents itself. The route goes to the other side of the mountain range, and there is obtained an extensive view of Eidsvåg, with its wooded mountain crests and the characteristic scenery of the west coast. At **Ytre Arne** there is another wonderful outlook. The route continues through an undulating and beautiful district to **Birkelund** (restaurant), from which Fantoft Stave Church is visited. Thence the route is along Gamleveien *viâ* **Årstad** to Bergen.

Further information respecting this and the following motor tours may be obtained at Bennett's or Cook's Office, where also seats can be booked.

4. **Round Fantoft and Birkelund.** A motor run of about 20 km. (12½ miles).

5. **To Solstrand and back.** About 65 km. (40 miles).

6. **Round Blomsterdalen and Rå.** About 35 km. (22 miles).

The following excursions are made by train or by steamer:

7. **To Os,** on the Samnangerfjord, by train (several a day). The distance is 36 km. (25 miles). At Nestun (10 km.) one must change. Os affords good opportunities of bathing, boating and fishing, and from it there is a magnificent view of the fjord and the Folgefonn Glacier. Half an hour's walk from the station is the Solstrand Hotel. A steamer runs on certain days between Bergen and Os, so that the journey can be made one way by train and the other by boat.

8. **To Ådland,** at the head of the Samnanger fjord, by steamer, taking from 3 to 5 hours.

As the steamer calls at Os, the excursion to that resort can be combined with this.

From Ådland there is an excellent road to Trengereid Station on the Bergen-Oslo Railway, from which Bergen can be reached in 1¼ hours. From Ådland also there is an excellent road to Norheimsund (*Sandvens Hotel*) and Öystese in Hardanger (p. 85). The route lies through grand scenery.

9. **To Asköy,** an island opposite Bergen. It is the site of many summer villas belonging to inhabitants of Bergen. Steamers run to it in an hour three times a day.

THE BERGEN-OSLO RAILWAY.

STEVENSON once wrote that the best way to see country was from the window of a railway train. Perhaps some of the best country to be seen in this way is that traversed by the Bergen-Oslo, or Bergen Railway, as it is commonly called. This line is one of the engineering wonders of Europe; it is also one of the greatest scenic railways of the world. It has been compared with the Riviera railway and with some of the mountain railways of Switzerland, but in reality it stands quite alone. The difficulties it presented are as great as and greater than those encountered elsewhere; and the scenery it unfolds, though as fine as anything in the Alps or along the south coast of France, is of a character quite its own. All the features which combine to make the scenery of Norway so alluring to visitors are unfolded along this line in panoramic succession.

If this journey is made before the end of June, the traveller will do well to take a pair of blue or smoke-tinted spectacles, as the glare from the snow between Myrdal and Geilo is very severe.

The route of this wonderful piece of railway lies across the high mountain chain that runs in a long ridge parallel with the western sea-coast of Norway, and it connects the eastern sides of this range with the western fjords, thus rendering the western coast directly accessible from Oslo and the eastern coast directly accessible from Bergen. The first section built was that from Bergen to Voss, begun in 1875, and completed in 1883. The whole line was completed in 1909. It cost roughly about £3,000,000, nearly one-third of which was for the mountain section.

Before the construction of this railway the journey between the two great cities it connects occupied 54 hours. Now the distance, 307 miles, is covered in from 11¾ to 13½ hours. The time by even the fastest train appears long, but the train has to be hauled from sea-level to an altitude of 4,267 feet, and as the traffic does not warrant the running, even in summer, of more than one through train by day and one by night in each direction, the stoppages are necessarily frequent.

There are buffets at several stations which will be indicated on the pages which follow. There is a restaurant wagon on the day through trains and for a convenient portion of the journey on the night train which leaves Bergen about * 6.20 p.m. on certain days

* *See* footnote, p. 12.

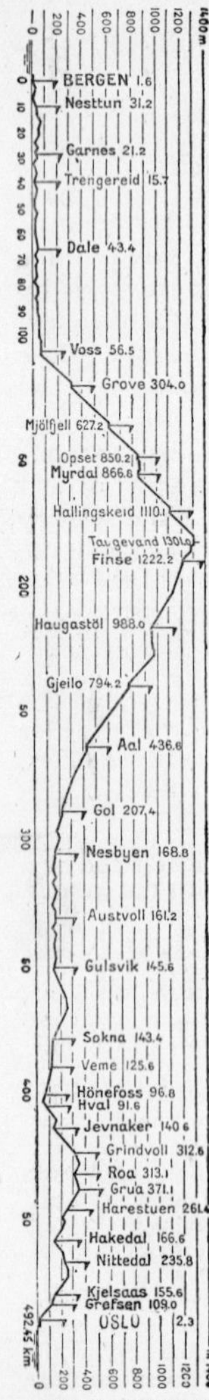

PROFILE SHOWING HEIGHTS ON BERGEN - OSLO RAILWAY.

but not on that which starts later on the other days of the week to connect with the steamer from Newcastle.

For sleeping accommodation and the observation coaches see p. 16.

Unlike those Alpine railways which cross the mountain chain through long tunnels, the Bergen Railway runs over the plateau, for more than 60 miles above the limit of the growth of pines and for half that distance above all tree growth. There are tunnels of course—178 of them with a total length of 23 miles. The longest is that at Gravehalsen between Upsete, 150 km., and Myrdal, 157 km. from Bergen. Its length is 3 miles 514 yards, and trains run through it in 8 to 9 minutes.

In spite of the deep snowfall to which a great part of its route is subject, the line is kept clear even in mid-winter. To protect it from the snow there are some 20 miles of screens and half that length of sheds. Snow ploughs as used in England and Scotland are useless. Special rotary snow machines of 1,000 horse power are employed. The engine of the machine is only concerned with putting in motion the great plough wheel which makes 140 revolutions a minute. The propulsion of the machine is a separate undertaking, often requiring two and even three locomotives.

Leaving **Bergen** station, the line skirts the base of Flöifjellet on the left, and on the right affords a good view of the beautiful suburbs of the town and the snowy mountains to the south. Very soon we are among farms and orchards, lakes, streamlets and waterfalls are passed, and wooded mountains rise about us, becoming higher and higher and more and more snow-covered as we advance.

From **Nesttun** Junction a line runs southward to **Fana** for **Lysekloster** (once a Benedictine nunnery), and **Os** (p. 60). Near Os is the pretty seaside place of **Solstrand** (*Solstrand Hotel*), which can also be reached from Bergen by steamer.

From Nesttun the line turns northward past Heldal and Haukeland, through the most varied scenery of hills and heather, rocks and marsh, with stony streams fed by mountain runnels. At Arna we strike the shore of the **Sör Fjord,** an arm of the Bergen fjord. **Arna** is but a group of wooden houses among the grass slopes that fall away to the level of the fjord ; but the engineers who built the line to Voss had cause to know it well, for it was from Arna to the head of the fjord that they encountered their greatest difficulties. The walls of rock fall almost sheer to the fjord, and the difficulties of running a line along them must have been stupendous. Tunnel succeeds tunnel ; the slightest ledge is taken advantage of, and where there is no ledge embankments have been built. So it continues for some 20 miles. Garnes (29 km.) is beautifully situated on the shore of the Sőr Fjord of which we have a view as the line winds along the inlet past rocky islands to **Trengereid** (40 km.).

At Trengereid motors await passengers who wish to pass over the mountains which separate the Sör Fjord from the Hardanger Fjord—one of the finest motor runs in the country. It is a run of less than three hours to **Norheimsund** (*Sandvens Hotel*) (p. 85) from which Hardanger may be explored. The road, 51 km. long, lies through **Ådland** (*Ådlands Hotel*), at the head of the Samnanger Fjord, and through *Tysse*, passes the beautiful **Eikedalsfoss** coming from the Eikedalsvann, at the end of which is the *Kvamshaug Hotel*. The road follows the lake and then ascends to **Kvamskogen** (*hotel*), a tableland some 1,200 feet above the sea level. Thence it descends a wild ravine, the **Tokagjel.** Cut out of the face of the cliff, with the river hundreds of feet below and passing through a tunnel at two of the turnings, the road zigzags down into the Steinsdal, along which is its final section, a level stretch of 5 km. passing the *Öfsthusfoss*, a fall under which one can walk.

Still following the Sör Fjord, the line proceeds through a grim country of perpendicular rocks and tree-clad slopes, with only a few isolated patches of arable land, where hard-working peasants wring a bare existence from stern nature. At **Vaksdal,** 52 km. (*buffet*) there are several mills and a beautiful view over the fjord, which at **Stanghelle** (60 km.) we leave for a time, and following the Dale river strike across the peninsula to **Dale** (67 km.) (*Dale Hotel*), another town with factories.

There is a motor service between Dale and the mountain lake of **Hamlegrö** (*hotel*), 2,000 feet above sea-level. The road, cut on the face of the mountains, passes through the **Bergsdal**, an exceedingly fine ravine between mountains rising to a height of some 4,000 feet. Very far below the road rushes a great river coming from the lake and making five falls in its course. In the valley also is one of Norway's largest *jettegryter* (giants' cauldrons), bowl-like cavities formed by the action of water on the rock.

From Hamlegrövann a bridle path leads down to **Öystese,** a charming place on the Hardanger Fjord (*Öystese Turisthotel*).

Soon after leaving Dale, we strike the **Bolstad Fjord,** an arm of the Sör Fjord, narrower and still steeper. Soon we pass **Bolstadöyri** (78 km.), and wind by many tunnels along the Evanger river to **Evanger** (89 km.) (*Monsens Hotel*), where we finally leave the inlet. Next we reach **Bulken** (99 km.) (*Hotel Liland*) situated at the western end of the Vangsvann (Evanger lake). Here one can have good fishing and take pleasant walks.

From Bulken there is a fine route to Hardanger, but except for the short distance from Bulken to **Skjeldal** one must walk or go on horseback. From the end of the driving road there is a bridle path to *Hodnabergseter* on the Hamellgrö lake, from which a well-marked path ascends to **Lökedalsnut,** the site of a small shooting box and a magnificent view point. Three thousand feet below is the valley. Southward are the mighty walls of the **Fyksesund,** a narrow arm of the Hardanger Fjord. Also in view are the wooded peninsula of Öystese and in the background the Folgefonn glacier. A zigzagging path leads down to the valley to **Botnen** or **Flatebö** at the head of Fyksesund. Thence the route is to **Skåre** on the inlet, and then by a road across the peninsula to **Öystese** (see above). This excursion will take from 9 to 10 hours.

From Bulken the line skirts the Vangs lake to—

Voss.

Buffet.—At the Station.
Hotels.—*Fleischers*, at the Station; *Prestegårds*, *Vossevangen*, *Missions*, and several pensions.

Voss (107 km. from Bergen, and 385 from Oslo) is an important tourist centre, as it lies at a parting of ways. At the same time it attracts many visitors by reason of its charming situation, which is on the shore of a placid lake, surrounded by fertile slopes and pine forests, with the snow-covered crest of Gråsiden in the background. There is fishing for salmon and trout and shooting also may be had. In winter the ski association of Western Norway holds here its races, and a trotting match is held on the lake. The parish has what is something of a rarity in rural Norway,

Photos by] [*Wilse and Mittet & Co.*

SCENES ON THE BERGEN-OSLO RAILWAY.

Wilse,] [*Oslo.*

THE NÆRÖ VALLEY, FROM STALHEIM.

a stone **Church.** It dates from the thirteenth century, and by its size testifies to the importance of the place in past ages.

There are several interesting walks in the neighbourhood of Voss. One is that to **Finneloft,** about half a mile west of the church, a fifteenth-century wooden house, now turned into a museum of clothing, ornaments, furniture and other household articles of the district. Another is to the **Breidablik,** about a mile and a half from Voss on the opposite shore of the lake; from the chalet inn in the woods there is a fine view across the lake to Voss. There are several lesser peaks in the immediate neighbourhood to tempt rock-climbers, and the **Lönehorge,** a mountain to the north of Voss, can be ascended (4,670 feet) in about four to five hours. The **Hondalsnut** (4,780 feet) can also be ascended from Voss in about five hours.

From Voss there are daily motor services to **Stalheim, Eide** and **Ulvik.**

1. To **Stalheim** (for Gudvangen).—The distance is 32 km. (20 miles) and the time occupied is 1 hour 40 minutes. The road leads northward out of the village past the base of the Lönehorge. On the left **Tvinde** is passed, with the **Tvindefoss** falling from the mountain ridge beside the *Tvinde Hotel*. The drive proceeds through a romantic valley, which narrows and widens, and has many falls providing power needed by the slate works. Sometimes the cliffs rise sheer above the road, and threaten it with overhanging masses of rock, sometimes they recede into the distance and the valley becomes a smiling countryside. At 18 km. from Voss is **Vinje** (*Vinje Hotel*). The village is pleasantly situated, with lofty, light grey mountains surrounding it. About 3 km. farther is **Framnes.**

The road continues along the northern bank of the **Opheim Lake** past the *Opheim Hotel* near the church, and soon there comes into view the Jordalsnut, a conical mountain of grey syenite, rising to a height of 3,600 feet out of the Nærö valley, in the centre of a group of peaks. The road rises slightly to **Stalheim** (*Hotel Stalheim*), a good centre for walks and climbs, of which one is to the summit of the mighty **Jordalsnut,** a less difficult feat than it appears to be, and requiring only three hours for its accomplishment. Another attraction is a good trout stream.

From the garden of the hotel there is a wonderful view of the dark, deep **Nærö Valley.** Down 1,000 feet of sheer precipice one looks on the road which runs through the valley to **Gudvangen,** 15 km. (*Hotels Vikingvang and Gudvangen*), a calling place for steamers on the Nærö Fjord (p. 94).

The road between the lofty site of the Stalheim hotel and

the bottom of the valley winds in fourteen sharp curves on the face of the famous **Stalheim Klev,** up or down which one has to walk. Motor bicycles are allowed upon it but not cars, and none but the utterly impotent person would go up in a stolkjerre, which empty is a sufficient load for the horse.

During the descent two great falls are passed, the **Stalheimfoss** on the right, the **Sivlefoss** on the left, one of the most lovely although not one of the most famous in the country. From the other, which is less well seen, the hotel obtains its electric power. At the foot of the hill are motors and stolkjerres for the passage through the valley, one of the most imposing in Norway. Of the lofty and precipitous mountains which border it, the Jordalsnut, on the left, is the most dominating, but the highest is the **Kalafjell,** on the right, which has an elevation of 4,265 feet. There are numerous falls and in spring avalanches of stones are frequent. The narrowest part of the valley is at the lower end and is so overhung by mountains that between October and February the sun does not reach the bottom of it. On the opposite side of the river to Gudvangen is the **Kilefoss,** which comes from a height of 2,000 feet, but except in the periods of rain or melting snow there is little water. Anyone who is not going to sail on the fjord can obtain a good idea of it by walking along the path on the left shore from Gudvangen to Bakke (p. 84).

2. To **Eide,** about 30 km. (*Mælands Hotel*). It is a small but popular tourist resort charmingly situated on a narrow branch of the Hardanger Fjord. The road (soon to have a rival in a branch railway from Voss) crosses the Voss river and gradually ascends. It continues to ascend through the pine forest of Langskogen to the watershed, from which it descends in great curves into the gorge of Skjervet. On the left is the **Skjervefoss.** At the foot of the fall the stream from it is crossed. Looking back, the stream, bridge, river and rugged rocks make a most delightful picture. At the bottom of the valley is another fall, the **Skorvefoss,** on the left. Through grand scenery the road goes to the hamlet of Seim (or Övre Vassenden) at the northern end of the beautiful **Granvinvann,** which it then follows, in places being cut out of the rock. From the southern end of the lake the road follows the river through a prettily wooded glen to the sea.

3. To **Ulvik,** 45 km. (*Hotels*: *Brakanes,* close to the fjord, *Vestrheim* in a garden, and *Ulvik*). This small village is a very popular summer resort on the Osa Fjord, a narrow branch of the Hardanger Fjord. The route to it is that to Eide as far as the church of Granvin, whence it ascends to the left to **Lake Espeland,** 1,125 feet above sea level, where a grand view opens. In front is the snow-crowned **Mount**

Vasfjörö, 5,364 feet. To the left are the peaks of Stavskarnuten and Sotenuten. Skirting the small Lake Stokke, the road continues through the forest and along the river to a bridge where the stream by precipitating itself into a deep cleft forms the beautiful Verafoss. Passing through the pine forest and deep gorge we reach the gateway to the pass at Hyllaklöven, with splendid views of Ulvik, the fjord and the surrounding mountains.

From Ulvik there is an attractive walk to the **Solsi Lake** and Seter (farm), from which Vasfjörö can be ascended with a guide. Good walkers can go on from Solsi to **Upsete** on the Bergen railway.

At Voss we enter upon the mountain section of the line. At Voss the line is only 185 feet above sea level; 60 km. (37½ miles) farther it is at a height of 4,082 feet, and for that climb an extra engine has to be attached to the train. On the outskirts of Voss the line crosses the Strande river, passes through a fertile district to **Ygre,** 113 km., and beyond that we come to the wild gorge known as the **Sverreskar,** taking its name from King Sverre, who, with a band of his followers, made his way from Voss to Sogn, in the depth of winter, through this supposedly impassable pass. This took place in 1177, when he had not yet obtained full possession of his kingdom. When tunnels permit, one has a good view of the ravine on the right. **Grovu,** 121 km., is passed, and then we get a fine view of the **Lönehorgen** to the west, and to the south of the *Hondalsnut*, at the foot of which is **Reime,** 130 km. Hereabouts snow protections begin to be necessary, the air grows colder, and after Reime the pines begin to disappear and birches are the principal trees until they, in their turn, have to yield to the rigour of the climate. At **Mjölfjell,** 138 km., we have on our left the *Rjoandedal*. Continuing, we pass through snowsheds and may get a glimpse of the highest farm, *Kleivene*, far up on the hill side. Then we pass through the *Örnebjerg* mountain, through other tunnels and snowsheds, and at the *Langevann* we enter a treeless district, through which we pass along the banks of the lake to **Upsete,** 150 km. (*Opset Höifjells Hotel*). On leaving Upsete we enter the **Tunnel of Gravehalsen,** the longest on the line (it is 3 miles 514 yards, and took twelve years to bore). It leads through the mountain to **Myrdal** (157 km. from Oslo; 2,844 feet high; very good *station restaurant*. About 20 minutes' walk from the station is the *Valnahalsen Hotel*. Its stolkjerres meet the trains.)

Myrdal lies near the great **Storskavlen Glacier,** to which expeditions can be made. The valleys in the neighbourhood offer excellent ground for ski-ing, and it is the turning-point for travellers who are proceeding to the Sogne Fjord *viâ* the Flåmsdal.

Myrdal to the Sogne Fjord.—From Myrdal the road descends the Flåmsdalskleiva by a number of sharp winds into the **Flåm Valley,** the mountains on either side rising to a great height. The scenery on the road through the bottom of the valley is as fine as anything on the Stalheim road, some would say finer; travellers having descended the winding road should look back at the route by which they have come. The valley narrows, and the walls rise so precipitously that at one point they have had to be tunnelled; in places it widens among the picturesque farms and orchards. Two fine waterfalls, the **Leirfoss** and the **Rjoandfoss,** are passed as we near the mouth of the valley; then, proceeding through the village of **Flåm,** we come to the junction of the river with the Aurlands Fjord, and to the *Hotel Fretheim.* The distance from Myrdal is 20 kilometres.

A railway is in course of construction, but the road is the prettier route. The valley is so exceedingly beautiful that a good pedestrian would feel well paid for his walk through it.

Quite near Hotel Fretheim is the pier from which the steamer may be taken to Bergen by the Sogne Fjord, or to one of the many tourist resorts on the Fjord and its arms. Travellers making their way from Bergen to Oslo sometimes take the morning steamer from Bergen to Fretheim and drive to Myrdal, where they join the train.

Leaving Myrdal, we begin the grandest part of the route, the ascent of the great mountain range that divides eastern from western Norway. Between tunnels one catches glimpses of most imposing scenery. Down sheer precipices of 2,000 feet we look into the Flåm Valley. Then far below us, yet far above the valley, a glimpse can be had of the hotel at **Vatnahalsen,** occupying one of the most remarkable positions among the hotel sites in Europe. Often, as the train ascends past the Reinunga Lake along precipitous ledges from one high-lying valley to another, we look down into rocky gorges where an opalescent river, fed by mountain snows, rushes foaming through its boulder-strewn bed. A chain of mountain tarns among the snowy fjells provides a course for the line, which makes its way up to **Hallingskeid** (170 km.; *Fjellstova Hotel*), a lonely station at an elevation

Wilse,] [*Oslo.*

THE FLÅMSDALSKLEIVA.

Wilse,] *[Oslo.*

FINSE IN WINTER.

of 3,642 feet amid a mountain waste. Its sole attraction is a mountain route (difficult, and to be attempted by climbers only), *viâ* Osa to the Eid Fjord and the Hardanger. The great **Hardanger Jökul** (*jökul* means glacier), a series of dentine peaks, rough and jagged, comes into view as we leave the snowy levels of Hallingskeid; the train climbs steadily upward, the view ever increasing in the grandeur of the snows, as we pass along the fringe of the small mountain lakes of the Lågheller and round the edge of the Vossaskavl and the Osaskavl, with distant views of the Hallingskarv on the left. At **Taugevann** the highest point of the line is reached; it is marked by a cairn of great stones set up at a height of 4,267 feet. Only small points of black rock pierce the snow, while the view of the mountains stretches away in every direction, a blinding field of whiteness. Ice floes lie in the little lakes throughout the year, and it is less than winter here for a few short weeks only. Farming, of course, is impossible in these lofty tracts, but herds of cattle are kept at the summer pasturages and great droves of half-wild horses roam about.

The descent begins very gradually, and the line, skirting the Finsenut and the Finsevann, soon arrives at—

Finse

(190 km., 4,008 feet above the sea, *Buffet, Finse Hotel*). This is the highest station on the line.

It is winter nearly all the year at Finse, and the place has consequently a great reputation among the followers of winter sports. For one thing, it is situated above the tree line, and the runs are free from a terror that often confronts even the most expert ski-runner. For another, owing to the length of the days in spring, it enjoys more sunshine than any other winter-sport centre. On the glaciers, about three miles from the hotel, ski-ing is possible all the year round; but the best season is from February to May, when the daylight is long, the sunshine transforms the landscape into a scene of dazzling beauty and the keen air is a source of delight. The place affords as fine grounds for the beginner as for the expert, and for every grade between them. Even in summer one may obtain ski-ing instruction in the vicinity of the hotel.

For visitors staying at Finse warm windproof clothes are necessary at all seasons.

The principal tour is that to the *Demmevann Hut*, about

four hours distant from Finse. The lake is dammed up by the Rembesdals glacier, hence its name, of which the literal meaning is dam-water. The road is marked by cairns as far as the glacier; in another four hours the expert skier can reach Simadal on the Eidfjord, but is advised to take a guide.

Other expeditions from Finse are: to the *Steinbergdal Hut*, to the *Fagernut*, *Norenut*, the *Finsenuts*, and to the *Hallingskarv*. There are many others, a mere list of which would take too much space; but information is readily obtained at Finse, which exists primarily for the winter sportsman. At the same time it must not be forgotten that others who love alpine scenery, as climbers, as pass-stormers, as botanists, and even merely as admirers, will find Finse a wonderful place, and an entire change from Switzerland.

From Finse the train descends some 800 feet through the wild scenery that will now have become familiar. We pass from the Hardanger mountain district into the **Halling Valley,** the home of the race of Hallings, a race that from long separation from the rest of their countrymen—owing to the lack of communication with their valley—have maintained the curious customs of life and dress that have been developed during the centuries of their isolation. At weddings and other festive occasions the peculiar Halling dance, somewhat resembling a reel, is still a part of the proceedings. The girl is whirled round by her partner, who brings the dance to an end by kicking the rafters in a flying jump. The valley is now in touch with the railway and the world, but the tenacity of the Hallings for their dress and their dialect (which betrays their Western Norway origin, though geographically they belong to the East) is likely to continue.

Passing along the lower slopes of the Bergsmulnut we approach the shore of the **Stöle Fjord** and its continuation, the large **Ustevann,** on the north shore of which is the station of **Haugastöl,** 217 km., 3,240 feet (*Haugastöl Hotel*). There are sailing and rowing boats on the lake and Haugastöl also is a good winter sports centre.

A magnificent motor road, completed in 1928, connects Haugastöl with **Eidfjord,** on the Hardanger Fjord, 65 km. distant. It runs *viâ* **Maurset** and **Fossli,** passes the wonderful Voringfoss waterfall and goes through the wild **Måbödal.**

From Haugastöl the **Follarskarnut,** 6,406 feet, can be ascended in about 5 hours. The return occupies 3½ hours. Among the other excursions which can be made are—

(1) By boat to **Horneboseter** and thence to **Tuveseter**, about 1½ hour's walk.
(2) To **Krekjahytten Tourist Hut** (3 hours).

Continuing along the Uste Fjord, the train descends into the Ustedal, at the head of which is—

Geilo,

240 km., altitude 2,604 feet. (*Hotels : Dr. Holm's, Breidablik ; Ustedalen Sanatorium* and *Geilo.*) Geilo marks the end of the mountain crossing ; the landscape loses its forbidding aspect here, trees grow, corn ripens, and the scenery changes to that of Eastern Norway, with belts of conifers and fertile valleys. It is much frequented in summer ; and with the completion of the road into the Numedal is likely to attract even more visitors. It is a delightful place for a restful holiday or for walking excursions into the verdant hills that surround it.

From it all the principal mountains in the district can be easily reached, and it is a good centre for ski-ing and other winter sports.

From Geilo one can now conveniently visit the **Numedal** (p. 163). There is a good road with a motor service to **Rödberg,** 65 km. from Geilo, and from Rödberg there is a new railway to **Kongsberg,** 93 km., connected by rail with Oslo (see p. 162).

The descent is rapid through **Hol,** 251 km., to **Ål,** 264 km. *Buffet* (*Sundre Hotel*). Ål, 1,433 feet above sea level, is not much visited by tourists, though its surroundings offer many pleasant walks. Near the hotel, which stands on a hill on the opposite side of the river to the station, are two very interesting old buildings, both curiously carved. One is a Thingstue, erected in the eighteenth century and originally used for meetings of the Thing ; the other, called Gretestuen, is a typical Halling log-house. Continuing on the same side of the river we reach **Torpe,** 274 km. On the hill on the opposite side of the river stand a modern church and a **Stave Church,** probably dating from 1200. It is not now used. It has a very fine western doorway.

The descent through the Hallingdal is now very rapid, and the landscape increases in verdant beauty as we approach **Gol,** 290 km., altitude 678 feet (*Hotels : Rolfshus,* and several others. In the neighbourhood, *Kamben Seter Hotel.*) Gol is a pleasant village, with walks among the slopes of the Golsreppen and the Skogshorn. It is more important as a stopping-place for travellers by reason of its being at the junction of important road routes.

From Gol there is a motor service *via* **Hegg** and **Borgund** (p. 76), to **Lærdalsöra** (p. 76), on the Sogne Fjord (*Lindströms Hotel*), a day's steamer journey from Bergen. Also *via* Hegg, **Maristua** (*Maristuen Hotel*), **Nystua** (*Nystuen Hotel*) to **Tyin** (*Hotel*) and *via* **Skogstad** to the railway at **Fagernes** (p. 80). Also from Gol there are (1) a road *via* **Fjellheim** to **Björgo** station on the Valdres railway (p. 80); (2) a road *via* **Heslabro** to **Oset** on the Tisleia lake, and (3) a road thence to **Aurdal,** on the Valdres railway.

On leaving Gol the line goes towards the south-east, into the broad Hallingdal proper. At **Svenkerud,** 298 km., it crosses the river, and then runs through fine pine forests to **Nesbyen,** 307 km. (*Hotels : Öyes* and others; in the neighbourhood *Buvassbrenna Hotel*). Nesbyen is the administrative centre of the district and the site of **Hallingdals National Museum.**

There is a summer motor service between Nesbyen and **Tunhövd** on the fjord or lake of the same name.

Below Nesbyen we run for some miles through the fertile but rather monotonous valley. The river widens considerably as we near **Flå,** 340 km. (*Vik Hotel*), and soon we approach its junction with Lake Kröderen at **Gulsvik,** 352 km. (*Hotel Granheim*). The lake is a long winding stretch of water between the desolate Norefjell on the west and the Satefjell and Blodfjell on the east. There is a motor service between Gulsvik and **Kröderen,** at the southern end of the lake, and between the latter place and **Vikesund,** from which Oslo can be reached *viâ* Sandviken.

From Gulsvik the line goes along the eastern side of the lake, over which there are beautiful views, to **Örgenvika,** 364 km. Here the lake is left and the line goes through tunnels and passes **Rallerud,** 372 km., before reaching **Sokna,** 380 km., from which it goes through the *Soknadal*, wooded and monotonous, to **Veme,** 392 km. Thence it descends through **Nökleby** to **Hönefoss,** 403 km.

Hönefoss

(**Buffet. Hotels:** *Glatveds, Grand, Fönix.*)

is an industrial town of some 3,000 inhabitants, and an important tourist centre by reason of its surroundings and the many roads and routes that converge here. Millions of logs are pulped in Hönefoss every year for the manufacture of paper, and there are many subsidiary undertakings, such as saw-mills and cellulose factories. Through being used for industrial purposes, the **Falls** have lost their impressiveness except in spring, when the water is high. They are best seen from the bridge over them. At half an hour's walk from them on the road to Hen is the **Hofsfoss,** often worth seeking, and half an hour's walk farther is the **Svinefoss.**

The neighbourhood of Hönefoss abounds in pleasant walks and drives : to **Norderhov** (p. 153), on the Sundvollen road ; to **Ask,** on the western shore of the Tyri Fjord (p. 152) (the return can be made by train) ; to **Vik, Krokleiva** and **Sundvollen** (p. 152) ; through the Aadal to **Lake Sperillen** ; to the **Rands Fjord** (the return may be made by train) ; westward along the **Soknedal** and to the **Ringkollen,** a mountain about 5 miles east of Hönefoss, 2,270 feet, in about 2½ hours to the summit, which commands a fine view of **Ringerike,** one of the most beautiful parts of Eastern Norway. The motor route between Hönefoss and Oslo, 60 km., passes through it. Cars each way four times a day in 2½ hours.

The train, on leaving Hönefoss, takes a north-easterly direction, crosses the Randselv above the falls which give the town its name, and passing stations at **Hval**, 407 km., **Viul,** 409 km., and **Kistefoss,** 412 km., continues through the valley to the southernmost shore of the Rands Fjord by **Jevnaker,** 416 km., where there are pulp works, and turning eastward again joins at Roa the line from Fagernes and Gjövik to Oslo, having crossed the heights above the Rands Fjord at Hadeland.

The **Rands Fjord** is a lake notable in Norwegian history because one of the most respected of the early kings, Halfdan the Black, was drowned in it in the spring of 860, through the ice breaking beneath his sleigh. He was so very highly esteemed and was thought to have so much influence with the gods that each of the four provinces of his kingdom insisted upon giving him a grave. Civil war was averted by the provinces agreeing that the body should be divided into four parts, of which each province should have one. This is the reason why there may be seen to-day four burial mounds of Halfdan the Black.

From **Roa,** 435 km. (*Roa Hotel*) we go southward through woods and fine farming districts, passing stations at **Grua, Björgeseter, Harestua, Hakadal, Aneby** and **Nittedal,** 468 km., all on the borders of the great **Forest of Nordmark,** which stretches southward as far as Oslo, and is undoubtedly the most extensive and pleasant natural park possessed by any great city. Then, past the **Maridal Lake,** we descend through the suburb of **Grefsen,** 485 km., situated at the top of one of the high hills surrounding Oslo. From it the view includes the city, many of the suburbs, the wooded mountains rising around the city, and the Oslo Fjord with its charming islands. Seven kilometres farther we enter the Östbane station, the terminus of the line at **Oslo.**

THE FILEFJELL-VALDRES ROUTE.

Routes.—From Bergen to Lærdalsöra by steamer, either direct (pp. 90–95) or *viâ* Fretheim (p. 68) or Gudvangen (p. 65), one day. Lærdalsöra or Lærdal by motor service to Fagernes.

Alternative routes from Fagernes: Train to Oslo, train or drive to Bjorgö, by public motor to Sörum, steamer down Lake Sperillen to Sperillen, and train to Oslo. Or, train from Fagernes to Odnes, steamer down the Rands Fjord to Röykenvik or to Randsfjord station, thence train to Oslo.

Valdres is one of the principal valleys between Eastern and Western Norway. Its great scenic beauty has gained for it the proud title of "the Pearl of the Norwegian valleys." In it are many places suitable for a long stay either in summer or in winter and it gives easy access to the Jotunheim.

Filefjell is a mountain at the western end of the valley.

THE road over the Filefjell and through the district of Valdres is one of the oldest lines of communication between Western and Eastern Norway. It was known in the thirteenth century, and probably earlier. Mountain hospices existed in those early times, supported by, and belonging to, the State. The road in those days was little better than a cattle-track, and the crossing of the mountain ridge separating Western from Eastern Norway was doubtless attended with many dangers. It was from the earliest times the Royal route across Norway, and the farmers of its valleys enjoyed certain privileges of immunity from taxation in consequence of their liabilities in respect of it. The Valdres side, on the east, plays a considerable part in Norwegian history, and was visited by the kings in remotest times; but the Filefjell section, which was the real mountain crossing, must have presented extraordinary difficulties in the Middle Ages and even down to quite modern times.

Nowadays this has all been changed; the man who crosses the Valdres Route has no claim to be thought a great traveller, but merely one who knows where exquisite scenery is to be found combined with exquisite comfort. It is doubtful whether the intrepid men who crossed by this route even as late as the eighteenth century had the leisure to enjoy the views that change and charm throughout the valley; our more degenerate age gives us this advantage.

The westernmost portion of the route—that from Bergen to **Lærdalsöra,** at the head of the Sogne Fjord—is described on pages 90–95. From the broad plain formed of deposits of débris washed down from the mountain valleys, the road winds up through the valley, gently at first, but becoming gradually steeper. At 11 km. from Lærdalsöra it reaches the first village of any importance, **Blåflat.** The road continues alongside the river through a narrow and charming valley in which are many fine falls. On the opposite side of the stream may be seen the steep mediæval road called *Gallene.* Traces of two other ancient roads are found hereabouts. At **Husum,** 26 km. (*Hotel*), the wildness of the route begins. (Starting near Husum and following the telegraph poles one can walk to Borgund in about an hour, along the road which King Sverre used in 1177.) The driving road goes through a gorge, a splendid piece of wild country. Soon **Borgund,** 30 km. (*Borgund Hotel*), is reached. Here is a fine stave church, black with age. It dates from 1138 and is one of the most interesting of its kind. Originally there were no windows. The cloister (the *svalgang*) round the building is perfect. Over the doorway are runic inscriptions. It was in use until 1870, when the church near it was erected. Near the ancient church is its old belfry. The stave church is now under the care of the Norwegian Society for the Preservation of Antiquities. To see it, ask at the hotel.

After Borgund we follow the road, which still winds up through the river valley, with high hills on either side, until, at 39 km. from Lærdal, we reach **Hegg** (*Hegg Hotel*). The name of this place, like that of many others in Norway, is variously spelt. From Hegg a road with a motor service goes *viâ* Breistölen (*Hotel*) and Bjöberg to **Gol** on the Bergen railway (p. 71).

Now the valley mounts rapidly, past **Bor'ang** towards Maristua; here in this sharp rise we begin to leave the fresh vegetation of Western Norway and to ascend to the bare wastes of the Filefjell, the mountain crossing. Already at **Maristua,** 50 km. (*Hotel Maristuen,* open June 1 to Sept. 31 and at Easter), we are among the real mountain scenery. The situation of the place—formerly a Government hospice, founded about 1300, and still retaining obligations towards travellers that are reminiscent of its early origin—is very

Wilse,] [*Oslo.*

LÆRDALSÖRA.

Wilse,] [Oslo.

THE VANGSMJÖSA.

fine. It stands on a kind of plateau, 2,400 feet above sea-level, encircled with ranges of snow-capped hills, and commands a glorious view towards the Lærdal valley. For those who care to stay for a few days in high altitudes, Maristua is ideal. There is good trout-fishing near the hotel, also grouse shooting. On the neighbouring mountains herds of tame reindeer are often seen.

There are several easy climbs to be made in ascending degrees of difficulty, chief among which are the **Brunshöi** (in 2 hours), the **Bleia** (in 6 hours), and the **Suletind** mountain, 5,300 feet, and lake (in 6 hours), while there are many pleasant and easy walks along the main road in both directions, as well as along the old road between Maristua and Nystua, and in about 4 hours one can walk or ride across the mountains to Bjöberg on the motor car route between Hegg and Gol (*see* above).

After we leave Maristua the road leads upward through a barren wilderness beside a chain of fine lakes. The highest point of the journey, the road summit of the Filefjell, is passed on this stage of the journey; the altitude is 3,529 feet. The point is marked by a stone, but is also easily distinguishable by the fact that it is the watershed between the two sides of the "Keel." A slight drop brings us to **Nystua,** 67 km. (*Nystuen Hotel*), another of the old hospices, at the height of 3,000 feet. Its situation on the Utrovann, at the east end of the Filefjell, is very beautiful, and it rivals Maristua as a place in which to spend a mountain holiday. Big mountain trout abound in the Utro Lake, and during the shooting season ptarmigans are plentiful.

The principal excursion is the ascent of the **Stugunose** (4,300 feet, 3½ hours up and down, 33 km. distant), the Rigi of this part of the world. The view of the **Jotunheim,** the promised land of all Norwegian climbers and many English ones, should not be missed; the rugged peaks of that wild and entrancing "home of the giants" seem to beckon the tourist into their country. From Nystua, Bjöberg (*see* above) may be reached *viâ* Eldrevann.

After we leave Nystua the road drops with amazing suddenness, and we are swung down the steep and winding road into a well-wooded valley, which continues through the heart of the Valdres Country and into Eastern Norway. The first village is **Opdal.** (There are at least two other places with this name; see Index.)

Here goes off the **Östre Slidre Route** (*see* pp. 79–81) to **Tyin** and **Bygdin** and thence to **Fagernes.** That which the main road follows, and along which we will continue, is the **Vestre Slidre Route.**

The scenery becomes more and more friendly as we descend to **Skogstad,** 89 km. from Lærdal *viâ* Tyin, 11 from Nystua, (*Skogstad Hotel*), visited by those who wish to ascend the easy **Horntind** (4,770 feet); the descent continues to the western end of **Vangsmjösa,** one of the most beautiful of the Norwegian mountain lakes. The lake almost fills the valley. It lies at an altitude of about 1,500 feet, and is some twelve miles long. The rugged and rocky slopes of the mountains fall abruptly to the water's edge, and are reflected in the smooth waters. The ends are shut in by distant snow-topped mountains, and the views down the lake—especially towards the late afternoon—are very fine.

The lake widens as we approach **Grindaheim,** 106 km. (*Grindaheim Hotel*). The road at this part, and both before and after it is passed, presented some difficult problems to the engineers who built it. In many places they had to cut a way through the solid rock; and this they did in the face of stone avalanches, which even now are by no means uncommon, hence the road is partly roofed.

The **Grindene Mountain,** behind the hotel to the south, is the best climb in this district; it is not difficult, and can be accomplished in from 5 to 6 hours there and back. A path leads from Grindaheim up over the lower slopes to **Lake Helin.**

Near Grindaheim, on the high-road, is **Fagerlid** (*Fagerlid Hotel*), and about a mile on the road is **Vang** Church, built to replace a stave church sold in 1841 to the King of Prussia, who had it transported to Silesia. Against the wall of the churchyard is a stone with a runic inscription which states that "the sons of Gosa erected this stone to the memory of Gunnar, their brother."

Passing through the Kvamskleiva ravine amidst scenery of great grandeur, the road runs on the face of perpendicular cliffs, and is partly roofed to protect it from falling rocks and stones. The fine series of views lasts all the way to **Öylo**, 116 km. (*Hotel Öylo*), at the head of Vangsmjösa Lake.

Now we follow the river *Begna,* which here is a small stream. At the end of 10 km. we pass the pretty **Falls of**

Lo, and shortly after passing the stave church of **Lomen,** of which the portal should be specially noted, we reach **Löken,** 131 km. (*Löken Hotel*), on the eastern shore of the **Slidre Lake,** in which there is good fishing. The scenery is fine, but less imposing at this point.

From Löken can be made the ascent (easy) of the **Kvithövd** (3,322 feet).

Through beautiful scenery the road continues along the shore of the lake, passing the summer pension of **Einang** and, on the right, the old stone church of **Vestre Slidre.** At several points views of the mountains near Bygdin are obtained. At 145 km. from Lærdal we arrive at **Fossheim** (*Fossheim Hotel*). (*There is a Fossheim on the Ottadal Route,* p. 120.)

Fossheim, named from its waterfall, is in touch with several roads on both shores of the lake, and their churches, particularly those of Rön, Ulnes and Strande, are worth visiting. A driving road leads from Fossheim to **Fossheim-seter Mountain Hotel** (1½ hour), at an elevation of 2,800 feet. It is 21 km. from Fagernes Station. From Fossheimseter there is a pedestrian route to Gol, in the Hallingdal (p. 71). From Fossheim there are other routes to the Hallingdal for good walkers.

We proceed along the shore of the **Strande Fjord** to the head of the lake. At **Fagerlund** the road from the **Östre Slidre,** coming from the Jotunheim district, rejoins the main road, and a short piece of road brings us to Fagernes station.

THE ÖSTRE SLIDRE ROUTE

From **Opdal** (p. 77) at the western junction of the Östre Slidre and Vestre Slidre routes, **Tyin** is 5 km. northward (*Tyin Hotel*). It is situated on a beautiful lake of the same name, at an altitude of 3,529 feet. By motor-boat one can go to **Tyinholmen** (*Tyinholmen Hotel*), and thence walk or drive 4 km. to **Eidsbugaren,** at the western end of Lake Bygdin, from which a motor boat can be taken to—

Bygdin

(*Hotels, Bygdin Höifjellshotel, Bygdisheim* and *Fagerstrand*), right in the heart of the **Jotunheim Country,** the best touring-ground in all Norway for the walker and the climber, and which, thanks to modern conveniences of travel, may be visited by those whose journeyings do not claim independence of motor and boat. (For the routes through the Jotunheim district, *see* pp. 122–125.)

By a good road (motor service), Bygdin is connected with the railway at Fagernes, about 50 km. distant. The surrounding country is dry and moss-covered, so that one walks as upon a carpet. Among the mountains which can be easily reached and safely climbed are **Bitihorn** (4,800 feet) and **Synshorn,** affording a grand panorama of the Jotunheim peaks with their glittering glaciers and white snowfields. In the winding Vinstra river, between Lake Bygdin and Vinstervann, are good-sized mountain trout, and the Bygdin hotel has the fishing of several private trout lakes. The country abounds with ptarmigan, ducks, snipe and hares. Farther up in the highlands are wild reindeer. On **Lake Bygdin** there is a motor-boat service to Torfinsbu (1 hour) and to Eidsbugaren (2 hours). The lake, 25 km. in length, is surrounded by grand mountains and may remain frozen until the middle of June.

From Bygdin the road runs at the foot of the Bitihorn and thence across a plateau and along a good road, descending through **Beitostölen** and **Fjellheimen** to **Heggenes**, 22 km. (*Heggenes Hotel*). From it several paths lead into the mountains. In the neighbourhood are the remains of the stave church of Hegg. It has finely-carved doors. Thence the route is through **Fredheim**, 33 km., beyond which it crosses the northern end of the Sebufjord, and after running along its western side again crosses the lake, from which it gradually descends through **Fagerlund**, in a wood, to **Fagernes**, 55 km., 1,100 feet above sea-level (*Fagernes Hotel* and several others.) With its lake, neighbouring wood and small waterfall, the village is very pleasantly situated, and hard by is the *Fagernes View* (2,600 feet), which one can ascend and descend in a couple of hours.

At Fagernes the road journey ends, and the railway journey begins. The scenery throughout the whole of this trip is very fine ; passengers should sit to the right of the carriage. The route lies at first through the Valdres Valley. From **Björgo,** 18 km., a road, with a motor service, follows the course of the *Begna,* through a hilly country of pine and birch forests, passing Tollefsrud Hotel, to **Sörum** (*Sörum Hotel*), and onward to **Hönefoss,** 64 km. farther.

From Sörum an excursion may be made back along the road to **Hedalens Stave Church.**

Wilse,] [Oslo.

THE TÖRFINSTIND, LAKE BYGDIN.

[*E.N.A.*

THE LÅTEFOSS, NEAR ODDA.

The Legend of Hedalens.—Some centuries ago a man in pursuit of grouse traversed one of these formerly inhabited, but now almost deserted places. As he shot an arrow at a bird on one of the trees he heard a peculiar sound, as if the arrow had struck against something. Full of curiosity, he approached the place, where, to his astonishment, he came upon an old church. Mindful of the ancient idea that if this was a work of witchcraft it would immediately disappear if brought into proximity with steel, he seized his tinder-box and threw it over the church. On the spot where it fell a farmhouse was afterwards built, which to the present day bears the name of Ildjernstad (" the tinder-box place "). After taking this precautionary measure, he proceeded to investigate the church. The key stood in the church door, which was half open. In the middle of the floor stood a large bell, and at the foot of the altar a great bear had taken up its winter quarters. It was killed by the brave hunter, and its skin was hung up in the church as a memorial of this strange occurrence. In the church he is said to have found, among other things, some pictures, a little brass shrine, four large bells and one small one. It was against one of these that the arrow had struck and produced the sound which attracted his attention.

The little brass shrine is still preserved in the church. Its ornamentation represents the martyrdom of St. Thomas à Becket of Canterbury, and as the date of the reliquary is about fifty years after that of the martyrdom, it is possibly the earliest representation of the murder of St. Thomas. A copy of the reliquary is in the Bergen Museum.

The night is usually spent at Sörum by this route. If there is plenty of water in the river the steamer comes up to Sörum, and the rest of the journey is made to **Hen** by steamer, and thence by train to Hönefoss (7 km.); but there are many routes from Hen *viâ* Hönefoss and the Tyri Fjord.

The more ordinary route from Fagernes to Oslo is that by railway from Björgo *viâ* **Tonsåsen** (*Breidablik Tourist Hotel*, a favourite holiday resort), **Odnes** and **Eina**, where the Valdres Railway joins the line from Gjövik on Lake Mjösa.

Many travellers prefer to take the steamer down the Rands Fjord from Odnes to **Randsfjord** station. The journey down this fjord is a delightful progress through hilly country and dark forests; the fjord is hardly wider than a broad river, and the views, especially in the upper part of the lake, are very beautiful. The route from Rands Fjord to Oslo is the same as that from Hen.

The train journey from Eina to Oslo is fine, but the country does not compare with that traversed by the Bergen Railway, and it is not seen to the same advantage as from the deck of one of these comfortable little steamers. For those not pressed for time, the Rands Fjord is perhaps the best of the three routes.

THE HARDANGER FJORD.

Map.—Telemarken, facing p. 151.

Routes.—**1.** From Bergen (Pier: Holbergs Almenning) by the *Hardanger Söndhordland SS. Co.'s* steamer: there is a service three times a week calling at all the tourist resorts along the fjord.

2. Overland from Bergen. By train to Trengereid (p. 63) on the Bergen railway, and thence by motor to Norheimsund *or* train to Voss and thence go by motor to Eide (p. 66).

3. From Stavanger. (*See* page 181.)

4. From Oslo by rail to Voss (p. 64), thence by road to Eide.

5. From Oslo by the Telemarken Road to Odda (p. 161).

THE **Hardanger Fjord,** lying to the south of the Bergen railway, is the second largest fjord on the west coast of Norway, its length being about 114 miles. It has numerous arms, the most important of which is the **Sör Fjord,** which runs southward for some 20 miles to Odda. The fjord combines stern grandeur with luxuriant vegetation, for the climate is milder than this mountainous region would suggest.

Along the fjord are all the most typical features of Norwegian scenery. The bordering mountains uplift bleak grey peaks and have their lower slopes clothed with beautiful pine and birch woods, or with moors and verdant pastures. Leaping from the heights or descending in lace-like streamlets are innumerable waterfalls and cascades. There are lonely hamlets, still lonelier hillside farms, and well-known tourist centres offering every convenience and comfort to visitors who wish to linger amid the lovely scenery. The fjord has the two grandest waterfalls in Norway, the Vöringfoss and the Skjeggedalsfoss, and two great ice-fields, the Folgefonn and the Hardanger Jökul.

A narrow passage between the steep mountain wall at Vikingnes divides the fjord naturally into two parts, the Outer and the Inner Hardanger. The chief characteristic of the **Outer Hardanger** is the immense number of small rocky islands, grey, bare and austere, with distant views of the high peaks and glaciers of the inland mountain range. The **Inner Hardanger** approaches these peaks more nearly, and the scenery is more imposing. The mountain walls slope steeply to the margin of the fjord, so that the merest track, if any, has usually to suffice as a link between the scattered farms.

The people of the outer fjord are called *Söringer*. In dress and characteristics they differ little from the coast folk. The peasants of the Inner Hardanger, called *Haringer*, are a fine race, of strong individual character. They cling with great tenacity to their dress and customs. The dress of the women is the most picturesque that will be seen in Norway. It mainly consists of a red embroidered bodice over a white long-sleeved garment, a dark skirt and a white embroidered apron. The married women have a white linen headdress. The hair of the unmarried falls in two plaits over the back. The Harings are excellent wood-carvers and makers of far-famed violins, are very musical, and their national airs enjoy a popularity not confined to Norway.

For a note relating to travelling by steamer in Norway, *see* page 17. The fast steamers call at only a few of the principal places, and not at all those noticed in the account which follows. Local steamers supplement the service of the faster vessels.

On leaving Bergen the steamer passes the large island of Asköy, and then steers southward through the **Kors Fjord,** on the west side of which is the large island of **Sotra,** and on the left the entrances to the small Fane and Lyse Fjords. From the Kors Fjord, the steamer enters the **Björne Fjord.** Soon on the left there is **Os** (p. 60). On the opposite side of the fjord, at a point almost due south of Os, is the small island of **Godöysund** (*Godöysund Hotel*), a favourite place for holiday-makers who want to spend a quiet time. A favourite amusement is to row from island to island (many of them are uninhabited) in the narrow sounds, and there is excellent bathing. The neighbouring large island of **Tysnes** is also a popular summer resort.

From Godöysund we thread the narrow **Loksund,** between Tysnes and the mainland. A small island on the left, with a wooden castellated villa, formerly belonged to an eccentric Englishman; it was left by him to his daughter, who presented it to the Crown Prince Olav. Fast steamers usually proceed through the Kvinnherad Fjord direct to the Inner Hardanger, but the slower boats cross the fjord to **Heröysund** (*Bringedals Pension*), where steamers frequently correspond with those from Stavanger and passengers may have to change boats.

From Heröysund the boat goes to **Uskedal,** thence through the narrows to **Dimmelsvik** and **Rosendal** (*Skåles Hotel*).

In an extensive park is a noble mansion built in 1660–65 by Baron Ludwig Rosenkranz, from whose family it passed into that of the Rosenkrone, of whom there are many monuments in Kvinnherad Church, a stone building of the thirteenth century, situated near the pier.

The church is especially interesting to visitors from Scotland, through being the burial-place of Anna Throndson, the first wife of James Hepburn, Earl Bothwell, to whom she is said to have been married in Copenhagen in 1560. She survived Bothwell many years and died at Seim, near Rosendal, where her father had property.

From Rosendal some steamers cross the fjord to **Gjermundshavn,** then call at Varaldsöy, on the island of **Varaldsöy** (Beacon Isle), and thence go along the west side of the island to **Mundheim** and **Bakke**, from which there is a carriage road to Norheimsund, 28 km. Other steamers go along the east side of the island to Bakke, and there are some which go on from Rosendal to **Ænes,** at the mouth of the Mauranger Fjord. This village has one of the old thirteenth-century Norman stone churches characteristic of the coast. Slow steamers proceed up the Mauranger Fjord to **Sundal** (*Sundal Hotel*), from which place there are some very beautiful views of mountain and glacier.

From Sundal across the snowfield to **Odda** is an excursion of 25 km., occupying 8 to 9 hours and comprising riding on horseback, rowing across a river, a sledge drive and a walk. The view from the summit is very fine. Those who do not care to make the complete journey across the glacier should visit the **Bondhusbræ.** At the end of a 40 minutes' walk up the valley, a boat is taken across the lake, a passage of about 20 minutes (the guide rows), and on landing one has a quarter of an hour's walk to the glacier.

From Sundal or Ænes the route is to **Bakke,** mentioned above. Thence it passes Röirvik, on the opposite side of the pretty bay of Ljonæs on which Bakke is situated. On Vikingnes, the extremity of the promontory, are some fifteen Viking burial-mounds. Here the fjord becomes very narrow. The steamer crosses to the eastern side to **Jondal** (*Jondal Hotel*), from which an excursion occupying 10–12 hours (there and back) may be made to the **Skjördalsfoss** and the neighbouring **Juklevann** into which the glacier descends and which is frozen even in summer. Again crossing the fjord we soon reach **Norheimsund** (*Sandvens Hotel*), one of the most lovely spots in the Hardanger Fjord. The view southward, across the wide water, has for background majestic mountain peaks and the glittering **Folgefonn Glacier.** The fine road (motor service) between Norheimsund and Trengereid on the Bergen Railway has been described in the reverse direction on p. 63. It is but a short walk from Norheimsund to the **Öfsthusfoss** (p. 63). By a walk of 6 km. through attractive scenery one arrives at **Öystese** (*Öystese Hotel*), which is usually the next port of call. The view of the Folgefonn from this part of the fjord is perhaps as good as that to be obtained in any part of the journey. From Öystese one can walk or drive to **Skåre** on the Fyksesund, a narrow branch of the Hardanger Fjord. It is 10 km. in length and has magnificently wild scenery. The excursion can be continued to *Bulken* on the Bergen railway. The route is described in the reverse direction on p. 64.

Nearly opposite Öystese is **Herand,** at the foot of the Samlenut. Then on the north-west coast are **Steinstö** and **Ålvik,** which has sprung up round a factory and faces **Vines** at a pretty spot on the south-east shore. A short distance farther we cross a wide channel on the right and enter the narrow **Granvin Fjord,** at the head of which is **Eide** (*Mælands, Jansens*). The immediate surroundings offer few opportunities for excursions, and Eide is visited principally by travellers who are making for or coming from Voss. This route has been described on p. 66. (The lower portion of this route and of that to Ulvik make a very pretty walk or drive between Eide and Ulvik.)

From Eide the steamer returns down the Granvin Fjord, and crosses the main fjord to **Utne** (*Hotel Utne*). There are several mountains on this spur of land ranging in height from three to four thousand feet, for the ascent of which the hotel at Utne makes a good starting-place, and from Utne there is a good view up the three branches into which the main fjord here divides, the Granvin Fjord to the north, the Eid Fjord to the north-east, and the Sör Fjord to the south. Immediately opposite Utne is the *Oksen*, which rises to a height of over 4,000 feet, and can be ascended from Utne or Eide in 5 to 6 hours. The summit affords a very fine view and has upon it a stone with a runic inscription, which is said to mean " If you turn me round you shall see wonderful things." At Utne we enter—

The Sör Fjord,

the south fjord, as its name signifies. It runs southward for about 20 miles to Odda, and is perhaps the most beautiful of all the arms of the Hardanger. Although on both sides there are lofty mountains, and those on the west have glaciers, yet on the shores of the fjord there are flourishing orchards which justify the Orcharding and Agricultural School at Utne. The first calling-place is **Grimö,** 7 km. by land from Utne. The next is **Lofthus in Ullensvang,** on the opposite shore (*Hotel Ullensvang*), in a district often called the fruit garden of Hardanger. At a quarter of an hour's walk from the hotel is its fine stone church, dating from the twelfth century. It has been restored, and many of its relics are now in the Bergen Museum; but is still worth a visit for its fine west arch, with triple colonnade, and for the curious chancel window, with a sculptured figure of a bishop, laughing on one side of his face and crying on the other.

From Lofthus there is a good road northward to **Kinsarvik,** 10 km. It has an ancient church, and from the village there is a beautiful short walk through a pine wood in the Huse valley (Husdal) to two fine falls, the Tveitafoss and the Nyastölsfoss. At **Huse** is a house, probably of the fifteenth century, with a carved doorway.

From **Nå** the Folgefonn can be reached in a couple of hours. **Espe** stands in a district celebrated for its fruit and connected by a new road with Lofthus. From Espe there is about an hour's voyage, through scenery increasing in grandeur, to **Tyssedal** (*Tyssedal Hotel*), the site of the power station for generating the electricity required for the Carbide Factory at Odda, but its interest to tourists lies in its being the landing-place for the excursion to **Skjeggedalsfoss** (*see* below).

Only 6 km. farther is **Odda,** situated at the head of the fjord in one of the most picturesque spots on the Hardanger. Its hotels (*Grand, Hardanger, Hospitset*) offer opportunity for a long stay, and its environment is well worth a few days' exploration, but the smell often emitted by its carbide factories, which since the close of the last century have converted a picturesque village into a small town, has made the place a less busy tourist centre than it formerly was.

Among the excursions from Odda are—

1. To the **Skjeggedalsfoss,** one of the finest falls in Europe, remarkable for its height and for the grandeur of the chasm which receives it. The water has a sheer fall of over 500 feet, but the total height is about 1,300 feet. From Odda one goes by motor boat or motor car to Tyssedal, 6 km. From the power station there, a bridle-path mostly ascending alongside the river leads in about a couple of hours to *Skjegget,* the site of a small hotel. Here the river is crossed and then in about ten minutes one reaches the *Ringedalsvann,* a gloomy lake some 5 miles long and the source of the water power used at Tyssedal. The fall is at the end of the lake, upon which a motor boat plies. On the way to the fall one sees the dam works of the Tyssefallene, the biggest in Scandinavia.

By motor boat also the twin falls of *Tyssestrengene,* about half way up the lake, can be visited. Two streams fall separately but unite half way down the total height, which is some 600 feet. From this part of the lake there is a fine view of the Folgefonn.

2. To the **Buarbræ,** a spur of the great Folgefonn Glacier, the trip taking about five hours. One goes by boat to Jordal, or by the road round the edge of Sandven lake (¾ hour), and thence one walks for more than an hour along a broad bridle path up the Buar Valley to the small *Buar Hotel* which is beside the glacier. It is dangerous to enter the ice grotto or to stand near the glacier, as blocks of ice and stones often fall. The glacier alternately advances and recedes during a series of years. In 1878 the lower edge was about 1,000 feet above sea level. The glacier is now going through a period of diminution. A more difficult trip is the crossing of the Folgefonn Glacier to **Sundal.** This can be accomplished by good walkers in a day, but all except expert climbers should take a guide. (*See* reverse direction, p. 84.)

3. To the **Folgefonn.** As a guide is necessary, detailed directions are not needed. A good road leads round the head of the fjord to Tokheim and thence a bridle path ascends through the Tokheimsdal. The snow is reached in about 3 hours. The summit, 5,425 feet, commands a magnificent view.

4. To the **Låtefoss** and **Skarsfoss,** 15 km. distant. Drive to the Sandvenvann and follow the western shore to the end of the lake. Thence go along the valley, in which the Hildalsfoss will be passed on the right. Two km. farther, just beyond a narrow ravine containing a tablet in memory of a German officer who lost his life in a bicycle accident, the two falls will be seen on the left where they unite. There is a small hotel and from this a good road leads in 4 km. to the top of the Låtefoss, from which one can look down on

the falls and have a good view of the magnificent surroundings. Near these falls on the right is the beautiful Espelandsfoss.

5. To **Seljestadjuvet** a pass on the road to Breifonn. From the pass, which is about 26 km. from Odda, there is a magnificent view of the Folgefonn and the neighbouring mountains. At Seljestad, not far from the pass, are *Hotels Folgefonn* and *Seljestad*.

6. To **Utsigten** (i.e. The View). This is on the same road as *Seljestadjuvet*, but at only 20 km. from Odda. The principal features of the magnificent view are the Odda Valley and the Folgefonn Glacier (*Hotel, Utsigten*).

From Odda there is a motor service *viâ* Röldal (Breifonn) to **Nesflaten,** on the Suldals Lake, from which Stavanger can be reached *viâ* Sand. The route is described in the reverse direction on page 161.

From Odda also there is a motor service *viâ* Röldal (Breifonn) and Haukeliseter to Dalen. The route is described in the reverse direction on pages 157–159.

The Eid Fjord.

The steamer for the Eid Fjord, after leaving Eide, usually calls at **Utne** (*see* above) and then, rounding the point on the north shore beneath the Oksen, enters the **Eid Fjord**. The order in which the boat makes its calls at the various ports is sometimes varied. The principal place in this fjord is **Vik-i-Eidfjord**, often shortened to **Vik** (the *i* = in), but generally only the name of the fjord is used (*Hotel Vöringfoss*). The spot is visited chiefly for the excursion to the **Vöringfoss** at the head of the Måbödal. The road (daily motor service) passes through some imposing rock scenery, and is one of the many fine examples of the skill of the Norwegian road builders. A part of it is cut out of the solid rock, and at other points it passes through tunnels. The fall comes down in a single leap of about 470 feet, with a terrific roar that can be heard a long way off. Above the falls is the *Fossli Hotel*, 18 km. from Vik, surrounded by a birch forest, 2,300 feet above sea level. By motor boat or by the local steamers, which sometimes go up the Simadal fjord, a visit can be paid from Vik to the **Simadal,** at the farthest end of the Hardanger. The landing-place is at Sæ, 5 km., from which there is a road up the valley, passing Midthus and crossing the river to Tveit, from which a path leads into the Stykjedal in which, at 5 km. from the landing-place, is the **Stykjefoss,** falling nearly 700 feet. From its vicinity a path ascends to Stykjedals Terrace, commanding a fine view of the whole Simadal. At the farther end of the valley is the Rembesdalfoss, an even finer fall than the Stykjefoss, from which it is 3½ km. distant.

The church at Vik is worth a visit.

Fossli is a good place at which to spend two or three days. It is a centre for pedestrian excursions, there is angling, and guides are available for long expeditions. The path which leads through the mountains to the Rembesdalfoss and Lake (*Tourist Hut*) goes thence to Demmevann Glacier (*Tourist Hut*), and so over the Hardanger Jökul to Finse on the Bergen railway.

The car service is continued beyond Fossli to **Maurset,** 25 km. from Vik, and thence by a fine road, completed in 1928, to Haugastöl, on the Bergen railway, 65 km. from Eidfjord.

From Vik **or** from Simadal the steamer returns down the Eid Fjord, and then goes northward through the Osa Fjord to **Ulvik** (p. 66), on the western branch of the fjord. On the eastern branch is **Osa,** which may be visited by walking or driving to Öydvenstod, 5 km., and then by rowing 5 km.

From Osa a mountain path leads over the Hegranut and the Osaskavlen to Hallingskeid on the Bergen railway (guide advisable).

THE SOGNE FJORD.

Routes.—**1.** From Bergen *by steamer.* By the *Fylkesbåtane SS. Co.*; pier Mur Almenning. About twice a week fast day steamers leave Bergen in the morning, calling at Vadheim, Balholm, Leikanger. On other days there are slow boats and night boats. For dates and hours of sailing the *Rutebok for Norge*, local time-tables or a Tourist Agency should be consulted.

2. From Bergen or Oslo *by rail* to Voss and thence by road *viâ* Stalheim to Gudvangen (p. 65) *or* by rail to Myrdal and thence through the Flåm Valley to Flåm (p. 68), and steamer down the Sogne Fjord to Bergen.

3. Oslo by train to Fagernes, thence by the motor to Lærdal, steamer to Bergen *or* Oslo by train *viâ* Hönefoss to Gol and thence by motor to Lærdal (p. 95).

4. Steamer to Eide (Hardanger), motor to Voss, thence *viâ* Stalheim (p. 65) to Gudvangen, steamer down the Nærö Fjord and Sogne Fjord to Bergen.

5. By motor from Sandene on Nord Fjord to Vadheim on the Sogne Fjord, 122 km.

THIS, the longest of the fjords of Western Norway, has its entrance some 50 miles north of Bergen. It extends in an almost straight line from west to east for a distance of about 130 miles. Its width, greater than that of any other fjord of Western Norway, varies from 2 to 5 miles, and the inlet is remarkable for its great depth, which in places is about 4,000 feet. The mountains on either side descend for the most part sheer to the water's edge, varying in height from 2,000 to 5,000 feet, bleak and bare for the most part, some of them snow-capped at the summit, forbidding, and difficult of access. The Sogn has only a few large waterfalls, but it con ıins many glaciers, chiefly branches of the great snowfield of the **Jostedal** (580 square miles) northward of the fjord, and the farther one goes the more wonderful become the rugged peaks and deep gorges. On the western half of the fjord the offshoots are few and short, but the eastern half sends out long arms, dark and gloomy, their precipitous sides shutting out the sun for the greater part of the day, and in places for whole weeks in the year. It is here that is found the most striking scenery of Sogn. Only in a few places does it present the placid loveliness of Hardanger. The predominant scenery is grand and wild. Only here and there, at the edge of the waters, are there occasional stretches of flat land, and the number of towns and villages that find a hold against these sheer walls of mountain rock is small. But there are on the northern shores a few places where there are flat ledges of land facing south, and on these a number of tourist resorts have sprung up. These, owing to their position amid such superb scenery, and the variety of walks and excursions to be made from them, have made the Sogne Fjord one of the most popular touring grounds in all Norway.

The climate varies considerably. In the Outer (Western) Sogn, during the tourist season, it is mild and damp; in the Inner Sogn it is drier and warmer, and the summer heat developed among the steep mountains adapts the low-lying parts of the district to the growth of fruit. The people differ also, as in the Hardanger. Those of the Outer Sogn are, on the whole, placid and good-natured; those of the Inner Sogn are lively and excitable.

The route of the fjord steamers from Bergen lies through the narrow passages of a maze of islands. The large cruising steamers have to follow a course farther from the mainland.

The steamers usually make no call till they are almost at the mouth of the fjord, the first calling-place then being **Skjerjehavn.** Off the mouth of the fjord are the **Sulen Islands.** They are on the left as the vessel enters the inlet, and English passengers may recall that it was at those islands Harald Hårdråde, with Tostig, the brother of the English king Harold, by his side, assembled his fleet in 1060 to make war on Harold. Only the slow boats call at the unimportant stations. The inlets thus visited are pretty, but the chief charm in this part of the journey is the distant view of the snowfields and mountain ranges up the Fjord. Visitors do not miss much, therefore, by taking the fast boats, which make their first call at Vadheim, about 8 hours from Bergen. **Vadheim** (*Hotels Vadheim* and *Trædal*), situated at the end of an arm of the Sogne Fjord, is visited mainly as a junction for the motor route through Sunn Fjord to Förde and the Nord Fjord.

Leaving the little fjord on which Vadheim is situated, the steamer may call at **Kirkebö** and then at **Höyanger,** the site of a large water-power station and an aluminium factory, which in the course of a few years have transformed a bare spot into a small town. Then we reach **Vik** (*Hopstocks Hotel*) on the south side of the fjord. It has a fine long view across the fjord to the Balestrand, where the Fjærland Fjord comes down to the Sogne Fjord; in the distance is the **Jostefonn,** an offshoot of the great glacier.

Near Vik are two interesting churches. Both can be visited in an excursion occupying about a couple of hours. One is at **Hoppestad,** the other at Hove, a mile farther on. The former is the largest of Norway's stave churches. It dates from the twelfth century, has very fine carving, a baldachino with rude pictures painted on it, and the svalgang or cloister is in the main preserved. The church at **Hove** is of stone. It was probably constructed in the twelfth century and has been carefully restored. Services are not held in either of the ancient churches, but in a modern wooden church.

The boat now heads north for the **Balestrand,** passing on the right **Vangsnes,** a place that figures in Frithjof's Saga as Framnaes. The principal place in the Balestrand is—

Balholm

(*Hotels Kvikne* and *Kvamme*), 12½ to 13½ hours from Bergen, at the entrance to the Fjærland Fjord.

Careful note should be made of the fact that *Balestrand* is the name used in the time tables, while *Balholm* is the name displayed at the pier. A similar trap for the unwary is made by the like use of *Fjærland* and *Mundal.*

Balholm is of all places on the fjord most suited for a prolonged stay, although those who desire a quiet spot will prefer the neighbouring Mundal. There are motor boats and rowing boats for sea-fishing and excursions, there is trout fishing in the river and the mountain lakes and all the mountains surrounding the small **Ese Fjord,** which passes inward to the north-west, are easily ascended and guides are to be had at the hotels. In passing up the fjord one has the **Munkeggen** to the left (4,120 feet, in 10 hours), straight in front the **Vindeggen** (3,870 feet, in 8 hours), and to the right the **Toten** (4,590 feet, in 7 hours). From the peaks there are imposing views of the Sogne Fjord, of the steep precipices, rugged mountains and narrow inlets. As there is a road along each side of the Ese Fjord one can make a circular excursion by crossing the water by boat from Balholm and walking round the head of the fjord or crossing by the ferry near the head.

By the road alongside *Hotel Kvikne* or by either of the other roads between that hotel and *Hotel Kvamme*, one can reach in three minutes the English Church of St. Olaf, built in 1897, in the style of the ancient stave churches of Norway, and in ten minutes one will arrive at the *Tomb of King Bele,* a low mound on the left. On a similar mound a few yards distant is a statue of the King erected in 1913 by the ex-Kaiser, who also erected on the promontory of Vangsnes, on the southern side of the fjord, a colossal bronze statue of the legendary Frithjof (the Fearless), the hero of the saga familiar to English readers through Longfellow's translation from the Swedish of *Frithjof's Homestead* and *Frithjof's Temptation*. The road beyond the tomb is worth following. It skirts the fjord and passes between villas surrounded by rich grass land, orchards and fruit plantations. Raspberries are cultivated in abundance, and the meadow grass ready for the scythe reaches well above a tall man's thighs. At the end of half an hour one arrives at the café and restaurant *Jotunheim*, with its pleasant tea garden.

Two minutes short of this, curiosity may be excited by a skeleton wooden tower, with a man sitting at the top, from which hang down a number of lines. He is fishing for salmon by a method practised at other places along the coast. At the bottom of the water is a white painted board which makes visible any salmon which passes over it. When one is seen the watcher pulls lines which draw around the fish a net suspended from a number of barrels floating on the water.

A local steamer goes up the Fjærland Fjord from Balholm to **Mundal** (*Hotel Mundal*), steadily growing in favour with English visitors. It is a charming spot, about 22 km. from Balholm and 3 km. from the head of the inlet, one of the most interesting of the branches of the Sogne Fjord. It possesses both wildness and soft beauty. It narrows as we advance, the mountains, clothed with birch woods and verdure to the limit of vegetation, become higher and steeper, and the glaciers at the head of the fjord make the scenery more imposing.

From Mundal one may take easy, pleasant walks, go on foot or by motor to the **Suphelle** and **Boya Glaciers,** two great arms of the vast Jostedal snowfield and glacier, or with guides, obtainable at the hotel, make excursions to difficult mountain passes.

The two glaciers visited from Mundal present entirely different features. **Boya** is broad and majestic; **Suphelle** narrow and wild. The former is generally considered the more beautiful. It is about 100 yards wide at its base and the wall in which it ends from 30 to 40 feet high. Its appearance is that of a frozen cascade, very broken and tormented by the rocks in its bed. One can walk to it and back again in about 4½ hours, and a car can reach a point within a twenty minutes' walk of the ice-wall. The Suphelle Glacier, in view from the hotel, can be reached in 2 hours on foot and a motor can go right up to it.

A more ambitious excursion is that to the **Frudals Glacier**

(6,030 feet, in 10 hours); this can be extended to the summit of the **Jostedal Glacier** (6,400 feet, in 14 hours). A guide (from 8 to 10 kr.) is recommended. A favourite excursion is to climb up by the Boya Glacier to the summit of the **Skjeidesnipa** mountain, descending by the Suphelle; it is not a difficult feat, and is often accomplished by ladies. The Jostedal Glacier can also be crossed from Mundal to Sunde in 8 hours; good roads have been made on either side by the Norwegian Tourist Club.

Fjærland is the original home of the handweaving industry, mainly a winter employment, and as such is being encouraged so that it is now widespread and everywhere the products are displayed for sale. Large carpets, rugs of various sizes and chair coverings are made. Both sides are exactly alike. The articles will last a lifetime, and as the price compares very favourably with that of factory-made goods, they meet with a ready sale among tourists. No needle or shuttle is used. The wool is manipulated by the fingers only. The designs are for the most part ancient, some going back a thousand years.

The return to Balholm is made by steamer. Thence the route eastward passes the *Kvinnafoss*, very lofty but having little water, beyond which is the Sysstrand, with large fruit gardens. The steamer calls alternately at **Leikanger** (*Hotel Leikanger*) and **Hermansverk,** the latter at the entrance to the short and narrow Sogndal Fjord. Near the head is the village of **Sogndal** (*Hofslund Hotel*). From the church, which stands on a hill outside the village, there is a fine view of the valley, and near the churchyard is a stone with the runic inscription: "King Olaf shot from between (or among) these stones."

From Sogndal there is a motor-car service to **Fortun,** 70 km. (p. 124), and also to **Kroken,** 70 km., in Jostedal. In each case the car ascends the famous Gildreskrea, winding up the face of the mountain, near the top of which is **St. Olav's Well,** under a rock. According to tradition its water is a sovereign remedy for any disease, if a small cross is erected when the water is imbibed.

The fast steamers usually steer straight across the Sogndal Fjord to the mouth of the Aurlands Fjord. Entering this dark and gloomy fjord, they turn westward into the still darker and gloomier **Nærö Fjord,** at the head of which is **Gudvangen** (*Hotels Gudvangen, Vikingvang*). This fjord is sometimes described as the grandest of all the branches of the Sogne Fjord, but its claim rests on the fact that its walls are the steepest, most threatening, and its waters the darkest and most mysterious of all the inlets. The route from Gudvangen to Voss *viâ* the Nærödal and Stalheim has been described in the reverse direction (p. 65).

The **Aurlands Fjord** is wider and altogether less gloomy; at the head of the waters is the *Hotel Fretheim*. The road from it to Myrdal on the Bergen railway is described on page 68.

Returning, the steamer calls at **Frönningen** on the south shore, at the foot of the Bleia mountain (5,650 feet), at **Amla** (*Amla Posting Station*) on the north shore and then enters the **Lærdals Fjord,** at the head of which is **Lærdal** (*Hotels Lindström, Kvamme*), 15 minutes from the pier. It is the most important place in the upper Sogne Fjord, principally by reason of its being at the terminus of the Valdres and Hallingdal routes between the Sogne Fjord and Oslo. On each are motor services. The Valdres route is described on pages 75–81, and the Hallingdal route on pages 71–2. Owing to the proximity of the high mountains the air at Lærdal is hot and oppressive in summer.

The two upper arms of the Sogne Fjord—the wild and bleak Årdals Fjord and the Luster (or Lyster) Fjord, the innermost and longest branch of the main fjord—can be visited from Lærdal by steamer thrice weekly. **Årdal** (*Årdal Hotel*) is the starting-point for the **Vettisfoss,** one of the highest falls in Europe. It is fed from the Mörke, drops over 800 feet into the gorge, throwing up a mist of spray, but usually the quantity of water is small. Very active persons can get to it and back in a day, but generally the excursion takes a day and a half. There is sleeping accommodation at *Vetti Tourist Station* (a farm) about ¾ hour from the fall. The excursion can be made by ladies.

From Årdal there is ¼ hour's walk to the Årdal Lake, which is crossed by motor boat to **Farnes** (in ½ hour). At Farnes (*Farnes Hotel*) a stolkjerre can be procured if desired. Those who elect to walk follow a new road which in many curves winds up the hill and goes thence to Lake Tyin (p. 96). From the confluence of the Årdalselv and the Utla, reached in ¼ hour, the latter stream is followed along its eastern bank for about ¾ hour and then the route lies over a bridge to the western bank, which, followed about ¾ hour, brings you to the Gjelle (or Hjelle) farm just after passing the Gjellefoss. At the farm the road ends. The river is again crossed and is followed upward for about ¼ hour to Johannebro, where it is crossed for the last time, the western bank being followed to Vetti farm, reached in about 1½ hours. Thence the route is through the Vettisgjel, a fine ravine between precipitous cliffs, down which fall avalanches of stone in rainy weather. The walk from the farm to the fall and back again takes about 1½ hours.

From the farm a steep zigzagging path leads in rather more than ½ hour to the top of the mountain and then there is ¼ hour's walk to the top of the fall.

From Farnes to Tyin. The route is along the new road, which soon comes to Tyinfallene, the site of a great power station, and thence, by many windings, ascends to the top of Mount Heirsnosi (about 12 km.) commanding a wonderful view of the western portion of the Jotunheim and the Årdal lake and district, some 3,000 feet below. At 12 km. farther the road reaches the Sletterust seter (mountain dairy) and in another 7 km. arrives at **Tyin.** (See p. 79.)

For walkers there is a mountain path through the Mörkedal to **Lake Bygdin** and **Lake Tyin,** in the Jotunheim country.

In the **Lyster** (or Luster) **Fjord** the calling places are Solvorn Luster and Skjolden. **Solvorn** on the west bank, and **Marifjöra,** higher up on the same shore, are connected with the road from Sogndal that runs up the valley to Fåberg, the highest farm in the Jostedal. From Solvorn the stave church of **Urnes** on the opposite shore can be visited by rowing across the fjord (about ½ hour). The church dates from about 1090, has beautiful carvings, an ancient rood, and old-time vestments and other articles. **Skjolden** (*Skjolden Hotel*), at the head of the fjord, is principally visited by mountain climbers on their way to **Fortun** (*Fortun Hotel*) and **Turtagrö** (*Turtagrö Hotel*), who come here to scale the peaks, glaciers and passes of the Sogne Fjell. The country has been well described by W. C. Slingsby, who explored it with great thoroughness, scaling many rocky heights previously unconquered.

THE NORD FJORD.

NORD FJORD, the third of the great fjords of western Norway, is one of the loveliest of the country's great inland waterways. It is about 60 miles in length from the sea entrance to Olden, its innermost village.

The mountains bordering it rise to heights of about 6,000 feet. Their slopes are covered with vegetation, and hamlets and farms are freely distributed along its shores, and yet it has well been described as the home of the glacier. Whether one's eyes turn right or left, the margin of the great Jostedal Glacier, which crowns the highlands that divide the Nord Fjord from the Sogne Fjord, overhangs the mountains, and wherever there is a cleft in the mountain wall, glaciers are seen descending. From the melting crowns of the snow and ice-covered peaks, the water descends in cascades and falls. The scenery at the seaward end of the fjord is similar in character to the Skjærgård, but as we proceed to its interior channels it becomes ever grander and more Alpine, rivalling in places the scenery of the two great fjords to the south.

Of the two routes to it from Bergen, the steamer route and the overland route, the latter is the more popular.

1. THE OVERLAND ROUTE.

The favourite route from Bergen to the Nord Fjord is *viâ* **Vadheim** (p. 91) on the Sogne Fjord, and thence by road *viâ* Förde and Egge to Sandane, on the Gloppen Fjord, a branch of the Nord Fjord. The drive lies through a fine piece of wild country of mountain and lake. The road winds up from Vadheim past the **Öksneland Lakes,** whence it descends to **Sande** (*Hotel*).

Here a road branches left to **Sveen** (**Bygstad**) (p. 99), a calling-place of the Sunn Fjord steamers to and from Bergen. There is also a road to the right, along the *Viksvann* to Vik's Church, 14 km.

The main road continues due north from Sande; it climbs steeply among higher mountains, with the **Kvamshest** (4,060 feet) as the outstanding peak, a strangely shaped mountain somewhat resembling the head of a horse. At **Langeland,** from which the road rises to the **Langeland Lakes,** a by-road branches off to the left, leading also to Sveen (p. 97). The main road follows the shore of the lake, and after climbing the watershed, a ridge of about 1,000 feet above sea-level, descends in sharp elbows to **Förde,** 11 km. from Langeland (*Hafstads Hotel*, on the road), a pleasant village beside the Förde Fjord. Steamers ply between Bergen and Förde about twice weekly in each direction, in about 18 hours.

After leaving Förde the road turns eastward, and enters a pleasant and well-cultivated valley, between high mountains. About 6 km. from Förde the Mo lake is reached, and the road lies along it to the village of **Mo,** where it forks. At this end of the lake is the **Huldrefoss,** of insignificant height, but with a great volume of water, and where the road leaves the lake is the Mo Agricultural College. The right arm leads to Holsen and the Haukedal. We follow the left branch, leading north-east to the **Jölster Lake** at Nedre Vassenden (*Vassenden Hotel*), 20 km. from Förde. The road runs alongside the lake, passing Ålhus Church and then **Ordal.** Affording a fine view of the Lundebræ, on the other side of the lake, it passes Helgeim Church, so to **Skei** (*Skei Hotel* at the pier).

From Skei one can go by motor boat up the Kjösnes Fjord, an arm of the Jölster Lake, to **Lunde,** and thence by half an hour's walk to the *Lunde Glacier*. It is an excursion through very pretty scenery.

The route from Skei to the village of Förde, on the left, and thence by the Brehimsvann almost to Sandane, is now never used, having been superseded by a fine road through the picturesque Våtedal to **Egge,** 14 km. from Skei (*Hotel Egge*). The steep walls of the Svenskenipa, on the one hand, and the Botnfjell on the other, prevented the road from being carried along the shore of the lake at this part; but from **Red,** 12 km. from Egge (*Gordon*, a simple but comfortable inn) to **Eide,** near Sandane, we follow the margin of the **Brehimsvann** by a road that is a marvel of engineering. It is built partly by tunnelling the rock, and partly by terraces built upon the mountain side, and is altogether a feat compelling wonder. We pass the Eidsfoss just before reaching Eide, and then descend into **Sandane** (p. 100), with a fine distant view all the way down.

2. THE STEAMER ROUTE

From Bergen by *Fylkesbåtane* steamer, starting from the Nykirke Quay. Four times weekly. Bergen to Sandane 17 hours, 19½, 28 or 38 according to the day on which the start is made. The steamer which does the voyage in the shortest time arrives at Sandane at the inconvenient hour of 2 in the morning. The boat taking 19½ hours leaves Bergen at 3 o'clock on Saturday afternoon and is due at Sandane at 10.30 on Sunday morning.

From Sandane there is a local steamer to the places east of it on five days of the week. Tuesday and Friday are the days omitted.

As all these arrangements are liable to alteration, current time tables should be consulted.

The steamer route from Bergen as far as the Sogne Fjord is the same as that described on p. 91. Soon after we have crossed the entrance of the Sogne Fjord, the scenery becomes more mountainous, while the lower slopes are more wooded and the islands show more signs of habitation. The steamer passes inside the large **Indre** (Inner) **Sulen.** Then comes the entrance of the pretty **Dals Fjord,** up which goes another service of steamers from Bergen, the farthest point being **Bygstad** (*Hotels Bygstad* and *Lundes*), from which it is a short drive to **Sande** (*Hotel*) or **Langeland,** on the main road between Sogn and Nord Fjord.

Beyond the entrance of the Dals Fjord is Askvoll, north of which is the narrow **Förde Fjord,** having at its head the village of Förde on the route (p. 98) between Sogn and Nord Fjord.

Proceeding northward, the steamer comes to **Florö,** thence keeps to the east of the islands of Batalden and Aralden, and crosses a small open stretch to Kalvåg, at the south-west point of the large island of **Bremanger.** At its eastern extremity the vessel passes directly beneath the famous **Hornelen,** a rugged and stony peak 3,000 feet high, the top of which overhangs the base, which is littered with falls of rock. It has been climbed on several occasions. The steamer after passing beneath Hornelen enters the **Nord Fjord** and calls at **Bryggja,** a small village at the mouth of the fjord. There is a small hotel here, visited sometimes by those who are driving to Åheim, 20 km., on the Vannelvs Fjord, whence there is a steamer once a week to Ålesund. It is one way of avoiding the passage round the dreaded Stat.

Farther eastward, on a pretty bay on the south shore, is **Davik,** and then on the north shore are **Kjöllestad, Stårheim** and **Naustdal,** the last two on the Eids Fjord (*Smördal Posting Station*).

At **Nordfjordeid** (*Hotel Yri*) the steamers call. It is a very pretty place, suitable for a short stay; it is within easy reach of the Hornindalsvann, whence the **Glitteregg** (4,100 feet) may be ascended. A local steamer goes from end to end of the lake.

The steamer returns down the Eids Fjord, and rounds the sharp promontory on which the Mörkeseterfjell rises steeply. Thence it crosses to the narrow Hyen Fjord, at the head of which is **Hyen,** sometimes visited by climbers for the ascent of the **Sessegg** (4,493 feet), the **Ålfotbræ** and **Gjegnalund Glaciers** (53 square miles in extent), a stretch of icefields quite distinct from the Jostedalsbræ, and as yet hardly explored.

Returning down the Hyen Fjord, and calling sometimes at **Hestenesöyra,** we turn sharply to the right into the **Gloppen Fjord,** at the head of which is **Sandane** (*Hotels Sivertsens* and *Gloppen*), an important place by reason of its being the point where the overland route from the Sogne Fjord comes in. The surroundings of Sandane are very beautiful. Hills, backed by high mountains, enclose it on every side except that of the shore, and from these heights foaming streams, waterfalls and cascades descend, but in the immediate neighbourhood of the village the land is open and pastoral, with fir and birch woods through which the visitor can ramble at will. The place offers a variety of excursions by road and by water, and bathing and angling can be enjoyed. In consequence of its varied attractions many visitors make it the headquarters of a long stay in summer. Among the excursions possible are visits to the lovely Brehimsvann, the Olden and Loen lakes, the Briksdals and Kjendals Glaciers (pp. 102, 101), the ascent of the **Svinestrand** (3,700 feet), which can be climbed in about four hours, the ascent of the Rysdalshorn (5,000 feet), to the Eidsfoss and to Gjemmestad Church, 400 years old, against Rygg on the western shore of the fjord.

Returning down the Gloppen Fjord, the steamer follows the southern shore of the main fjord to **Utvik** (*Hotel Britannia*), a small village at the water's edge.

The fjord now bends northward, and we cross to **Faleide** (*Faleide Posting Station*), whence a road leads across to Hellesylt (p. 115) and another to Visnes, 9 km. From Faleide the steamer goes eastward to **Visnes** in Stryn (*Visnes Hotel*). It is one of the most important places on the fjord, as it is the centre for two important routes, one through the Hornindal to Hellesylt, 71 km., on a short western arm of the Stor Fjord and onward to Öye, 27 km.; the

Valentine & Sons, Ltd.,] *[Dundee.*

LOEN LAKE.

Wilse,] [*Oslo.*

THE KJENDALSBRÆ GLACIER, LOEN.

Wilse,] [*Oslo.*

OLDEN LAKE.

other *viâ* Grotli to Maråk (Geiranger) on a long narrow eastern arm of the fjord. These roads form alternative portions of the overland route to Molde, and are described on pages 104–107. Tourists who are not going to Grotli should from Visnes or from Loen go along the road as far as Videseter (p. 106); the excursion can be made in a day and includes some of the finest scenery in Norway.

Visnes is also on the motor road which goes round the head of the Nord Fjord and links Visnes with Loen and Olden (*see* below).

The remaining portion of the steamer route is short. Leaving Visnes, the vessel ascends the last part of the Nord Fjord, which at its farthest end forks left to Loen and right to Olden. Both are favourite places (they are linked by a motor service).

Loen (*Alexandra Hotel*), delightfully situated, offers excellent fishing in lake, river and sea, and several very fine excursions.

Chief among these are the excursions to the **Bödals Glacier** and the **Kjendalsbræ.** The latter is the more popular. One first walks for forty minutes or drives beside a salmon stream to the lower end of the **Loen Lake,** about 12 km. long, upon which a small steamer plies. The lake lies between snow-capped mountains, between which glaciers, waterfalls and mountain torrents descend. One of these glaciers is the **Helseterbræ** seen on the right coming from the Ravnefjell, about half-way up the lake. On the opposite side is Gården Hugrending (Hugrending farm) at the entrance of a valley leading to the Bödalsbræ. Next on the right, not far from the head of the lake, is the hamlet of Nesdal. A few yards short of its first houses is a hollow in the face of the cliff. It dates from January, 1905, when the rock which until then had filled it slipped quietly into the lake. It caused such a tremendous wave that sixty-one persons and a great number of horses and cattle were drowned and the lake steamer was thrown high up on the land, where remains of it may still be seen, 600 yards from the spot where it was immediately before the time of the disaster.

At the landing-place at the head of the lake, the proprietor of the *Alexandra Hotel* has a restaurant. Here stolkjerres are waiting to go to the glacier, about 5 km. distant. The road ends at a ¼ hour's walk from the ice.

To the **Bödals Glacier,** an excursion occupying 8 to 9 hours. The Kjendalsbræ route is followed to Bödal on the Loen lake. Thence there is a bridle path to the Bödalsseter Tourist station, 5 km. Here one gets fine views in which are included seven branches of the Jostedal glacier. From the Seter there is a ½ hour's toilsome walk to Bödals Glacier.

This is the starting point for the ascent of the **Lodalskaupa,** 7,000 feet, the highest mountain in Western Norway.

From Loen climbers often make the ascent of the **Skåla,** 5,700 feet. On the summit is a stone hut, in which one may pass the night in order to see the sun rise. The ascent and descent can be accomplished in 8 hours.

From Loen through the Fosdal to Hjelle (p. 105) is an easy passage, occupying 4 to 5 hours.

Olden (*Yri Hotel*) is the last place on the steamer route of the Nord Fjord. It lies at the foot of the third of the great glacier valleys that run down from the Jostedal to the Nord Fjord, and the surroundings of the peaceful village are very majestic and beautiful. It is half an hour's steamer journey from Loen, with which, as already stated, it is connected by a good road (motor service). There is trout fishing in the Olden lake and salmon fishing in the river. There are daily steamer and motor-boat connections with Sandane, Sogne Fjord and Bergen, and motors run daily to and from Hellesylt, Öye, Grotli, Geiranger (Maråk), and Otta.

The principal excursion from Olden is that to the **Briksdal Glacier.** The route is less picturesque than that to the Kjendals Glacier, the distance from the lake is greater and the road is uphill. From Olden one walks or drives about 5 km. to Eide on the Olden Lake, from which a steamer goes daily to Rustöy, 11 km., passing **Ceciliekrone,** 6,000 feet, and the **Melkevoll Glacier.** From Rustöy one drives or walks up the valley to Briksdal farm, 7 km. from Rustöy. Near the farm are a small hotel and a large restaurant, both belonging to the proprietor of the *Yri Hotel.* From this point one has a walk of 40 minutes along a good road through birch woods to the **Briksdal Glacier,** of which the lowest part is seen through the trees. If one walks all the way from the lake the time occupied will be at least 2 hours.

Excursions may also be made to the *Melkevoll Glacier* and to the three peaks named *Onsdagsfjell, Larsnebba* and *Middagsnebba,* all about 6,000 feet above sea level. Authorized guides can be obtained at the hotel.

BERGEN TO MOLDE.

MOLDE is a small west-coast town, considered to have the prettiest situation in Norway. Its luxuriant vegetation has gained for it the title of "the town of flowers," and its many attractions have made it a favourite summer resort.

I. The Sea Route.

Length, about 380 km. or 240 English miles. Time occupied, 21 to 24 hours.

Molde is a calling-place for all the steamers between Bergen and Trondhjem. Their course northward has been followed as far as the Nord Fjord (pp. 91 and 99).

The steamer turns westward after passing beneath Hornelen (p. 99), threads the **Skateström,** and so enters the Sound of Ulve. On a small island at the southern end is situated **Moldöen** or **Målöy** (*Hages Hotel*), a simple village of few attractions; it is sometimes visited by those who are changing here to pick up the steamer from Bergen to Olden and the Nord Fjord. The steamer continues through the **Ulvesund.** At the head of the sound the vessel enters the open Silde—Gapet or herring channel—too open often for the comfort of the unaccustomed. The channel lies between the northern end of the island of **Vågsöy** and the peninsula of **Stat,** which the vessel has to round.

Off the base of the peninsula lies the island of **Seljöy,** once the seat of a bishopric and upon which, visible from the steamer, are the tower and ruins of a Benedictine monastery probably erected early in the eleventh century in honour of St. Sunniva, whom legend declares to have been an Irish princess.

The story goes that she was to have been wedded under compulsion to a Viking, but with some companions escaped in an open boat, which drifted on the current from the North of Ireland to Seljöy. Attacked by the heathen, they took refuge in a cave. A stone avalanche closed the entrance and all perished. When their remains were discovered, the body of the princess bore all the marks of saintship and was therefore reverently treasured. In the twelfth century the bishop's stool and the relics of St. Sunniva were transferred to Bergen, where the relics were preserved in the cathedral until the destruction of that building in 1531. Other examples of boats coming across from Scotland and Ireland on the drift are recorded, so there is nothing wildly improbable in the legend.

Most travellers are glad when they are round **Stat.** It is a peninsula, high and rugged, jutting some 18 miles into the sea. The rolling waves come in here from the Atlantic with unbroken force, and beat against the steep walls of angular mountains that fall sheer to the sea. Bare and jagged headlands jut out, with only a sparse moss finding hold among the heaps of debris—an inhospitable shore that has known many wrecks. Fortunately, the rough passage is soon over; the vessel steers at once for the smooth water on rounding the headland, and picking its way among the islands, crosses the wide **Breisund** and enters the harbour of **Ålesund** (*see* page 107).

Here passengers who are going on to Molde by sea are but 70 km. from the end of their voyage, and the vessel's course is over a smooth sea. It lies between pretty islands and the mainland, over which it affords some charming views with the Sunnmöre and the Romsdal mountains in the background. And then, after Molde has come into sight, the beautiful scene it presents, as the vessel draws nearer and nearer, attracts and holds all eyes.

The town is described on page 108.

II. The Overland Route

from Bergen to Molde is not wholly in accordance with its name, but there is at any rate a greater proportion over land than over water.

A considerable portion of the route has already been described, as it comprises the route from Bergen to Vadheim outlined on page 91, the route from Vadheim to Sandane sketched on pages 97–8, and the short passage from Sandane to **Visnes** (Stryn) described on page 100.

From this point we go over new ground, either *viâ* Hellesylt or *viâ* Grotli. Upon each route is a motor service.

(*a*) **The route via Hellesylt.** By this route Molde can also be approached *viâ* Öye.

The road begins by going westward from Visnes (Stryn) along the shore of the fjord, but soon rises and gives beautiful views of the snow-capped mountains. By windings it ascends to a height of 850 feet, and then descends to **Kjös,** a small place on the **Hornindal Lake** 10 km. from Visnes.

Motor service between *Kjös* and *Nordfjordeid*, 31 km. to the west, and also from Nordfjordeid to **Kjöllesdal** still farther westward. This runs alongside the Eids Fjord and passes through **Naustdal** and **Stårheim.**

Passing the foot of the steep Kjöshammer, we skirt the east end of the lake, over which there are charming views, and at the end of 7 km. reach *Grodås*. Ascending, we pass Hornindal's Church, and go through a well-cultivated district to **Indre Haugen,** 9 km. from Grodås, a small place from which the apparently unclimbable *Hornindalsrok*, 5,300 feet, to the left, can be ascended with a guide in 10 hours up and down. Not much more than half that time is necessary if the ascent is made from **Kjeldstadli,** 6 km. farther, and situated at a height of 1,430 feet above sea level.

We now enter upon a long downhill road, which at **Tryggestad,** 7 to 8 km., goes over the narrow gorge through which the river is rushing far below the bridge. Then a beautiful view of the Stor Fjord opens out and the road, winding down, crosses a fine fall which enters the fjord, shortly before we reach **Hellesylt,** described on page 115.

At Hellesylt we have a choice of routes :—

1. By car to Öye, 30 km., and thence by steamer along the Norang Fjord and the Hjörund Fjord to Ålesund. The road, the fjords and Ålesund, are described on pp. 111–113 and 107, and the route from Ålesund to Molde on p. 108.

2. By steamer through the Sunnelvs Fjord and the Stor Fjord to Ålesund, pp. 114–115.

(*b*) **Visnes to Molde** *viâ* **Grotli and Maråk.** The road to Grotli, the famous **Stryn Route,** lies through a glacier valley, an offshoot from the Jostedalsbræ. It begins by a level stretch alongside the river issuing from the Stryn Lake and then along the southern shore of the lake to **Hjelle,** 29 km. (*Hotel Hjelle*), reached just after passing the Glomsfoss.

Once a day on four days of the week a steamer traverses the lake between Hjelle at the east end and Mindre Sunde at the west end. The scenery of this lake is at first rather tame, after the upper reaches of the Nord Fjord, because the view is very much shut in by the **Flofjell** (4,400 feet). As the lake bends in a southerly direction the view opens out, and the peaks and glaciers recede into a more harmonious perspective. The arms of the great glacier here fork high above the two valleys of Erdal and Videdal; between them is the **Hjellehydna** (4,900 feet).

The road from Hjelle leads through the Viadal to **Skåre,** 7 km.; thence it climbs in zigzags. By a narrow bridge it crosses one of the finest gorges in the country. At the bridge it is only a few yards wide and the Skjæringsdals river is 270 feet below. From **Viaseter** or **Videseter** (*Hotel*), 2,000 feet above sea level, the view is indescribably grand. To the left of the hotel, as one mounts to it, is a fine waterfall, fed by a torrent coming by a long and winding course from the Nuken mountain. The mountain can be ascended from Videseter, from which its summit, however, is not in sight.

From Videseter the road continues to ascend the Via valley. It passes within an hour's walk of the **Skytod Glacier**, on the right, and skirts the Lande Vann into which the Tystig glacier descends. Soon afterwards we reach the highest point of the route, 3,740 feet (height of Snowdon, 3,560 feet). The descent to **Grotli** lies over a long and wide mountain moorland. Small lakes on the right are passed, also Lake Heilstugu, before reaching *Grotli Hotel*, 32 km. from Videseter. In the neighbourhood of the hotel a large herd of tame reindeer may sometimes be seen.

From Grotli a road (see pp. 119–121), goes eastward to **Otta,** from which Oslo can be reached by rail, as described in the reverse direction on pp. 138–140.

Our route runs westward. Gradually rising, it passes along the northern shore of the Breidalsvann, 8 km. in length, and past several small lakes to the shore of the Djupvann, covered with ice even in summer, and having waterfalls and glaciers around. Here is the *Hotel Djupvasshytten*, much frequented, and here also is the highest point of the road, 3,400 feet up. Soon we come to the finest part of the route. The road goes down steeply by hairpin bends, and in one place makes a complete circle under itself, and forms a knot, the famous **Knute** which the chauffeur will point out. Stones marked 1,000 metres (over 3,000 feet), 800, 300 and 100 are passed. The descent affords delightful views of the **Geiranger Fjord,** and of the deep valley into which torrents rush through gorges draped with ferns. Indeed, the vast amphitheatre formed by the mountain walls of the valley is one of the most impressive spots in Norway, and the variety of the scenery of this road one of its chief attractions. The actual distance from the brink of the cliff to Mårak (also Merok, Geiranger) would be barely 5 km., whereas the zigzag road distance is about 18 km.

A short distance above Maråk's first hotel in this direction (*Hotel Utsigten*—the view) is a railed-in platform on the edge of the **Flydals Juv** (or gorge), a view-point at which the cars make a brief halt. The descent is continued to the *Union Hotel*, in **Maråk,** 52 km. from Grotli (*see* p. 116).

The next portion of our route is by water and extends to Ålesund. We can either go direct through the Geiranger Fjord and the Stor Fjord, or from the former we can pass into the Sunnelvs Fjord and call at Hellesylt before going along the main fjord. A description of these fjords, taken in the reverse direction, is given on pp. 114–116.

Ålesund.

Hotels.—*Scandinavie* and several others.
Population.—About 18,000.

Ålesund as we see it to-day is a mushroom town, for it was burnt out on January 22, 1904, when every building perished except the hospital. But Ålesund profited by the lesson, and is now almost entirely built of stone. The old Ålesund had a history dating from the time when Rolf the Ganger, expelled from his country by Harald Hårfagre, sailed to conquer France, and founded Normandy. Its shape, on a long narrow slip of land, with the sea lapping almost its very streets, suggests a life of war with the waves, and this is indeed Ålesund's story. Shipping and fisheries are its main—almost its only—occupations. It is the principal commercial centre of Stor Fjord and the west coast fisheries. Its principal street, in which there are some good shops, runs the length of the peninsula. From the park, which lies on a hill, there is a view of the town and harbour, and from the summit of the Flöifjell or **Akslå,** a massive hill which rises in a cone about 500 feet, there are fine views in the direction of the Hjörund Fjord (south) and the Langfjell.

Ålesund to Molde.—1. Daily steamer connection with Molde, 70 km.

2. Motor service to Vestnes, 70 km., from which a steamer goes to Molde, 12 km.

3. Local steamers ply every day through Hjörund Fjord to Öye (pp. 111–112).

Through Stor Fjord and Sunnelvs Fjord to Hellesylt (pp. 114–116).

Through Stor Fjord and Geiranger Fjord to Maråk (pp. 114–116).

The motor run from Ålesund to Vestnes occupies from 3¼ to 3½ hours. The route lies through beautiful scenery, including alpine views. Beyond the outskirts of Ålesund, it passes **Borgund** Church and an arm of the fjord, and then proceeds along the Brusdalsvatn, crosses the Skodje stream and then passes through the fertile district of Skodje, lying alongside the Stor Fjord. At 40 km. from Ålesund it arrives at Sjöholt or Örskog (*Söholt Hotel*), very pleasantly situated, where a long halt is made. Thence the route ascends through a charming valley to the plateau of Örskog-fjell, which it crosses to the Skorgedal and from this lies along the Tres Fjord to Vestnes.

The journey from Ålesund to Molde by sea lies wholly through smooth water, and the traveller approaching the latter by this route will be quite disposed to endorse its title to the epithet, "The Paradise of the North."

Molde.

Hotels.—*Alexandra*, *Årõs*, *Missions* and others. Accommodation at all prices can be found.
Post Office—On the eastern side of the town.

This deservedly popular little town is beautifully situated on a promontory on the north shore of the entrance to the Romsdal and Fane Fjords, a peaceful haven of villas in a frame of verdure. Facing south, it looks across the fjord, dotted with forest-covered islands, to a wonderful mountain panorama, chains of high mountains that include peaks behind the Tres Fjord and in Sunnmöre to the south; and bordering Romsdal the Vengetinder, the aiguilles of the Trolltinder and the conical cap of the Romsdalshorn—a view that can vie with the best in Norway. The site of the town is a fertile slope exposed to the sun and well sheltered against winds from the north, a position that enables the gardens of the pretty wooden houses to be made bright with flowers. The town, though it has a small fishing trade and some coasting, depends chiefly upon the traffic of tourists; it is beautifully clean and well kept. The **Church** is generally visited for the world-famous altar-piece of the Women at the Sepulchre, by the Norwegian painter *Axel Ender*.

The fjord abounds in fish, and there is good trout fishing in mountain lakes.

The **Park,** the *Rekneshaug*, on a hill behind the town, is a pleasant resting-place.

A better view-point is the **Varden,** a hill about 1,500 feet high, at the back of the town, marked by a weathercock which can be reached by active pedestrians in 1½ hours. One may go to it through the park or by going inland, past the church,

THE WOMEN AT THE SEPULCHRE (*Axel Ender*).
(Altar-piece, Molde Church.)

Wilse,] *[Oslo.*

ÅLESUND.

and then turning to the left. The road is steep. It passes through a fir wood with green undergrowth. On the way a signpost indicates that Storlien, Varden and Moldheien are all in the same direction. Varden means the cairn or beacon; Moldheien, Molde's mountain ridge. An alternative name is Moldhöi, Molde's hill. **Storlien** is the site of a café and a good view-point, about three-fourths of the way up. A short distance beyond this the road divides. The branch to the left should be followed.

(The branch to the right descends gradually to the Molde river. From the bridge which crosses the stream a good road to the left leads to the Molde Valley and on the left bank of the river a road leads to the town.)

Among longer excursions are the following:—

1. A walk or motor run along the **Fanestrand,** a road going eastward from Molde along the Fane Fjord. It affords fine views of the Romsdal mountains, and 7 kilometres of it are an avenue of hazel, birch and mountain ash. It leads to **Batnfjord,** at which steamers call, and which is much used by travellers going to Trondhjem and desiring to avoid the bad stretch of open sea across Hustadvika, off the coast between Molde and Kristiansund. Daily motor service between Molde and Batnfjord.

2. **Round Fræna,** a motor run of about 2½ hours. The route is along the Fanestrand, up the wild Årödal, down the steep Malmedal and alongside the Fræne Fjord to Julsund and thence alongside the fjord to the town.

3. **To Trollkirken,** the Witches' Church, a cave with stalactites going more than 50 yards into a mountain. It is 30 km. distant by way of Julset. The last 4 km. must be walked along a river bed. Strong boots and candles or lamps are needed.

4. To the summit of the **Tusten** (2,290 feet), north-east of Molde, from which it may be ascended in about three hours. The path has been staked.

5. Motor boats may be obtained in Molde, and many excursions made to the surrounding islands. On **Veöy**—the Island of the Holy Place—is a well-preserved church, about 700 years old.

Molde is also the centre for excursions to the Fane Fjord, Lang Fjord (to Nauste), Romsdals Fjord (to Veblungsnes and Åndalsnes), and to Vestnes (p. 108) for the overland route to Ålesund and the Sunnelvs Fjord.

1. The Fane Fjord.

As there is a good road along the north shore of the narrow **Fane Fjord,** leading to **Eidsöra** on the Sunndals Fjord (part of the overland route from Molde to Trondhjem), the steamer route is not much used, except as a means of making excursions from Molde. As the Fane Fjord has some of the best scenery of all the fjords in this district, the traveller is advised to make a trip up it by water.

2. The Lang Fjord and Eris Fjord.

The **Lang Fjord,** though not much frequented by tourists, is nevertheless well worth visiting. It is almost as narrow as the Fane Fjord, but the shores are less steep, and upon them are several villages. After calling at **Visdal,** in a small bay on the south shore, the steamer runs up to Eidsvåg. From **Eidsvåg,** 55 km. from Molde, on the road to Eidsöra, there is a good road to Nauste. The distance from the junction is 19 km. Thence the steamer goes to the **Eris Fjord,** a short arm of the Lang Fjord having a southerly direction. Here the scenery becomes grander, as the waters narrow. At the southern end is **Nauste** (*Ness Hotel*). From Nauste can be made the ascent of **Skjorta,** 6,000 feet, 11 hours up and down. In clear weather Galdhöpigg and the Glittertind, about 120 miles distant in the Jotunheim, are among the mountains of the extensive panorama.

If time permits a day or two could be pleasantly spent amid the magnificent scenery of the **Eikesdal** and its mountain lake, 19 km. in length. From Nauste there is a good road to **Överaas,** 8 km., at the northern end, from which a small steamer goes to **Reitan** at the southern end. (*Hotel* about 200 yards from the pier.) About halfway along the lake is a pier from which a path leads up to the twin falls **Mardals.** They can also be reached by an hour's walk from the Reitan Hotel.

From Reitan there is a cart road to Finset, 11 km., and thence a bridle path to *Bjorli* (p. 147) on the Romsdal railway. There is also a path to Ormeim, near *Verma* (p. 147), on the Romsdal line. Time occupied, 8 to 10 hours.

3. The Romsdal Fjord.

The fastest boat, which goes direct to Åndalsnes, leaves Molde half an hour after midnight and arrives at Åndalsnes shortly before 3 o'clock in the morning. Another boat leaves between 3 and 4 in the afternoon and calls only at **Vestnes** (*Vestnes Hotel*) at the termination of the overland route from Söholt. On these occasions Åndalsnes is reached in about 3 hours. It is after leaving Voll that the scenery of the Romsdals Fjord really begins. Soon the two giant peaks of the **Romsdalshorn** and **Trolltinder** become visible as we near **Veblungsnes,** at which only slow boats call (*Hotel Romsdal*), and the more important village of **Åndalsnes**—also called Nes—the terminus of the famous Romsdal Road and Romsdal Railway (*see* p. 149). *From Molde* there is a daily motor-car service to *Eidsöra* from which steamers cross to *Sunndalsöra*, whence there is a motor-car service to *Opdal* on the Dovre Railway.

There is also a daily motor-car service to *Batnfjord* in connection with a steamer crossing to and from *Kristiansund N.* (p. 183).

ÅLESUND TO ÖYE

viâ The Hjörund Fjord.

During the tourist season there is a steamer daily. The time occupied is from 3½ hours to 4 hours.

This is the best route to the Hjörund; but it can be approached from Eastern Norway by the route from Otta to Maråk, thence down the Geiranger Fjord, and by driving from Hellesylt to Öye, routes mentioned in greater detail later.

The **Hjörund Fjord,** although one of the smaller fjords of western Norway, is certainly one of the most interesting. It is only some 25 miles long, mostly only ½ mile wide, and nowhere is its width more than two miles, but there is in this restricted area some of the grandest and most imposing scenery in Europe. On each side is a chain of mountains with peaks from 4,000 to 5,000 feet above sea-level.

The small steamers from Ålesund thread the narrow **Vegsund,** separating the island of **Sula** from the mainland, and steer across the **Stor Fjord** to the mouth of the Hjörund Fjord, calling at **Festöy.** The larger boats come round by the wider **Sule Fjord,** between Hareidland and Sula, passing near **Liavåg** the ancient **Hjörungavåg,** where, in the tenth century, Håkon, Jarl (Earl) of Lade near Trondhjem, who then ruled Norway, defeated in a great sea-fight the Jomsburg Vikings, whose name was then known with terror in all corners of maritime Europe.

According to legend it seemed at first as if the Vikings would be the victors, so Håkon went ashore and offered his little son as a sacrifice to his gods, Odin and Thor. When he had regained his ship, a fierce storm of hail broke in the face of his enemies, a sign that his sacrifice had been accepted.

Before the narrow fjord is entered there is seen the range upon range of jagged peaks which crenellate the summits of the abrupt cliffs. These are the famed **Sunnmöre Alps,** the rugged and almost inaccessible peaks that have long attracted climbers from England. The surroundings of the lower walls—slopes they can hardly be termed—are somewhat gloomy, as though still mindful of their past. For the legend goes that in the Black Death the population of the valley was absolutely wiped out except for one woman, whose name was Hjörund. The valley is said to have been re-peopled from Scotland, and the inhabitants, dour as their surroundings, have certainly some of the characteristics of the Scots.

The steamer passes **Hundeidvik** ; the high mountain on the left is the **Skopshorn,** that on the right the **Jönshorn.** Next we come to the **Standals,** Great and Little, as they are called, not meriting in particular either term. Here the view of the fjord is at its best. The **Kolåstind,** or Gluggentind (first ascended by W. Cecil Slingsby and Mohn in 1876), lies on the right. It has been ascended several times since from the west and north. On the opposite shore is the **Ringsdalstind,** and ahead on the same shore rises the grim **Saksa** ; while far down the fjord one sees dozens of peaks and pinnacles rising one above the other, or in rows like the upper edge of a jag-saw.

The steamer calls at **Sæbö,** where a road comes down from Örstavik and Volda, on the Volden Fjord. A short distance beyond Sæbö the steamer enters the **Norangs Fjord,** the only branch of the Hjörund, and there is opened up a wonderful view of the Sunnmöre Alps, including the peaks of Slogen, Smörskredtind and Skruen, all over 5,000 feet. After calling at, or passing, the village of **Urke,** the steamer reaches **Öye** (*Hotel Union*). It lies at the edge of the fjord, and at the foot of the towering Mount Slogen, 5,120 feet. There is boat and salmon fishing, but climbing is the chief attraction.

Many ascents can be made from Öye without sleeping elsewhere if use is made of the morning and evening steamers and motor services. These make Kviteggen, Råna, Kolåstind and De Tre Söstre nearly as much Öye mountains as **Slogen.** An accurate survey of the immediate surroundings of Öye is in the possession of the Union Hotel and photographed copies are available. Slingsby's *Northern Playground* contains a Sunnmöre section and Oppenheim's *New Climbs in Norway*, 1898, is entirely devoted to the subject but has long been out of print.

By courtesy of] [*R.M.S.P.*

THE GEIRANGER FJORD AT MARÅK.

Wilse,] [*Oslo.*

THE ROMSDALSHORN.

That experienced mountaineer, Mr. C. W. Patchell, has said—

" For a guideless party with some experience Sunnmöre is absolutely ideal. There is trustworthy information to be had at Öye, and distances are not so great as to make it impossible to retrieve an error in route-finding. Six a.m. is considered an early start and in July the slowest party cannot be benighted. There are yet first ascents to be made, and there are new routes and variations without number."

Motor-car service between Öye and Hellesylt, 23 km., in about an hour. The tourist steamers usually drop their passengers at Öye and steam round the headland to Hellesylt, while the passengers make their way overland to rejoin there. The road crosses the brawling stream and ascends among a series of fine views of the **Skruen** (5,285 feet). About 7 km. from the hotel is the scene of the great landslide in 1908. It was over 400 yards wide at the bottom and 40 yards in height. The debris dammed the river, which formed a lake, 600 yards long and 300 yards wide, submerging the old road and a number of houses. When the water is clear the track of the road can be seen, together with the roofs of the houses, at the bottom of the lake. In earlier days a couple of other lakes in the valley were formed in the same way. We enter the **Norang Valley,** a wild pass littered with rock between snowy slopes. The scenery, as the road rises, becomes stern, wild and gloomy. The road rises to a height of over 1,100 feet among the precipices, and on the heights the snow lies throughout the year. The summit is at **Fibelstad-haugen,** where there is an hotel; this is the most important climbers' centre of the Alpine district, lying as it does close to the Kvitegg, Fibelstadnut and other mountains.

Now we descend into the Nebbedal, and the scenery becomes less forbidding; soon we pick up the rushing Sunnelv, turn eastward past Tryggestad, and, following the course of the river, as it roars through the gorge, reach **Hellesylt** (p. 115), at the head of the Sunnelvs Fjord.

The steamer returns down the **Norangs Fjord,** and rounds the point on which stands the **Jagta** (5,115 feet), entering again the Hjörund Fjord. Passing the villages of **Viddal** and **Leire,** on the left, we come to **Bjerke,** at the head of the fjord. The village lies at the foot of a range of forbidding mountains 5,000 feet high, and is frequented mainly by climbers. The two principal peaks of the district are the **Kvitegg** and the **Hornindalsrokken,** but Bjerke serves as a good base to explore the many other peaks and passes of the two peninsulas between which the Hjörund Fjord lies. Those who contemplate doing so would do well to consult Slingsby's *Norway, the Northern Playground,* the publications of the Norwegian Tourist Club, and the pages of the *Alpine Journal*.

ÅLESUND TO HELLESYLT AND MARÅK

viâ **the Stor Fjord, the Sunnelvs Fjord and the Geiranger Fjord.**

(**Note.**—*All steamers do not call at every place mentioned below. The local time table of the steamers—their "Sommerruter"—should be obtained.*)

The first part of the steamer route from Ålesund to the Geiranger Fjord is the same as that to the Hjörund Fjord already described, the smaller boats passing through the Vegsund, the larger skirting the Sula. The slower boats on this route call at **Hundeidvik,** at the mouth of the Hjörund; the fast boats turn directly east along the **Stor Fjord,** and, passing several villages, call first at **Söholt** (*Söholt Hotel*), a rising village growing in favour as a resort for tourists. It lies prettily situated at the head of a bay, and offers many charming excursions, as well as several mountain climbs that are not too difficult for the beginner and the amateur. The **Snaufjell** (2,880 feet), the **Lifjell** and the **Storhorn,** however, are heights that offer the charm of difficulty.

Motor service runs from Söholt through the valley between the Næremstind and the Trolltind to **Vestnes,** 30 km. (p. 110), whence the steamer can be taken to Molde. This is really a section of the through route from Vadheim to Molde.

Motor service also between Söholt and **Ålesund,** 40 kilometres. The scenery the whole way is very fine (*see* p. 107).

The steamer continues through the Stor Fjord, past the village of **Stordalen,** on the left, and **Stranden** on the right, at the entrance of the Stranddal.

The **Stranddal** is sometimes visited by walkers, but the good road ends before the head of the valley is reached, and only a cattle-track carries it on to **Ljöen,** on the Sunnelvs Fjord.

Opposite Stranden are the **Ringsetklov** and the **Gamtind** (about 4,500 feet). The fjord narrows here. After we pass Liabygden it forks left and right of the towering **Skrenakhorn,** which stands on the promontory. The northerly arm is the **Norddals Fjord,** which later becomes the Tafjord. The most important place on this fjord is **Sylte** (*Hotel Sylte*), at the mouth of the Valdal.

From Sylte there is a driving road to *Fremmergröning,* 23 km., the last farm in Valdalen, and thence to **Nedre Stölseter,** 2 km. farther, from which there is a path to **Åndalsnes,** reached in 9 hours, and one to **Ormheim,** reached in 12 hours.

The southern arm of the fjord is the more important, since it leads to Hellesylt and Maråk. The view of the **Sunnelvs Fjord** is very fine; it lies between the **Blåhorn** (5,018 feet) and the **Skrenakhorn** (4,887 feet). The shores of the fjord have but a small population. A few houses cling to the steep mountain side, and the inhabitants derive a living by toil among such patches of soil as the rain does not wash out from among the stones. **Oaldsbygda,** on the left, is almost the only village. The Geiranger Fjord branches off to the east before we reach **Hellesylt** (*Hotels Grand, Norangsdal, Missions*), a favourite resort for a long stay. It lies among some of the best mountain scenery in the Norwegian Alpine district, and is within easy reach of the principal peaks. It is at the same time on the important road which connects Öye, described in the reverse direction on pp. 104–5, Visnes, Grotli, and Maråk. Most tourist steamers call here. It is in consequence of these advantages a favourite centre for excursions, and there is variety of routes from Hellesylt sufficient to fill a long holiday.

The steamer returns down the bay in which Hellesylt lies, and makes eastward for the **Geiranger Fjord.** The character of the scenery changes a little; here the fjord is less open—in fact, it is as closed in as any fjord in the district. The Geiranger Fjord is at once of great grandeur and great loveliness. It is about 11 miles long, and hardly anywhere is it a quarter of a mile wide; while, on either hand, the mountains rise in sheer cliffs to a height of three or four thousand feet. The sides are scored with the tracks of numerous waterfalls, fed by the snow deposits and small glaciers that lie on the hollows of the mountain tops. High up, too, on both sides are small patches of cultivated fields, with farm-houses which look inaccessible, but winding paths connect them with boat houses on the shore. Near the entrance of the fjord is the great **Nokkenibba,** on the right, having the appearance of a gigantic arm-chair. The next height but one on the same side is the pointed **Lysurnibba,** roughly pyramidal. Then soon on the left is the **Bridal Veil,** a fall of which the upper part descends clear of the rock and has a lace-like appearance. A very short distance beyond it, and on the same side, is the celebrated **Seven Sisters** fall; the "sisters," although not always seven, shine like silver against the black and broken rock. The farm above it is Gården Knivsflå. On the opposite shore is another high-lying gård by the side of a fine waterfall, and a little farther on the right shore is a projecting rock called the **Prekestol** (pulpit). At the head of the fjord is **Maråk,** or **Merok,** a cluster of little wooden houses and some fine hotels, lying at the foot of the **Blåhorn** (not to be confounded with the Blåhorn on the Sunnelvs Fjord). Maråk (*Utsigten*, some way from the fjord, on the main road; *Union*, on the hill above the church; *Geiranger*, near the pier) is much visited by those who are crossing Norway by the Ottadal route to Otta, whence the railway runs to Oslo. This route is described on pages 119–121, but visitors who take their journey comfortably will be well advised to spend a day or two in **Maråk.**

The principal excursion is to **Djupvasshytte,** the frozen lake (*see* p. 106), and visitors whose time is limited are advised to take this in preference to any of the others, among which are trips to the **Storseterfoss,** a fine fall, an excursion of 2½ to 3 hours; to **Flydals Juv** (p. 106); to the farm Grande, a walk along the fjord (a couple of hours there and back); and to various peaks including the **Såthorn** and the **Blåhorn.**

THE ROMSDAL ROUTE.

From Åndalsnes to Dombås by Road.

ALTHOUGH the railway through the Romsdal (pp. 146–149) has almost entirely superseded the road, for travellers passing between Åndalsnes and the Dovre Railway the road route must have at least a brief note.

Rightly considered one of the finest travelling roads in Norway, both as regards scenery and in respect of accommodation, it may be said that its principal charm lies in the first 20 or 30 miles. For this reason many travellers content themselves with a journey as far as Bjorli, which comprises the best the route has to offer, with the additional advantage that the journey can be made from Åndalsnes there and back in one day. The character of the scenery on the other side from Bjorli is typical of that of Eastern Norway, and unlike the country west of the mountain range.

We may start either from **Åndalsnes** (p. 149) or from **Veblungsnes,** on the other side of the outlet of the River Rauma. The roads unite about 3 kilometres from either place. The main road then ascends a fine valley, past the *Halsa Hotel*, and the *Park Hotel*, near **Åk,** one of the beauty spots of the valley. Lady Beauclerk, in her book, *A Summer and Winter in Norway*, says: "Åk will always be to me the pearl of Norway, and the gem of my imagination. No description can do it justice." Let us therefore not attempt it, but, having enjoyed this matchless view, pass on beyond the Isterdal to the giants of the valley—the **Vengetinder** (5,958 feet), the **Romsdalshorn** (5,104 feet), and the **Trolltinder,** or Witches' Peaks, some 800 feet higher.

The road ascends less steeply to **Horgheim** (hotel); the valley is here strewn with boulders that come down in stone avalanches from the Trolltinderne in winter, and, whatever their past danger, they now add to the picturesqueness of the river scene. We pass the **Mongefoss,** a fine waterfall, apt to lose much of its splendour in dry weather;

next we pass **Kors Church,** and soon reach **Flatmark,** a small station. This is often the terminus of the journey made by steamer visitors. Climbers come sometimes to ascend the **Kalskråtind** (5,890 feet).

Continuing to ascend, we reach the **Vermafoss,** one of the finest falls on the route; it comes down some twelve hundred feet, fed from the **Verma Lake,** high up in the mountains. We pass many smaller falls—the **Styggefonnfoss,** the **Gravdefoss,** and on the right hand the **Dåntefoss.** The next station, **Ormheim** (*Ormheim Hotel*) is the last in the Romsdal. The village is much frequented as a resort, and occasionally climbers come here for an attack on the **Storhetta** (5,940 feet), a not very difficult ascent, made in 4 hours.

A little beyond Ormheim is the **Slettafoss**; here it is as well to leave the vehicle and go down to the little bridge near the road. Every driver on the road knows it, but the roar of the fall is itself guide enough. Now the road winds up the Björneklev, high above the river; we pass a road on the right leading up to Horgheim Seter, Tunga Seter, and the path through the Ulvådal to Muldal on the Tafjord. A steep winding ascent brings us to **Stuguflåten** (*Hotel*), 2,050 feet up, a good place for the night's stay. We pass several farms on the way to Bjorli (*Railway restaurant*), beyond which is a mountain-path leading north-west to Finset and the Eikesdal country. Farther on in the valley is the farm of **Einbu**; a monumental stone by the roadside records the story that Olav, King and Saint, halted here in his flight before Canute the Great in 1029.

The character of the country is now somewhat changed and rather less interesting. We pass **Lesjekogen Church,** close to which is *Mölmen Hotel.* From here the ascent of the **Storhö** (6,550 feet) may be made.

The hotel is at the west end of the **Lesjekogen Lake,** a gloomy sheet of water, the watershed of the valley; from it the *Rauma* flows westward through the Romsdal valley, while from the eastward end begins the *Lågen,* which we follow for the rest of the journey. The road follows the north shore of the lake to **Lesjaverk** (*Hotel*), a rest station dating from the eighteenth century. We next reach **Holset** (or Hoset), an old posting station.

After **Holåker** (*Hotel*) the road begins to mount as we come towards the Dovre mountains; and at **Dombås** (*Dombås Hotel*) we reach the highest station on the road (*see* p. 141).

THE OTTADAL ROUTE.

Route.—Both Bergen and Ålesund are at the western extremity of the Ottadal Route, which can also be approached from various points between those two towns, as a reference to the map will make plain. The meeting-point of all the western portions of the route is **Grotli** (p. 106).

From Bergen the route to Grotli lies through Visnes on the Nord Fjord, reached directly by steamer, as on pages 99 and 101, or *viâ* Vadheim (page 97). For the route from Visnes to Grotli, *see* pages 105–6.

From Ålesund Grotli is reached by steamer to Maråk as described on pages 114–116, and thence by the road described in the reverse direction on pages 106–7.

From Grotli there is a daily motor service to Otta, on the Dovre Railway, and the route thence to Oslo is described in the reverse direction on pages 138 and 140.

THIS route across Norway has been in great part described on foregoing pages. We shall here deal with the central portion from Grotli to Otta.

Leaving **Grotli,** we go through a country of rugged and wild scenery, with a near view of the **Skridulaupsbræ** (ascent and descent 8 hours) and a more distant glimpse of the **Jostedal Glacier,** the blue-white snowfield that backs the mountains in the foreground. We cross the mouth of the Vulu Valley, and pass small **Vulu Lake.** The view of these distant mountains is occasionally shut out, as happens as we cross the **Torsdal,** a valley on the left. A path, practicable only for good walkers, ascends this valley and descends to the Tafjord.

At **Billingen Seter** the road turns south, and, at 20 km. from Grotli, we reach **Pollfoss** (*Pollfoss Hotel*). The hotel is in a fine fir forest, 2,750 feet above sea level, and rushing down past it is a pretty waterfall, the Pollfoss, at the west end of the **Poll Lake.**

This is a starting-place for the path south-westward to Framrust Seter, and thence westward to the Raudal Lake, and the route to **Hjelle** (p. 105). In the opposite direction a path leads over the mountains to Nyseter, where a branch goes northward to **Bjorli**, on the Romsdal Railway, while the main line of the path is continued to Lesja on the same railway.

The main road lies along the north shore of the Poll Lake. At the east end of the lake the river *Otta* flows from it, and we follow its course for the rest of the journey. The road turns south below **Hegerbotn Seter,** which stands up on the hillside, and we reach **Bråten,** or Broten, at the mouth of the **Bråtedal.**

The **Tundredal Valley** branches off to the south-west from this point, and the Bråtedal road goes a little to the north of it, ascending past Åmot and Mörk to **During Seter,** whence a path leads along the Liavann to the *Sota Seter Tourist Hut,* in the Jotunheim.

We continue past **Nordberg Church** (18 km. from Pollfoss), near which, on the right, a path branches off to **Tundredal Seter,** by which the Grjotabræ may be reached. At **Flekköy,** or a little beyond it, we cross the river; we cross again, and then, passing Skjåk Church, come to **Ånstad,** at the head of the Otta Lake.

A mountain-path ascends to the north, leading to the Lordal at Nyseter, mentioned above; this route is sometimes followed by those intending to climb the Leirhö. Southward a route leads through the Lunderdal to the snowfields of Hestbræ and Grjotabræ.

The road follows the south shore of the Otta Lake, past the church of **Lom** (*Norddahls Hotel*), an old stave church which has been over-restored, and somewhat spoilt by the addition of a new ceiling. However, at the time of its restoration there was nothing else for it, so perhaps it is captious to criticize the restorers. A little farther is **Fossheim** (*Hotel Fossheim*) (*not to be confused with the Fossheim on the Vestre Slidre Route, p. 79*).

From Fossheim the ascent of the **Lomsegg** (5,980 feet) can be made. A guide can be obtained at the hotel. Up and down, 5 to 6 hours.

From Fossheim a road, on which is a motor-car service, runs up the Bövra Valley to **Röisheim** (*hotel*) and Elveseter (23 km.) for the Böverdal and the Jotunheim.

On the opposite side of the Otta Lake are the peaks of the **Lomshorungen** (5,560 feet).

The journey is continued along the **Otta Lake,** past several villages. The scenery is magnificent, especially the view back in the direction from which we have come. At **Frisvoll,** 15 km. from Fossheim (*Hotel Frisvoll*), the Otta Lake becomes merged into the **Våge Lake.** Having passed **Garmo,** we soon cross the Tesse River, which flows from the Tesse lake into the green waters of the Otta. Beyond **Tessand** we pass through **Volden,** where the road to Randsverk and the Sjödal, one of the entrances to the Jotunheim, branches off to the south (motor service between Vågå and Bessheim). Then the road, turning suddenly north, crosses the Våge Lake to the small town of **Vågå** (*Sörem Hotel, Svee Pension*). Vågå Church is an old fabric, presumably dating from the twelfth century, but enlarged, in the seventeenth, into its present shape. From the church we approach the attenuated village of **Sörheim,** in a prosperous farming district. After we leave Sörheim the valley begins to contract; soon we leave the lake and enter the Otta Valley, following the course of the river through Brovik and Björkheim into **Otta** (*see* page 140).

THE JOTUNHEIM.

Travel.—The Jotunheim is a walker's country. On some of the approach routee are motor services, and motor boats ply on some of the lakes, but the inner wilds are only possible of exploration afoot, and through these trails have been cut and staked. Guides are not necessary on the trails but must be engaged for the ascents. The tariff of fees is exhibited in the tourist club quarters.

Accommodation.—On the outskirts are excellent **hotels,** but in the mountain solitudes accommodation for tourists is provided by Mountain Huts. Some of them are privately owned; the majority belong to the *Norwegian Tourist Club*, and members of the club have priority. The prices are considerably below those of the hotels, but the accommodation is proportionately simpler. In the remoter parts of the Jotunheim the traveller must depend on the *Seters* (mountain dairies); as a rule he will find the occupants ready to give him the best they have at a ridiculously low rate, but these highland folk live on the simplest of fare and in the roughest of huts. The Jotunheim is no place for those who are inclined to be fussy or particular.

THE **Jotunheim,** an Alpine region of some 2,000 square miles formerly the "giants' home," as its name implies, to-day the "playground of Norway," lies between the valley of the Otta on the north, the upper parts of the Valdres on the south, and of the Gudbrandsdal on the east, and the Sogne and its branches on the west, but it has no sharply defined boundaries. On the west it merges into the Jostedal Glacier, and on the east into the lower mountain districts. In it are Norway's highest and finest peaks and most attractive mountain scenery. Streams and lakes abound, and on every hand gleam magnificent glaciers and waterfalls. Of vegetation there is little, as most of the valleys are about 3,000 feet above sea level. Many of the peaks, including the two loftiest, Galdhöpigg and Glittertind, are not difficult to ascend even by those persons who have never climbed a mountain, and the views are among the finest in the world.

It would require a guide-book of considerable dimensions to do justice to the claims of the Jotunheim as a tourists' playground, and we can here give only the merest outline of a few of the many routes among this group of mountains. Further information will be found in Slingsby's *Norway, the Northern Playground,* and in the many papers in English contributed to the Norwegian Tourist Club's year-books. That amusing book, *Three in Norway, by Two of Them,* deals with the country as it was in the early eighties, and those who go to-day will find it not very much changed. There is room for a good deal of local development before the charms of the country will begin to be spoilt.

Of the various approaches to the Jotunheim, the easiest is from the Valdres Route (p. 75). The route from **Nystua** (p. 77) across Lakes Tyin and Bygdin is available to the most indolent of tourists. Close to **Tyinholmen** (*large hotel*), at the head of Lake Tyin, is **Skinegg** mountain (5,216 feet), which affords a fine view of Jotunheim.

The ascent can be made in a couple of hours, and the descent may be made to **Eidsbugaren** (*large hotel*), at the western end of Lake Bygdin. From both Tyinholmen and Eidsbugaren the **Uranåstind** can be ascended. It presents so little difficulty that those inexperienced in climbing need not hesitate to attack it. The descent may be made to **Skogadalsböen** Tourist Hut. There is a marked path to it from Tyinholmen and Eidsbugaren, but it is prudent to take a guide.

From **Bygdin,** at the eastern end of the Bygdin Lake (*hotels*, p. 79), the **Bitihorn,** 5,200 feet, can be ascended in 4–5 hours. Also from Bygdin one can go in 6 or 7 hours to **Bessheim** or to **Gjendesheim** (large hut). From the hotels at or near either end of the lake the **Stölsnostinder** can be ascended with a guide. From its summit there is one of the finest views in Europe. From **Nybod,** about the centre of the north shore of Lake Bygdin and reached by motor boat, the Torfinstind can be ascended with a guide, and one can go down the **Torfinsdal** and over the **Svartdalsvann,** affording fine views northward, to the hut at **Gjendebu.**

From the western end of the lake also a path leads north-easterly to *Gjendebu Hut*. It lies at the west end of **Lake Gjende,** some 3,000 feet up. Gjende has been described as " an unfrequented and awfully desolate Lake of Lucerne." On the north shore of the lake (motor-boat in July and August) is a hut at **Memurubu,** from which a path north-east leads to the **Russvann,** and thence to the *Glitterheim Hut* (35 beds). A path leads north-west from Gjendebu through the **Uladal,** one of the finest valleys of the Jotunheim, to *Spiterstulen Hut* (plenty of accommodation), a merry and much-frequented place in the climbing season. Many climbers start out for the ascent of the Galdhöpigg (8,400 feet) from this place, descending to the *Gjuvass Hut,* on the north side of the mountain (plenty of accommodation) ; and also for the ascent of the **Glittertind** (8,383 feet). Farther on the valley becomes the Visdal, and leads to Röisheim and Lom.

From **Gjendesheim,** at the east end of the lake, a path leads north to **Bessheim** (*Bessheim Hotel*) on **Upper Sjodals Lake,** whence a good road leads to Randsverk and Vågåmo. Another leads east along the **Sikkildals Lake,** and thence to Vinstra station, on the line from Oslo to Otta.

Among other approaches are :

1. From the Luster Fjord and Årdals Fjord, branches of the Sogne Fjord.

From **Sogndal** (p. 94) a public motor runs along the western side of the Luster Fjord, through Skjolden, at its head, to **Fortun** (*hotel*), a short distance farther, but 70 km. from Sogndal. Thence one ascends to **Turtagrö** (*large hotel and Skagastöl hut*), an excellent starting-point for the ascent of the Horungtinder peaks, both to the mountaineer and to the tourist. A favourite excursion is to the *Skagastölsvann,* at the foot of the glacier. From Turtagrö one can go across the Jotunheim, to the Ottadal Route. One mounts to a desolate tableland, passing the *Oscarhaug,* a stone commemorating a visit of Oscar II in 1860. An altitude of 4,000 feet is reached, and then one descends to the Herrevann, from which one must mount again to a height of 4,500 feet, and then descend to **Krossbu** (*Tourist Station*), and 7 km. farther is the **Bövertun seter,** from which the route goes on to Röisheim *Hotel* (*see* below).

2. From **Årdal** (*Hotel*), reached by steamer from Lærdal (p. 95), thence ¼ hour's walk to Årdals Lake, on which a motor-boat goes to **Farnes** (*Hotel*), whence one can go to **Berdals Seter,** a small tourist hut (reached also from Turtagrö in 3–4 hours) for the ascent of the **Horungtinder** peaks.

From Farnes there is a path to **Tyin** and to **Vetti** (*Tourist Hut*), an hour's walk from the Vettifoss. The water falls more than 800 feet. In dry summers there is little water, which then has the appearance of a delicate veil as it goes over the cliff. Vetti is a starting-point for the ascent of the **Austabottind** and for crossing the Horungerne. It is also a good point of departure for the ascent of the **Skagastölstind** (7,874 feet), at the foot of which is the *Skagastölstind Hut.* From Vetti there is a good route to Tyinholmen. Northward of Vetti is the large *Skogadalsböen Hut,* from which a path leads westward beside the Skagastölstind to Turtagrö, and north-eastward to *Leirvassbu Hut*, amid high mountain scenery and in the heart of the Jotunheim.

3. From the Gudbrandsdal by way of **Lom,** on the Ottadal Route (p. 120), and **Röisheim,** connected with it by motor (sleigh in winter).

Here are excellent quarters in an old-fashioned Gudbrandsdal farm built in 1260 and opened as a posting station in 1858. It stands 1,700 feet above the sea, in a valley in which the mountain rivers Bövra and Visa meet in magnificent surroundings. Here one can have ski-ing in the winter, shooting in the autumn and winter, fishing in its season, and mountaineering. The trip to the Galdhöpigg can be made in a day, but it is better to spend a night at the Gjuvass hut, 4½ hours from Röisheim. The ascent of the Glittertind takes one day, the Lomsegg 7 to 8 hours, the Lauvhö 6 to 7 hours, and the Sulheimstorhö 5 to 6 hours. In the summer Röisheim is accessible from Geiranger or Nord Fjord in 11 and 13 hours respectively, from Otta in 4 hours.

4. Another much-used approach from the Ottadal Route starts from Vågå (p. 121), from which public motors run through Randsverk (*Hotel*) to *Bessheim Hotel*, from which a good road goes to **Gjendesheim** (*Hotel*) already mentioned. These last two places are in the very heart of "the Peer Gynt Country," the famous knife-edge ridge of Besseggen, across which Peer attempted to ride on a reindeer-buck, lying just above them.

5. From **Vinstra** on the Dovre Railway, a motor goes to **Kampeseter,** 18 km. (*hotel*), whence the road goes on to **Sikkilsdals seter** (*hotel*), from which a guide should be taken to **Gjendesheim.**

OSLO.

Approaches.—By sea, wholly or in part, *see* pp. 12–14. By train from Bergen in 13½ hours. From Trondhjem in about 15½ hours. From Åndalsnes (near Molde) in 13¼ hours. From Otta in 10 hours. From Fagernes in 7 hours.

Banks.—Bennett's Travel Bureau, Cook's Tourist Office and various Norwegian banks.

Baths.—*Oslo Baths,* in Munkedams Veien. Warm sea-water baths below the Victoria Terrace. There are Communal Baths in the Torv Gate and Pilestradet (Bislett Swimming Bath and Medicinal Baths). For open-air bathing it is best to go to Bygdöy. (*See* p. 136.)

Boating.—Pleasure boats can be hired at Bygdöy. There are rowing clubs at Dronningen and Frognerkilen.

Cafés.—There are excellent cafés in Oslo. At the best of them English papers are to be seen. Most are restaurants as well as cafés. The principal are the *Grand,* in the Karl Johans Gate; the *Bristol,* behind Karl Johans Gate; the *Theatre Café,* attached to the Hotel Continental, in the Stortings Gate; the *Frimurerloge* (Freemasons' Café) in the Stortings Gate; *Dronningen, Kongen, Skansen, Humlen* and *Möllhausen* (Confectioners, Karl Johans Gate).

Consulates.—*British Consulate,* 7 Kirke Gaten. British Passport Office, 2 Sehesteds Plass. Hours, 10 to 1.

U.S. Consulate, 1 Strand Gate.

English Church.—Möller Gaten. The hours of the services are shown on cards in all the hotels.

Excursions.—*See* under separate section, "The Environs of Oslo."

Hotels.—Prices in Oslo are slightly higher than those at other places in Norway for the same accommodation.

For British and American visitors, the three principal hotels are the *Grand,* on Karl Johans Gate; the *Bristol,* near Karl Johans Gate; and the *Victoria.* Others are: the *Norge,* near the Karl Johans Gate; *Savoy,* near the Karl Johans Gate; *Nobel,* Karl Johans Gate; the *Rose,* on the Drammensvel; *Missions,* centrally situated; *Pension Ritz,* in a quiet and select part of the city; and the *Westminster,* Karl Johans Gate.

In addition there are many private hotels and boarding-houses. The prices are more moderate, and the accommodation is quite good of its kind. Information regarding these can be obtained from the Tourist Traffic Association, 2 Stortings Gate, Oslo. The establishments are too numerous for details to be given here.

Music.—Bands play in the Gardens during the summer.

Places of Interest.—The *Royal Palace,* a classical building, opposite the western end of Karl Johans Gate. Not shown to the public.

Storting Building (Parliament House). Apply to the caretaker at the entrance in the Stortings Gate. A small fee is expected.

Museum of Art, Universitets Gate. Sculpture and collection of pictures. Open free on Sundays from 12 to 3 and 6 to 8 and Tuesdays and Thursdays 6 to 8. On Tuesday, Wednesdays, Thursdays and Fridays, 12 to 3. Admission 50 öre. At all other times apply to the custodian, when a small fee is expected.

Museum of Industrial Art. In the Ullevoldsvei. Daily, free, 12 to 3.

Historical Museum, in the Fredriks Gate, behind the University. Antiquities and Ethnography. From June 1 to September 1, weekdays, 11 to 3; Sundays, 12 to 3. Remainder of year, Tuesdays, Wednesdays, Thursdays, Fridays, 1 to 3; Sunday, 12 to 3. Admission free. *The Oseberg Collection, see* p. 131. In the Historical Museum. Days and hours as above, but admission 50 öre except on Sundays.

The *Gokstad Viking Ship*, in a shed, behind the University. Entrance from the Universitets Gate. Admission as for the Oseberg Collection.

Population.—About 256,000. With suburbs, 350,000.

Porters in the stations wear the words *Faste Bærere* on their caps, outside and at other places in the town porters wear the word *Bybud*. Their charges for luggage or messages vary with the distance and quantity; the porters are bound to produce a list of charges on demand.

Post Office.—At the corner of Prinsens Gate and Dronningens Gate (southward from Our Saviour's Church). Open week-days, 8 a.m. to 7.30 p.m. There are sub-offices in the various quarters.

Telegraph Office near the Post Office, open for telegrams only day and night.

Quays.—The quays where the passenger steamers from England are moored are on the east side of the town. The local tourist steamers start from the *Piperviks Quay*, reached from the Karl Johans Gate by the Tordenskjolds Gate, leading from the Stortings Gate to the Tordenskjolds Plass, where the quays and the West Station are situated.

Railway Stations.—The principal station is that in the Jernbanetorv, on the east side of the town, called the *Östbane* (East Station). This is the station for the trains for the North, to Trondhjem, to Bergen, to Åndalsnes and to Fagernes. The West Station, for Drammen, Skien and the southern districts, is called the *Vestbane*. It is on the river-front, near the Piperviks Quay. The terminus of Holmenkollen and Tryvanns Electric Railway is near the National Theatre.

Shopping.—There are plenty of fine shops in Oslo, notably in Karl Johans Gate, and in the district lying between it and the Fortress—the principal business district.

Sightseeing.—Motors with an English-speaking guide leave each of the Tourist Offices named below daily.

Taxicabs.—Cabstands in all the principal squares and at the quays and railway stations.

Theatres.—The *National Theatre*, in the Stortings Gate, seats 1,268 persons; *Central Theatre*, Akersgate 38 (comedy); *Tivoli*, Stortings Gate (variety); the *New Theatre*, adjoining the Grand Hotel in Rosenkranz Gate. Variety performances, or café concerts, are also given at many of the lesser cafés. The principal Cinemas are in or near Karl Johans Gate and Stortings Gate.

Tourist Offices.—*Bennett's*, Karl Johans Gate 35; *Cook's*, Karl Johans Gate 20; *Berg-Hansen*, Dronningens Gate.

Trams.—These run all over the city and to the suburbs. Fare 15 öre for any distance on the same line.

View Points.—Akershus Castle, St. Hanshaugen, reached by tramway in 10 minutes, and Kampens Vandbassin, in the eastern part of the town, reached by tramway in 20 minutes.

SEEN from the fjord which bears its name, Oslo conveys the impression of being a grand and imposing capital. It lies at the head of the waters, the sea lapping up to its streets, with high fir-clad hills rising on either side and beyond. Its tall spires and broad streets give an impression of grandeur and spaciousness that is indeed its true note. For the city enjoyed the advantages of town-planning at its very beginning. It adjoins the site of the ancient Viking city of *Oslo*, which the sagas say was founded in 1048 by Harald Hårdråde (The Hard-ruling), who, eighteen years later, invaded England to aid Tostig, the English king Harold's brother, and met his death in battle at Stamford Bridge, near York.

It is interesting in passing to recall that rather more than 500 years later, Hårdråde's city was the scene of an event connected with British history. This was the marriage which there took place in 1589, of James VI of Scotland, afterwards James I of England, with the Dano-Norwegian Princess Anne. Through this marriage Scotland became possessed of the Orkney Isles, of such great strategic importance during the Great War. Thirty-five years after the marriage Oslo was burnt out.

King Christian IV hurried from Denmark to the devastated spot and planned the new city that should be built, not on the site which Harald Hårdråde had utilized, but on the Akersnes peninsula where, for more than 300 years, had been standing the Akershus fortress, built to protect the city that fire had destroyed. King Christian laid out his city with broad straight streets, and gave it the royal name of Christiania (modernized to Kristiania), which it bore for just 300 years (1624–1924), and then the Storting decided that the capital should bear its ancient name.

Ancient Christiania set an example to the new city that grew up round its old boundaries, and carried on the tradition of spaciousness, with the result that it is one of the airiest, cleanest and healthiest of the capitals of the North. A broad garden runs through the centre of the city, forming a grand promenade where all the life and fashion of the capital assembles ; this garden runs to the foot of the hill on which the Royal Palace stands, and from it depend in formal regularity the principal streets and squares. As the starting-place for tours in Telemarken, the Valdres Route, or the Gudbrandsdal, to say nothing of its own immediate surroundings, the capital is largely visited by tourists. It can be seen thoroughly in three days, but those who have the time to spare will find plenty to occupy a week or more.

The following brief itinerary takes in the principal sights of Oslo :—

Oslo's main street is **Karl Johans Gate.** It runs from the **Östbane** (East Railway Station) through the liveliest business quarter up to the Royal Palace. Starting from **Jernbanetorvet** (the Railway Square), we soon have on our right the chief station of the Fire Brigade, behind which is **Vor Frelsers Kirke** (Our Saviour's Church), built in 1697, but so restored in 1850 that little of its old character is left. Over the altar is a painting of *Christ in Gethsemane*, by Steinle. The

Wilse,] — [*Oslo.*

KARL JOHANS GATE, OSLO.

[*Wilse and E.N.A.*

OSLO.

The Royal Palace—The Akershus—The Storting.

massive tower is used by the firemen as a watch tower. Facing the Church is the **Stortorv** (Great Market). In the centre of the Square is a *Monument to Christian IV*, the founder of the city.

Christian IV was born at Frederiksborg in 1577, and ascended the throne of Denmark and Norway in 1599. He made war on Sweden in 1611, and again in 1643; he also took part in the early stages of the Thirty Years' War. His military successes were few and insignificant; but his genius for organization found scope in developing the navy and overseas commerce of his country, and in breaking up the restrictive methods of the Hanse League's trading stations. His reforms in the internal administration of the country underlie the progress of Norway as we know it to-day.

From the **Market Place** Möller Gate, going northward, soon leads to the **Norwegian Home Industries** and then to the **English Church.**

On the opposite side of Karl Johans Gate to the Fire Station is Dronningens Gate, leading to the **Post Office,** one of the most modern in Europe, ranking among the sights of the city. A short distance westward of the Post Office is the **Telegraph Office** in Prinsens Gate.

Continuing along the Karl Johans Gate, we soon have on our left Cook's Tourist Office. Opposite it is Akers Gate, leading to the **Roman Catholic Church,** the **Museum of Arts and Industries,** and beyond these, **St. Hanshaugen.**

A few steps farther we come to the **Storting,** or Norwegian Parliament House. It is not an imposing building; in fact, it is rather dingy with its yellow brick exterior, and seems to reflect the period (1866) in which it was built. The only interesting thing in it is the picture by Wergeland of the drawing-up of the Norwegian constitution at Eidsvoll in 1814, and even that is quite an indifferent piece of work. In front of the building is the attractive little Eidsvold Plass, separated only by Rosenkrantz Gate from **Studenterlunden** (The Students' Park), in which a band plays at noon during the summer. These pleasant gardens lie between the Karl Johans Gate and the **Stortings Gate.** In these two promenades are the principal cafés, the offices of the chief tourist agencies, and some fine shops. The gardens widen towards the west end, where is the **National Theatre.** It will seat 1,268 persons, and such is the love of the Norwegians for the drama that it is generally full. Before the main entrance are

Statues of Ibsen and *Björnson.* Behind the theatre is a *Statue of Brun,* the actor.

Hard by the theatre is the underground terminus of *Holmenkollen and Tryvanns Electric Railway.*

On the opposite side of Karl Johans Gate is the **University,** forming three sides of a quadrangle, with colonnades and pediments—heavy-looking buildings, and not of any interest in themselves except for the *Aula.* The University was founded in 1813. Beyond the University Karl Johans Gate passes into **Slotsbakken** (The Palace Hill) at the top of which is the **Royal Palace,** occupying what is one of the best positions for a palace in the whole of Europe. Its **Park** is a pleasant place of rest, and the views are worth climbing the hill for. In front of the palace stands an equestrian *Statue of King Karl Johan,* the work of the sculptor Bergslien.

Karl Johan, King of Sweden and Norway, is better known to history under his real name of *Marshal Bernadotte.* He was one of Napoleon's Generals, and the part he played in the Napoleonic wars needs no recapitulation. The children of Karl XIII of Sweden and Norway having died, and also the elected Crown Prince, Charles Augustus of Holstein-Sonderburg, the Swedes offered the status of Crown Prince to Bernadotte, who succeeded to the throne in 1818, and was crowned at Stockholm and Trondhjem.

We can leave the Park at the north-east corner and, descending the slope, we shall come to the monument of *Richard Nordraak,* the composer of the music to the National Anthem. With back to this we have before us the Geographical Survey Office, separating St. Olavs Gate (left) and Kristian IV Gate (right). Taking either of these, a few yards bring us to Fredriks Gate. At its junction with Kristian Augusts Gate is—

The Historical Museum.

Admission.—*See* p. 126.

On the ground floor is an excellent collection of antiquities from the Stone, Bronze and Iron Age and the Viking times. On the second floor are coins, etc. On the second floor also and on the third are various ethnographical collections.

There is an interesting collection of objects illustrative of the life and handicraft of the Lapps. The skill of these primitive people, as illustrated in the Lapp sleigh, ski and trappings, is remarkable, and not less noteworthy are their carvings on reindeer horn, their spoons, charms, loom and woven work. There is, of course, no pottery; the Lapps in their enforced simplicity make very good substitutes for pottery by the deft use of horn and wood. Notice should be paid to the Lapp method of weaving bands. Anthropologists will find at the far end of the exhibition some Lapp skulls and plaster casts of heads.

The Amundsen Collection of Esquimaux ethnological objects is one of the best of its kind. But to many visitors the most interesting collection is that of articles found in the **Oseberg Ship,** now exhibited at Bygdöy. These include a four-wheeled wagon, three sledges, an oak chest, a richly hooped bucket, a bucket called the Buddha bucket on account of two enamel bail-end mounts suggestive of Buddha figures, a loom for a mode of weaving still existing in Norway, implements belonging to women's occupations, kitchen utensils, including little hatchets, small wooden dishes, a knife, scoop, lamp, pot chain, handmill. Other objects are an iron cooking pot suspended from a very fine jack, big water casks, a pair of shoes of fine leather, two beautiful carved bed posts, specimens of the cordage, bone combs and smaller articles used by the great lady to whom the ship belonged and in which she was buried some eleven hundred years ago.

Eastward from the Historical Museum, at the corner of Kristian Augusts Gate and Universitets Gate, is the **National Gallery.** It contains little of the older schools to attract the student of painting. The more modern collections have, however, an interest of their own. There is a good *Monet*, and a landscape by *Anders Zorn*. Room II is devoted mainly to the older school of Norwegian painting, and contains work by *Tideman*, *Gude*, *Fritz Thaulow*, and *Christian Krogh*. In the remaining rooms is a collection of works by the more modern school of Norwegian painters, and it conveys the idea of a national tendency in course of vigorous development.

From either of the institutions just described it is but a few steps to the building in the University grounds, in which is temporarily housed the celebrated **Viking Ship** which was dug up at Gokstad, in the south of Norway. It is identical with the warships used by the Northmen in their raids on Britain in the tenth and eleventh centuries. Either this vessel or that at Bygdöy should be visited.

At its northern end Universitets Gate, as well as Fredriks Gate, communicates with St. Olavs Gate, which, followed eastward (to the right), soon leads to the **Roman Catholic Church of St. Olav** and the **Kunstindustri Museum** (Museum of Arts and Crafts) at the corner of the Ullevålsvei.

It contains a fair collection illustrative of the development of Norwegian craftsmanship in the seventeenth, eighteenth, and nineteenth centuries. The drinking vessels are good, though they are hardly typical of Norway, being rather influenced by German ideas; the furniture is more representative. There are specimens of workmanship from foreign countries; note the piece of French tapestry of the seventeenth century, and do not fail to see the *Painted Room* (Room I), taken from a farm in Southern Norway.

From the Museum a tram runs northward to **St. Hanshaugen,** a hill on which is a public park. It has a restaurant and a bandstand and at the highest point is a reservoir. From the vicinity of this, and especially from the summit of the building, there is a most beautiful view of the city and of the fjord.

The tram passes the **Vor Frelsers Gravlund,** the largest of the Oslo cemeteries. In it are buried Ibsen, Björnson, Wergeland, Sverdrup, Nordraak and other celebrated Norwegians. Here, as in other Norwegian cemeteries, will be observed the curious practice of placing privately owned white garden seats by the side of graves, for the convenience of relatives and friends. Opposite the northern end of the Cemetery is the **Gamle Akers Kirke,** built in the twelfth century and restored in 1861, when the tower was added.

Returning to Karl Johans Gate we can go by tram or on foot along Rosenkrantz Gate to **Piperviken Pier,** from which small steamers go at short intervals to Bygdönes, where are sea baths, and to **Bygdöy.**

A short distance to the south-east of the pier rises the old fortress of **Akershus,** once of vital importance to the town, but now useful chiefly as a military store, prison and military museum. From the upper ramparts the views of the city and the fjord are very fine.

The fortress was founded in the thirteenth century by Håkon V, was rebuilt early in the seventeenth, and was a royal residence down to the beginning of the eighteenth. It withstood many sieges, the last being carried on by Charles XII of Sweden, who ineffectually bombarded the fortress from what is to-day the Great Market Place.

To visit the west end of Oslo, take a westward-bound tram from Stortings Gate. **Drammensveien,** one of the city's handsomest thoroughfares, comes from the foot of the Palace Hill, runs along the base of the Abel Mound, the site of Vigeland's monument to the mathematician, *Nils Henrik Abel,* and is continued to Skillebekk, whence there is a steam ferry to Bygdöy (p. 134).

We pass on the left the Government Offices of Victoria Terasse and then, on the same side, at the corner of Arbins Gate, we have the house, marked by a tablet, in which **Ibsen** spent the last years of his life. Beyond the Palace Park we have, on the right, the **Nobel Institute,** with library and reading rooms open to the public. A little farther we come to **Solli Park,** with a statue of *The Man with the Key,* a fragment from Rodin's group "The Burghers of Calais." Obliquely opposite the park is the University Library. Behind it is the Observatory.

At Solli Place is the junction of the important thoroughfares named **Bygdöy Alle** and **Frognervei.** The former, very wide and adorned with fine trees, forms the chord of the arc upon which Drammenveien now enters. Along Frognervei runs a branch of the tramway by which we soon reach **Frogner Park,** the most beautiful of the city's parks. In it are the **Oslo Municipal Museum** (Bymuseet), formerly Frogner Manor House, and the bust of *Abraham Lincoln,* given to the city in 1914 by Norwegian-Americans. Near the south-west corner of the park is Vigeland's Studio, converted into a **Vigeland Museum,** in accordance with the condition on which the building was presented by the city to the eminent sculptor. Instead of retracing our route from the centre of the city we can return by the tram which follows Kirkeveien, on the east side of the park, to Bogstadveien, goes eastward along that and finally arrives at Karl Johans Gate.

THE ENVIRONS OF OSLO.

THE capital of Norway is, in respect of pleasant surroundings, almost ideally situated. There is a wide selection of tours to be made, the complete enumeration of which is impossible. A few, however, are here briefly indicated.

Worthy of first place is the peninsula of—

Bygdöy.

Access.—The peninsula may be reached by ferry steamer from the Piperviks Quay (p. 132); by tram to Skillebekk or to Skarpsno (both westward of Piperviks Quay), and thence by ferry or by motor from any part of the city in about half an hour.

But those spending only a day or two in Oslo will be well advised to join one of the sight-seeing parties, setting out each morning in motors from Cook's and Bennett's Offices.

The great attraction of Bygdöy is the **Norsk Folkemuseum**—an open-air museum of Norwegian antiquities. Charmingly placed along forest-bordered roads and paths are ancient homesteads, storehouses, etc., removed from various parts of Norway and fitted up with their original furniture or with furniture of their period, the whole giving a very comprehensive idea of how the Norwegians have lived from Viking times onward. And in their midst is the fine Stave Church erected eight hundred years ago at far-off Gol, in the Hallingdal. It contains specimens of ecclesiastical art and craftsmanship from the middle of the sixteenth century to about the end of the eighteenth.

The entrance gate is a copy of the old town gate at Bergen, dated 1628.

It is impossible to guide the visitor from one building to another, or to say in what order the buildings will be visited by a conducted party. We can only name them. They comprise a *Telemarken loft and storehouse*, with fine carving. A *Setesdal house*, in quite different style; the Setesdal keynote is heaviness and solidity, a characteristic shared by, and perhaps derived from, the inhabitants of this remote valley. Two houses from Numedal; the one, an old *Rökstue* (smoke-house) from Rauland in Opdalen is *the oldest wooden house in Norway*, dating probably from the thirteenth century.

[*E.N.A. and W..se.*

OSCARSHALL—FROGNERSETER RESTAURANT—GOKSTAD VIKING SHIP.

Wilse,] *[Oslo.*

OSLO FJORD.

The other, though not less interesting, is of a much later date —seventeenth century, with eighteenth-century additions. A *Valdres house*. Two houses from the *Österdal*, a winter-house and a summer-house, giving a good idea of life in a country where extremes of climate and variations of light have moulded national habits to such a marked degree. A *Telemarken storehouse*, illustrative of farm life in that province in the eighteenth century. A *loft from Gudbrandsdal*, with galleries. A *louvre house* from Kjelleberg, Setesdal.

In a building specially constructed for it is—

The Oseberg Ship,

the Viking vessel named from the place of its discovery in 1903, in a fenny district midway between the coast towns of Tönsberg and Sandefjord, respectively about 45 and 60 miles south of Oslo. The mound in which the vessel was found was about 120 yards in circumference and about 20 feet high. From the discoveries made when the mound was opened, it was clear that the method of burial was to haul the ship high and dry into a hollow place; then, having placed the dead person within, to roof it over, and cover it with stones, earth and peat. In the ship two skeletons, both of women, were found, and it is conjectured that one of these was that of a lady of high rank who had died, and the other that of a maidservant who had been compelled to accompany her mistress in death. Many objects had been buried with them. Some of these have been named as exhibits in the Historical Museum (p. 131). Any gold and silver articles which had accompanied their owner had been carried off by robbers, probably in the eleventh century.

"The ship," writes Professor G. Gustafson, in an interesting pamphlet on the subject, "is entirely of oak, and the timbers have kept so well that they were able to bear being steamed and bent back into their original shape. . . . Even the steaming of the ornamented stem and stern timbers was ventured upon, in order to straighten them after their bending in the barrow. With all this work, the ship has been successfully restored to its original form; and nothing has been spoiled. With the exception of a piece about half a yard long, five or six little bits let in, and one of the beams, that are new, the whole ship, from end to end, consists of the old, original woodwork. Even two-thirds of the rivets are the old ones."

The dimensions of the vessel are: Length about 70 feet 6 inches, beam 16 feet 6 inches. There are twelve strakes, and the ship was propelled by fifteen oars. (The oars now in the holes are not the old ones.) She carried a mast amidships for the big square sail. "The ship," says Professor

Gustafson, "is rather flat-bottomed, but has a fine sheer and must have been both stiff and easy-going; but she has certainly not been a vessel for long voyages."

From the ornaments and other things the date of the ship can be fixed at about the year 800. It is thus over 1,100 years old.

A booklet giving in English a detailed description of the vessel and its contents is on sale in the building.

In the grounds is a good restaurant and on the same island is the restaurant *Dronningen* (the Queen), opposite which is *Kongen* (the King), at the club houses respectively of the Royal Yacht Club and the Rowing Club.

Not far from the Folkemuseum is the **Bygdöy Kongsgård,** a wooden building used as a summer residence by the royal family. The oldest part dates from 1652, being a portion of a shooting-box erected by Christian IV. Another notable building is **Oscarshall,** built in 1850 as a royal summer residence. In the banqueting hall is a series of paintings by Tidemans depicting Norwegian peasant life.

An **Agricultural Museum** belonging to the Folkemuseum is another of Bygdöy's attractions.

Mention has already been made of the **Sea Baths** (p. 126).

Bygdöy also has an **open-air theatre,** and on those evenings when plays are given or there are folk dances and numerous electric lamps are shining, the peninsula is especially delightful.

Holmenkollen, Voksenkollen and Frognerseter.

These places, in the pine-covered hills on the north-west side of Oslo, are the playgrounds of the city. They are seen at their best in winter, when the tobogganing and ski-ing sports are on; but they are also delightful in summer. A favourite approach is by a taxi or a private motor or by motor-car from one of the tourist agencies. The usual route is by the electric railway to **Holmenkollen** (*trains about every quarter-hour*). (The city terminus is underground behind the National Theatre, pending the extension of the line to the Östbane station.) Having an elevation of 1,018 feet above sea level, Holmenkollen affords a magnificent view of the city and the fjord. In winter, as already stated, it is the scene of the celebrated international ski-ing competition. The **Besserud Lake** is admirable for skating. Holmenkollen has a good restaurant, and a *Sanatorium* open all the year round. From Holmenkollen station the line goes on to

Voksenkollen and Frognerseter. Also from Holmenkollen a pleasant road winds among the hills to a point where it forks left to Voksenkollen and right to Frognerseter. For good walkers the best route is by road or through the woods to **Voksenkollen** (*Anne Kures Hotel*). Voksenkollen is but half an hour's walk from Holmenkollen, and, rising 500 feet higher, gives a more extensive view. Near by is the statue of Mr. H. H. Krag, the engineer responsible for the construction of some of the best of Norway's roads. As the hotel at Voksenkollen has no restaurant one should follow the road to **Frognerseter,** where there is a good restaurant. The view from Frognerseter (1,434 feet) is more wonderful than that from Holmenkollen. Another attraction is the **Ski-museum,** the only one of its kind in the world. Among its contents are the outfits of Captain Amundsen and other Norwegian polar explorers.

From Frognerseter to Midstuen station on the electric railway runs the **Corkscrew** (Korketrekkeren), Norway's most famous toboggan road.

Also from Frognerseter a walk of 20 minutes in a north-westerly direction will take one to **Tryvannshöiden,** the site of a powerful radio station and of a tower commanding a wonderfully wide view.

Other excursions in the neighbourhood of Oslo are :—

(1) To **Ekeberg,** a wooded hill on the east side of the town, reached by electric railway from Stortorvet. Over the harbour and Bundefjord is a fine view, made particularly pleasing by the range of beautiful islands just off the coast.

(2) By motor boat plying regularly between Vippetangen (S.E. of Akershus) and **Hovedöy,** an island on which are the ruins of an Abbey founded by English Cistercian monks in 1147.

(3) By small steamers running regularly from Jernbane-bryggen among the numerous islands on the east side of the fjord.

(4) By steamer among the beautiful islands on the west side of the fjord.

These by no means exhaust the places of interest in the neighbourhood. On both sides of the Oslo Fjord are watering-places, all speedily reached by steamer, rail or motor. Some of the more notable are Larkollen, Hankö, Skjærhalden, Åsgårdstrand, Nötteröy, Tjöme, Larvik, and Sandefjord.

OSLO TO TRONDHJEM.

Map facing p. 75.

Routes.—Since 1921 there have been two railway routes between the capital and Trondhjem. The older route lies through the **Österdal,** the valley of the Glommen river, as far as Elverum. Its line is broad-gauged to Hamar—rather less than a fourth of the way, and thence is narrow-gauged, so that at Hamar, by this route, one has to change trains.

The newer line goes through the **Gudbrandsdal** and over the Dovre mountains. On both lines express trains* are run to Trondhjem, once a day on the older route, twice daily on the newer route, one being at night, sleeping cars for the three classes (*see* p. 16) being provided. *Viâ* the Österdal the distance is 562 kilometres (nearly 350 miles), over the Dovre Mountains 553.

The newer route is the more beautiful and for that reason shall be the first described.

A. THE DOVREFJELL ROUTE.

THE train leaves Oslo from the **East Station** (Östbanegård), crosses the Akers river, and then ascends rapidly, affording a fine panoramic view of the city, of the hills stretching away east and west, and of the charming Oslo Fjord. Then for about 40 miles it runs through a region of fine forests and rich farms, small lakes and beautiful streams.. At the small but prosperous factory town of **Lilleström** (*buffet*), on the banks of Lake Öieren, a branch goes off to Kongsvinger, Charlottenberg and Stockholm, and the main line takes a more northerly direction to **Eidsvoll,** 68 km. (*buffet and hotel*), where on May 17, 1814, the Constitutional Convention, in the face of the menace of war with the greater part of Europe, reiterated the independence and sovereignty of Norway and adopted the present Constitution. The building in which the delegates met (6 km. from the station) is carefully preserved.

Immediately after the arrival of the train a steamer on **Lake Mjösa** starts for **Lillehammer** (p. 139), where the railway may again be joined. In fine weather this trip agreeably breaks the long railway journey for those who are not in a hurry to arrive at the northern terminus. The railway ticket is valid on the steamer, and on board there is a first-class restaurant. The lake, 62 miles in length and 10 across at its widest part, is the largest in Norway. The scenery

* See footnote, p. 12.

[E.N.A.

THE BYGDÖY KONGSGÅRD.

Wilse,] [*Oslo.*

A TELEMARKEN STOREHOUSE.

Wilse,] [*Oslo.*

VENGETINDER (5,958 FEET), ROMSDAL.

is very pleasing, especially as one proceeds up the lake, but is apt to fall a little flat after one has seen some of the mountain lakes on the western side of Norway.

From Eidsvoll the line runs along the eastern shore of Lake Mjösa to Lillehammer. Midway is **Hamar** (*good restaurant at station, Grand Hotel opposite station, and others in the town*).

Hamar is in the midst of a rolling pastoral country. The town has one or two large factories, and is an important centre for the agriculture of the district. About half an hour's walk from the station are the ruins of its **Cathedral,** built in 1157 by Nicholas Breakspear, the only English Pope (Adrian IV). In its prime it must have been an imposing Norman building, but only a few bays of an arcade remain to testify to its fallen greatness. Its destruction was brought about by the Swedes, during the invasion of 1567, and it afterwards served as a sort of quarry for local road-menders.

Pleasant trips may be made by steamer from Hamar to **Gjövik,** on the opposite shore, whence there is direct railway communication with Oslo; to **Lillehammer,** and to Eidsvoll.

Lillehammer (*Station Buffet, Hotels Victoria, Breiseth, Grand, Turist hotellet, Sole Pensionat, Fru Wieses Pensionat*) is a small town of about 4,000 inhabitants, which serves as a sort of capital to the district. By reason of the great beauty of the environs, it has an international artists' colony. On the Maihaugen is the *Sandvig Collection,* at a mile from the station. It consists of old buildings, utensils and costumes, forming a most interesting and very complete Gudbrandsdal museum in beautiful surroundings. The way to it is indicated by "*Til De Sandvigske Samlinger.*"

Lillehammer offers excellent facilities for winter sports, and the district is a paradise for the hunter and angler.

There are many fine walks in the neighbourhood. Excursions can be made to all parts of the lake by steamer, and to many charming spots by motor.

From Lillehammer, Balberg, Skeikampen, Gausdal, Lauvåsen, and other leading highland resorts of Eastern Norway may conveniently be reached.

The first station beyond Lillehammer is **Fåberg.** From it a road goes north-westward up the Gausdal valley, in which are several summer resorts, and **Aulestad,** which was the home of Björnson. The valley has a regular service of motors.

Near Hunder station, a fine waterfall, the **Hunderfoss,** comes in view as the train crosses the river Lågen. 243 km. from Oslo is **Ringebu** (*buffet*), with a partially modernized Stave Church, mentioned at the end of the thirteenth century.

At **Hundorp** is a great mound said to cover the remains of Dale Gudbrand, the great chief of the valley named after him, and the champion of heathenism when King Olav the Saint (commemorated by a monument erected in 1907) entered the valley about 1020 to Christianize it.

Having passed Breivegen we reach **Harpefoss,** 260 km., close to the waterfall of the same name, seen just below the line. In the neighbourhood is *Golå Höifjellshotel.* A run of about 4½ miles brings us to **Vinstra,** where the Vinstra river joins the Lågen. It is the station for *Fefor Höifjellshotel,* a favourite place for ski-runners. The Jotunheim can be reached from Vinstra by the Vinstra valley road to Kampeseter and on to Sikkilsdals seter, to which motors run.

Onward we go through Kvam to **Sjoa,** at the mouth of a river of the same name. From it a road leads into the Jotunheim by way of the hotels at Bessheim and Gjendesheim (p. 124).

After passing Sandbu we reach **Otta** (*Grand Hotel* and *Björkheim Turisthotel*), situated about 900 feet above sea-level in the heart of the **Gudbrandsdal,** close to the best mountain scenery the country has to offer; but its surroundings, being of the character of Eastern Norway, lack the sombreness and forbidding aspect generally associated with Norwegian mountain resorts. It offers a variety of excursions. The ascent of the *Pillarguri* (1,650 feet) does not take more than a couple of hours, and only 20 minutes south of it is the historic **Kringen** where, in 1612, a body of Norwegian farmers overwhelmed a detachment of Scottish mercenaries. The scene of this event is marked by a stone with a Norwegian inscription signifying " In memory of the peasants' bravery."

At the time of the incident there was war between Christian IV of Denmark and Norway and Gustavus Adolphus of Sweden. The latter had sent an officer over to Scotland to raise a force of mercenaries. A portion of these under Colonel Sinclair were landed in Romsdal, from which Sinclair marched through the Gudbrandsdal, foraging as he went. As he came through the valley, his troops straggling somewhat, and utterly unprepared for an attack, he was surprised by farmers on the hillside. They rolled logs and boulders down upon the unsuspecting Scots, charged them, took sixty prisoners and killed the rest, except one man, who is said to have escaped; and the prisoners were afterwards killed in cold blood. Sinclair's wife, it is said, accompanied the troops. A Norwegian girl, the sweetheart of one of the young farmers, desiring to warn her, sent the youth to her for that purpose on the night before the attack; but the lady, not understanding the purport of the visit, shot him dead.

There are motor services from Otta to Maråk (or Merok) on the Geiranger Fjord, Öye on the Norangs Fjord, and Visnes, Loen and Olden on the Nord Fjord. Otta is also one of the best starting-places for trips to the Jotunheim. Norway's highest mountain, the *Galdhöpigg*, may be reached in one day. In winter there are splendid ski-ing grounds in the vicinity of the town.

Continuing the railway journey, we pass through Sel. Beyond it the line enters the wild and narrow pass of Rosten, in which it traverses several tunnels. **Brennhaug** station is the first in Dovre and affords a fine view of **Storkuven** on the eastern side of the valley, while on the opposite side of the line rises **Jetta,** of which the ascent may here be begun. Its summit, 5,400 feet above sea-level, commands a magnificent prospect of the Jotun and other mountains.

Through fir woods, lovely landscapes, and a wider part of the valley, the line ascends to **Dovre** station, passing on the left Dovre Church, roofed with large slabs of stone. The line continues to ascend, and at the next station **Dombås,** 343 km., we are 2,110 feet above the sea. The extensive views westward include, in the background the snow-capped Horungfjell. At the station is a restaurant and a quarter of a mile away is the *Dombås Tourist Hotel*, much visited by those seeking rest and the pure mountain air, by sportsmen and by those who are making excursions into the Dovrefjell, which offers excellent opportunities for ski-ing in the winter and mountain-climbing in summer. Björnson, the Norwegian novelist, was born not far from Dovre, and has described the scenery of its desolate mountain wastes and the lonely lives of its inhabitants in his story *Blakken*.

From Dombås a line goes through the famous **Romsdal Valley** (pp. 117–8), to the west coast, while the line to Trondhjem strikes across the mountains. It at once passes through a short tunnel, beyond which are first a vast pine forest and then a mountain ridge with the river Gröna in a narrow cleft far below. On emerging from the Grönbogen Tunnel, we pass through one of the prettiest parts of the route. Far down in the east may be seen a portion of the line over which we have travelled. Then, having passed Fokstua marshes, we reach **Fokstua** station. Only ten minutes from it is the large *Fokstua Hotel*, more than 3,000 feet above sea-level. It is on the site of one of the Fjellstuer (mountain hospices) established by King Öystein in the twelfth century for the benefit of pilgrims visiting the shrine of St. Olav at Trondhjem. This almost treeless region is of the highest interest to botanists and geologists, and in autumn and winter there is good shooting.

We have a level run to **Vålåsjö,** at the far end of the lake of the same name, and then pass through birch woods and a short tunnel to **Hjerkinn,** the highest station on the route (3,250 feet). Here was another of the Fjellstuer, now represented by the *Hjerkinn Höifjells Hotel*, about half an hour's walk from the station.

For the ascent of **Snöhetta,** which has been in view westward, one drives from Hjerkinn to Reinheim, where is a roomy Tourist Club hut, and thence the summit (7,550 feet) can be reached in about 3 hours. A guide is necessary.

From Hjerkinn the line, protected by many snow sheds, continues to ascend until it reaches **Passet,** a long pass at an elevation of 3,260 feet, affording a magnificent view westward. From the pass the line descends, and at **Kongsvoll** station the height is only 2,720 feet. The place takes its name, which means King's grassy plain, from a royal visit in 1704. The spot is an excellent centre for mountain excursions, fishing, shooting and winter sports. Near its hotel, *Kongsvoll Fjellstue*, is a fall above which the river has cut a tunnel through the mountain.

We now pass over a section of the line exceptionally costly to construct, long tunnels being necessary as a protection against avalanches. The *Högsnyta Tunnel* is 1,000 yards long and the *Hestekrubben* 1,530. This is the longest tunnel on the Dovre line.

By the time we have reached **Drivstua** station, we have descended another 500 feet and see meadows and cultivated fields as well as birch and fir woods. About half a mile from the station is the last of the Fjellstuer—the *Drivstua Hotel*. Continuing we pass *Magalaupet* (the throat), a narrow gorge through which the river rushes, arrive at **Engan** station, and then at **Driva,** where the line leaves the river and goes through a well-cultivated district to **Opdal**, 429 km. At the station is a large restaurant in connection with the adjacent *Opdal Turisthotel*, one of the most comfortable and up-to-date hotels in the country. Around are fair fields, fine forests and gently-flowing streams, the whole surrounded by snow-capped mountains. The site is 1,500 feet above sea-level, and the spot is admirable alike for a holiday of pure repose in bracing air, or of the greatest activity, as shooting, angling, mountain-climbing and all kinds of winter sports may here be enjoyed. As there is another Opdal in Numedal, the postal address of the town here is " Opdal i Sör-Tröndelag."

Between Opdal and Sunndalsöra on the Sunndals Fjord is a most interesting road with a motor service (p. 185).

From Opdal we go through Opdal Forest and across monotonous wooded plains to **Fagerhaug,** in a pine forest. Beyond this we pass through a tunnel nearly half a mile long, cross the Orkla river by a fine stone bridge, 1,600 feet above it, and affording a splendid view down the Orkla Valley, and reach **Ulsberg,** from which there is a good road to Tynset (p. 144). We follow the Orkla river to **Berkåk,** whence motors run to Lökken, connected by a short railway with Thamshamn on the Trondhjem Fjord.

Through a wooded valley we go on to **Garli,** which is followed by Soknedal, Snöan and **Stören,** 501 km. (*buffet*, and near by the *Stören Hotel*). To this station comes also the Oslo-Trondhjem line through the Österdal (pp. 144–5), and from here to Trondhjem the two lines take the same route, as the railway, originally only narrow-gauge, was reconstructed to take both the standard and the narrow-gauge trains. The section runs through a cultivated valley country. Rather more than half-way is **Melhus.** Near the station is the ancient farm of Rimul, on which, in an excavation under a pigsty, the great Earl Håkon sought to hide from King Olav Trygvåsön. While asleep he was killed by a trusted slave, who then took the Earl's head to the King, who rewarded his treachery by condemning him to be instantly hanged.

A short distance beyond **Heimdal** station a glimpse may be obtained on the right of *Lille Lerfoss*, one of two great falls between 3 and 4 miles south of Trondhjem. Having passed through a tunnel we may see the city ahead. Another tunnel is traversed and then we enter Trondhjem station, after a journey of 553 km. (nearly 350 miles). For a description of Trondhjem, *see* pp. 186–192.

B. OSLO TO TRONDHJEM *viâ* THE ÖSTERDAL.

The route as far as Hamar coincides with that described on pp. 138–9. At **Hamar** it is necessary to change trains, as on this route the line between Hamar and Trondhjem is narrow-gauged. Then for 20 miles we go eastward through a rather monotonous district to **Elverum** (*Buffet* at station, *Hotels Central, Borrebæks* and others), whence the Solör Railway goes southward to Kongsvinger for Stockholm.

At Elverum we enter the beautiful **Österdal**, the easternmost of the great valleys of Norway, noted for its fine farms and vast forests and much frequented by Norwegians as a holiday district. Through the valley flows the River Glommen, upon which, at certain seasons of the year, huge floats of timber may be seen being carried by the stream on their way to the pulp and paper mills of the world.

After passing a number of small stations, we come to **Rena** (*Buffet* and *Hotel Trudvang*), at the mouth of the *Rendal*, the largest lateral valley on the route, leading up to the **Storsjö,** a long and pretty lake, and to the Rendalsölen mountain (motor service up the valley as far as **Sjölisand,** 50 km.).

The next important station is **Koppang,** 247 km. (*Buffet* and *Hotels Hansens* and *Koppang*). Thence we proceed through wilder scenery and far above the river flowing in a rugged bed. After Björånes comes **Atna,** 272 km. (*Storfjellseter Pension*), where the river Atna comes down from the picturesque Atnedal (motor service from Atna *viâ* Storbekkmoen to Brenna, 50 km.).

Thence we continue up the narrow valley to **Hanestad** (*Hotel Hanestad*), situated 1,275 feet above sea-level. On the left is the mountain **Gröttingsbråtten,** 5,000 feet. From Hanestad a good and interesting road goes over the mountains to **Övre Rendalen.**

In the neighbourhood of **Barkald** is *Jutulhugget,* a ravine about 600 feet deep. **Bellingmo** follows and then **Alvdal,** 324 km. (*Steien Hotel* and *Tronsvangen Pension*). From Alvdal a road, with public motor service, leads to **Hjerkinn,** 75 km., on the Dovre railway.

Having passed **Auma,** we arrive at **Tynset** (347 km., *Buffet* and *Hotels Björnsmoen* and *Sevaldsen*). In the neighbourhood are pleasant walks, and *Tronfjell* (7,300 feet) and other mountains may be climbed. (From Tynset there is a motor service to Ulsberg on the Dovre railway.)

The scenery is less interesting as we run towards **Röros** (*Buffet* and *Bergstadens Hotel*). The town is at a height of 2,050 feet, has some 5,000 inhabitants, and a fine large church. It is noted for its copper mines, discovered in the time of King Christian IV and still worked.

A road (motor service) runs from Röros through birch woods and magnificent scenery to **Skotgården**, 18 km., and across the Swedish frontier to Fjålnes sanatorium. Skotgården is said to owe its name to Scottish settlers who came to it in 1717. In its neighbourhood families of wandering Lapps may sometimes be seen.

There is also a motor service between Röros and **Sönderviken, at** the head of the Femund Lake, 36 km.

Leaving Röros we run through stretches of sand and moor, a district of the wildest and barest description, and the Glommen is but a tiny stream which, after we have passed **Nyplass,** we cross to enter **Jensvoll,** 412 km. Between this and **Tyvoll,** 420 km., the line reaches its highest point, 2,198 feet, and from Tyvoll goes down in great curves to Reitan, 432 km., from which it descends less rapidly and through more interesting scenery to Holtålen and then quickly to the bottom of the valley. In the neighbourhood of **Singsås,** 480 km. (*Buffet*), the scenery is a very beautiful rolling stretch of pine-clad hills and sloping valleys. We pass through tunnels and by Björgen, Kotsöy and Rognes, and then across a covered bridge to **Stören,** from which the route is described on p. 143.

OSLO TO THE ROMSDAL AND MOLDE.

THE greater part of the journey is on the Dovre Railway, on which one travels as far as Dombås (*see* pp. 138–141). Here a junction is effected with the Rauma or Romsdal line, which has made it possible to get from Oslo or from Trondhjem to the Romsdal Fjord and to Molde in a day. The distance from Oslo to the terminus at Åndalsnes is about 280 miles, and from Trondhjem 345 miles. The railway follows the course of the river *Rauma*, one of Norway's most famous salmon streams, and the valley through which it flows contains some of Norway's most beautiful scenery. There are snow-clad mountains, great waterfalls and whirling rapids. The line winds among these features and curves along the sides of precipices. For nearly the entire distance the line is far above the bottom of the valley, thus affording the opportunity of remarkable sight-seeing. The upper part of the valley is quite narrow, but as it advances the valley broadens out. In its lower part it is fertile, well cultivated, and partly covered with birch woods.

At **Dombås** the line is at its highest point, 2,110 feet above sea-level. Less than a mile south of **Lesja** station, 18 km. from Dombås, is its church, notable for its altar-piece, which dates from 1697.

The fences seen in many fields hereabouts have been erected to prevent the snow being blown away. The farmers wish it to lie and give moisture to the ground, which in this district is exceptionally dry.

Through a rather uninteresting tract we go on to **Lora,** where a river of the same name joins the Lågen. A short distance farther we have our first view of the Romsdal mountains, and after running through woods we reach **Lesjaverk**, in beautiful surroundings, at an altitude approaching 2,000 feet. We pass Lake Lesjaskog, a gloomy sheet of water 11 km. long, its shores sparsely clothed with verdure. This is the watershed of the valley; from it flow both the Lågen and the Rauma, the former going through the Gudbrandsdal to Lake Mjösa, and the latter north-westward to the coast. At the farther end of the lake is **Lesjaskog** (*Mölmen Hotel* and *Kvam Pension*), whence may be made, in from three to four hours, the ascent of **Storhö,** 6,800 feet, commanding a magnificent view. **Degervarden,** about a thousand feet lower, is also worth climbing. More and more into view come the Romsdal mountains as we proceed, and the line begins to go to a lower level. Snow protections tell of what the winter is expected to bring. At **Bjorli** station (large restaurant with dining-room for 200), we are just midway between Dombås and Åndalsnes, but are still at an altitude of some 1,865 feet.

Soon after leaving Bjorli the scenery changes. We are about to enter the Romsdal valley and so to begin the most interesting part of our journey. Before reaching the next station, the train takes an unexpected course. It enters a tunnel—the Stavem. This is natural enough, but when it emerges it has doubled on its track and is running southward instead of northward, as was the case a few minutes earlier, and the lines upon which it was then running are seen at a considerable height. A halt is made at Verma, 75 km., and then another circuitous tunnel, a quarter of a mile long, is entered. After that is left, the Rauma is crossed by the long and lofty Kylling bridge, from which the train again moves northward, and from the windows one can see the hairpin turn just left behind, one leg lying considerably higher than the other on the perpendicular wall of granite on the opposite side of the river. Between the two tunnels is the **Vermafoss,** a magnificent triple waterfall which, fed from the Verma lake, leaps 1,200 feet down the mountain side, and sometimes drenches passing trains with its spray. To secure the track against snow and rock avalanches, it has in many places been found necessary to blast away considerable parts of the mountains. Just below Kylling bridge the whole face of the mountain had to be removed along some 750 yards.

Onward from Verma to Flatmark, we pass many fine falls on the east side of the valley and on the western side is the fine **Dönfoss,** to the left of a bridge by which the main road is crossed.

At **Flatmark** we are only 400 feet above sea-level, having descended no less than 470 feet in the run of just over 8 miles from Verma. From a wider and more cultivated part of the valley we pass to a narrower section, with several fine falls, of which the **Mongefoss** on the right is the most notable. Shortly before reaching the next station, which is at **Marstein** (96 km.), the famous **Trolltinder Peaks** and the still more renowned **Romsdalshorn** come simultaneously into view. Nearer, facing the chaotic Trolltinder, as does the Romsdalshorn, are the vast bulk of **Mongejura,** down which the Mongefoss rushes, and the vaster and wilder **Kalskråtind,** which has been aptly described as "the Siamese twin of the Horn." Minor and harmless snow avalanches are of frequent occurrence among the Trolltinder, on which large masses of snow may be seen even in summer all the way down into the bottom of the valley. Marstein lies in the midst of farms on a broad and level tract from which the towering heights bordering it keep off the sun for five of the twelve months of the year.

The mountains just named enclose a great oblong bowl from which there seems to be no northern exit, but there is just room for the river, the road and the railway to squeeze through into a broad fertile plain, bordered by some of the finest peaks in Norway, one of which, the Romsdalshorn, gives its name to the last station but one (*Hotel Halsa*), 10 km. from Marstein and less than that distance from the terminus.

The cone-shaped **Romsdalshorn** rises to a height of 5,104 feet and is easily recognized by the terminating horn to which it owes its name. Behind it are the pointed peaks of the greyish white **Vengetinder,** 5,958 feet. The **Trolltinder,** on the other side of the valley, on which nature has carved fantastic peaks and pinnacles, lifts the topmost point 6,010 feet above sea level.

C. Hall climbed the Romsdalshorn in 1881, and it was then considered a first ascent; but Slingsby, whose services to mountaineers in Norway include that of historian, discovered subsequently that the mountain was first climbed in 1832 by two local farmers, Kristen Smed and Hans Bjærmeland, more as a piece of bravado than as a serious attempt at conquering the apparently inaccessible. They are said to have stayed two days at the summit before they dared to come down.

The Trolltinder was first conquered in 1870, and the highest peak of the Vengetinder in 1881 by Mr. Slingsby. The same intrepid climber placed the Mjölnir, in this district, to his credit in 1885; he describes it as the steepest mountain in Europe.

[E.N.A.

TROLLTINDER PEAKS, ROMSDAL.

Valentine & Sons, Ltd.,] *[Dundee.*

THE ROMSDALSHORN.

Åndalsnes,

114 km. from Dombås (*Buffet, Hotels Grand, Bellevue, Park* (4 km.) and *Victoria*), often called *Nes* by its inhabitants, who number about 900, is situated at the mouth of the *Rauma* and at the entrance of the Isfjord, a small branch of the Romsdals Fjord. The village is an excellent centre for mountain climbing, for which licensed guides are available, and from it several very interesting excursions can be made by steamer, motor, stolkjerre, or train. Daily service by steamer is maintained with Molde and other places on the Romsdals Fjord as well as with towns farther along the coast. The pier and the railway station are but a few yards apart. Hotel buses meet the boats and the trains. Many of the cruising yachts call here and stay long enough for their passengers to make a trip up the valley. Previous to the construction of the railway, passengers had to be satisfied with a small portion of the valley, but now they sometimes have time to go right through the valley to Dombås and return to the steamer the same evening. It is also possible for them now to go on from Dombås across the Dovre mountains to Trondhjem and pick up the steamer there for the journey to the North Cape. Those who stay long enough in Åndalsnes—and it is a delightful place for a stay—should make the tour up the **Isterdal,** to the foot of the Trolltinder.

The route to Åndalsnes by the Romsdal road is described on pages 117–118.

OSLO TO MARÅK (Geiranger) AND VISNES (Stryn) *viâ* OTTA AND GROTLI.

This journey between the capital and western Norway is by rail to Otta and thence by road. By leaving Oslo by the first express train one can reach Grotli very late the same day. Unless one is very pressed for time it is preferable to spend a night at Otta and to complete the tour next day.

The railway journey to Otta is described on pages 138–140. The route from Otta to Grotli is described in the reverse direction on pages 119–121, between Grotli and Maråk on page 106.

OSLO TO THE WEST COAST BY THE TELEMARKEN ROUTE.

Routes.—Telemark is a south central district with a richly varied surface. It is accessible from Oslo, Bergen and Stavanger.

From Oslo the best way of reaching it is by rail to Skien (*She-en*) and thence by steamer through the Bandak Canal and lakes to Dalen; or by rail to Lunde and thence by steamer, a route which avoids the locks; or by rail to Notodden, thence by public motor to Kviteseid and thence by steamer to Dalen. It can also be reached from the capital *viâ* Skien by going to that town by steamer instead of by rail.

THE journey across Norway by the Bandak Canal and the great Telemarken road is one of the favourite tourist routes of Norway.

The first section of the journey, from Oslo to Skien, can be made either by coasting steamer or by rail.

The second section is accomplished by the pleasant inland steamers traversing the chain of lakes linked by the Bandak-Norsjö Canal; the third section is that by road over the Haukeli Pass to Breifonn, and thence to Sand (for Stavanger) or Odda (for Bergen); and the last part from Sand across the Boknfjord to Stavanger or from Odda down the glorious Hardanger Fjord to Bergen.

(*a*) OSLO TO SKIEN BY STEAMER.

The best steamers are those coasting from Oslo to Bergen, but they leave Oslo at night (usually at 11 p.m.) and the tourist not only misses the scenery of the fjord, but arrives at Larvik tired, probably, the next day at 6.30 a.m. Larvik is 45 miles by rail from Skien or one can continue in the Bergen steamer to Langesund, reached at 8 a.m., and thence take a local steamer to Skien. Other steamers, smaller, but quite comfortable, run from Oslo to Skien direct at slightly lower rates. Regarding these, many of which run in the daytime, it is advisable to consult the weekly lists of sailings. The steamers start from the docks, near the East Railway Station. All have good restaurants on board. If the night journey is undertaken, early application should be made for berths.

The steamer proceeds down the beautiful **Oslo Fjord,** leaving the islands on the right. The first place of importance is **Dröbak** (*Holstads Hotel*). It lies on the eastern shore of the fjord, its pretty villas built in terraces up the sides of the pine-covered slopes, and is a favourite summer resort of the people of Oslo. Between Dröbak and the capital steamers run many times a day.

Crossing, we round the point of **Filtvet** (the Tönsberg steamers call here), and crossing the mouth of the **Drammen Fjord** (direct steamers to Drammen from Oslo) we pass or call at **Holmestrand** (*Hotel Societeten,* and many boarding-houses) a favourite seaside place, beautifully situated at the water's edge. Holmestrand is a small town of about 3,500 inhabitants, and owing to its railway connections it is a good centre for excursions to the Eidsfoss and Kvittingfoss.

From Holmestrand the steamer proceeds to **Horten** (*Hotels Central, Grand*), the principal station of the Norwegian Navy, with naval and military staff colleges, observatory and marine museum. Off the town lies the fortress of **Carl Johans Vern,** to which the public is not allowed access. The surrounding country is very pretty, with many charming walks.

Steamers between Horten and Oslo several times a day; also between Horten and Moss, on the eastern side of the fjord, in connection with the trains.

Next past **Åsgårdstrand** (visited by the Tönsberg steamers) we come to **Vallö** and **Tönsberg** (*Hotels Victoria, Royal, Klubben, Tönsberg Sjömandshjem*), prettily situated at the inner end of the fjord. Tönsberg, of about 13,000 inhabitants, is, in point of history, one of the oldest towns in Norway. In 1871 it celebrated its thousandth anniversary, though the exact date of its foundation is not really known. It finds frequent mention in the early Norwegian sagas. Harald Hårfagre was here, and Tönsberg was the scene of the pitched battle between Eystein and Magnus, when the Birchlegs were routed, as related in the Heimskringla. In the fourteenth century it was the most important town in Norway, with ten churches and a fortified castle. It was burnt out in 1536, and has never recovered its ancient consequence, but it is a pleasant place at which to break a journey.

A favourite excursion with Tönsberg as its pivoting point is that from Oslo to Tönsberg by steamer, thence by the Eidsfoss Railway to **Eidsfoss** on the **Eikeren Lake,** then across the Lake, returning to Oslo from Flesaker station *viâ* Drammen. The round tour can be accomplished in two days; the route lies through a pretty fertile country, and gives a good idea of the lowland scenery of this part of Norway.

Some steamers call at **Sandefjord** (*Hotels Sandefjord Bad, Atlantic*), a busy little seaport of about 5,000 inhabitants, developing rapidly as a watering-place on account of its sea-bathing and mineral springs. It lies deep in the fjord of the same name, with two jutting tongues of land running southward between the **Mid Fjord** and the **Tönsberg Fjord.** Few tourists stop here, but those who do should visit the **Jettegryter,** or giant's cauldrons. Near by is **Gokstad,** where one of the Viking ships (p. 131) exhibited at Oslo was found.

Thence to **Larvik** (*Grand, Hansens, Larvik Bad, Victoria*), built round the head of the fjord in tiers, with about 11,500 inhabitants. It has a very picturesque appearance when seen from seaward. Larvik, like many places in the neighbourhood, is much visited for its mineral springs, in connection with which is the *Kurhotel,* with baths and medical treatment. Above the town is a fine beech plantation, the *Bökeskog,* the only one in Norway, from which some pleasant woodland walks radiate.

Passengers by the Bergen steamers usually change at Larvik for Telemarken and proceed to Skien by train; but the local steamers proceed up the fjord to Skien.

(*b*) OSLO TO SKIEN BY RAIL.

Trains start from the West Station, near the Piperviks Quay. Fastest train takes 5 hours 30 minutes. Restaurants at Drammen, Kongsberg, and Nordagutu.

This route is usually taken by travellers making their way into Telemarken by the Bandak Canal, though many find the sea-route, above described, preferable. The train skirts the peninsula of Bygdöy at **Sköyen,** and runs between the wooded hills, with an occasional glimpse of the fjord, to **Sandvika** (*Hotel Sollihögda*), a playground of the Oslo people, much visited in summer. Only the slower trains stop here.

Motor service between Oslo, Sandvika and **Hönefoss,** 60 km. from Oslo. From Sandvika the road lies past the **Sollihögda,** 1,000 feet above sea level, whence is a fine view of the lakes and the **Hols Fjord.** It descends in curves to the rocky gorge of **Skaret,** beyond which the road is a magnificent piece of construction. Close to it is *Dronning Sophies Utsigt* (Queen Sophia's View). A little farther is Homledal, from which the road winds down precipices to the **Tyri Fjord.** Then it runs along the shore of the lake to **Sundvollen** (*Hotels Sundvollen, Krokkleiva*), whence in 1¼ hours the **Krokkleiva** (about 1,300 feet) can be ascended to *Kongens Utsigt* (the King's View). From Sundvollen the road goes past the farm Sten, where are the ruins of the ancient parish church, and there begins the long flat monotonous Stensgate. At 10 km. from Sundvollen it reaches *Norderhov Church*. On application to the sexton there may here be seen two embalmed bodies, said to be those of Jonas Ramus, the parish priest, and his wife, Anna Colbjörnsen, a Norwegian heroine. By a clever stratagem she brought about the capture of a large party of hostile Swedes in 1716. For Hönefoss *see* p. 72.

The train continues from Sandvika past unimportant stations and the more important **Asker, Heggedal** and **Röyken.** Beyond the last-named we get a brief glimpse of the **Drammen Fjord,** a vision of blue waters and sloping green hillsides.

From **Lier** a branch line goes north to *Sylling*, at the southern end of the Hols Fjord, an arm of the Tyri Fjord. Motor service between Sylling, Drammen and Lier.

After passing Lier the train crosses an open plain and reaches **Drammen** (*Grand*, in the Bragernes quarter; *Central* and *Britannia*, both near the station), at the head of the Drammen Fjord and at the mouth of the *Drammenselv*. The town is sheltered by high hills. The train crosses the river by means of a long bridge which connects the two quarters, Strömsö and Bragernes. Drammen is an important place in the district, with sawing and planing mills and paper and wood-pulp factories. It also has an extensive shipping trade. The population is about 26,000. The centre of the town is the *Bragernes Torv*, with the Exchange, Post Office and Courts. The *Church*, though important as a landmark to vessels coming up the fjord, is of little interest; it contains, however, a fine painting of the Resurrection by Tidemand. (Near Drammen is *Konnerudkollen Tourist hotel.*)

There is daily steamer communication between Drammen, **Horten** and **Moss,** on the Oslo Fjord, and motor communication with **Lier.**

From Drammen a line goes along the coast to **Larvik** and thence inland to **Skien**, but since the opening of the broad gauge line *viâ* **Kongsberg** (p. 162) and **Hjuksebö** (p. 164), the former route is never used by tourists. From Hjuksebö the route is southward to **Nordagutu Junction** (146 km.), from which the Sörlando Railway goes to **Lunde** (p. 164), and then, after passing four stations, **Skien** is reached, 180 km. from Oslo.

SKIEN.

Hotels.—*Grand,* in the Telemarken Gate ; *Höyers,* near the station, etc.
Population.—About 16,500.
Quay.—The Canal steamers start from Hjellebryggen Quay, above the Damfoss.

Though claiming a fourteenth-century foundation, and figuring often in Norwegian history, Skien must be regarded as a modern town, for most of it was rebuilt after a fire in 1886. Its charm lies wholly in its surroundings ; the green slopes of the valley, the wide expanse of water and the distant fir-covered hills. Its landmark is the new Gothic **Church,** standing on a hill, with two tall spires ; and its proudest claim is that it was the birthplace of *Henrik Ibsen,* the poet and dramatist (1828–1906), to whose memory there are a statue (in the square in front of the Church) and a park. The streets are busy, for Skien is an important industrial place, devoted to the export of timber and the manufacture of wood-pulp and cellulose.

The two waterfalls of **Damfoss** and **Klosterfoss** lie almost within the town ; they are reached by the Broerne, a narrow street beside the harbour quays. The falls are impressive, but grow yearly less and less through their power being captured for industrial purposes. On the estate of **Bratsberg,** behind the station, are the ruins of a church dating from the twelfth century. In the **Brekke Park** is a collection of ancient Telemarken buildings (15 minutes' walk).

It is quite possible to spend some time in Skien as an excursion centre, for it has several motor services, and excursions can also be made by steamer.

SKIEN TO DALEN.

Route.—By steamer through the Bandak–Norsjö Canal. The boat starts at 8.30 a.m. and is due at Dalen at 7.45 p.m. On the boat there is a good restaurant, with table d'hôte. The distance from Skien to Dalen is about 68 miles.

The steamer starts from the pier above the two lowest locks which allow vessels to reach the Skien river. It runs up the river to Grötsund and then turns to the right into the narrow **Löveid Canal** between high rocky walls. By four locks the steamer is lifted above the Skotfoss into the **Norsjö,** a magnificent lake, 28 square miles in extent, with wooded banks sloping to the water's edge. Very soon may be seen on the right, about 85 feet up the mountain-side, the *Mikalshule,* or St. Michael's Cave, used as a church in pre-Reformation times. Then, on the same side, a fine view of the snow-capped **Lifjell** (5,087 feet), opens out. Constantly the scenery changes in character, and not the least picturesque part is that where we pass the two islands of **Munken.** Half-way up the lake we arrive at **Ulefoss.** The steamers for Notodden continue northward on the lake. Those for Dalen enter the **Bandak-Norsjö Canal,** which has replaced the 22 km. of road between Ulefoss on the Norsjö and Strengen on the Flåvann.

The construction of this canal, linking the long chain of lakes of which Bandak is the most western, was a great feat of engineering; extraordinary difficulties had to be over-come to maintain the right level of the lakes, to deepen the channels, to divert enormous waterfalls and to construct locks, for the level of the Flåvann is about 185 feet above that of the Norsjö. The work was carried out between the years 1889 and 1892, at a cost of about £170,000.

The pier at Ulefoss is the stone wall of one of the three massive locks that lift the steamer to the level of the head of the fall after which the town is named. Then, through an embanked channel, we proceed to the fall of **Eidsfoss.** Two locks are necessary to overcome this fall. A little higher is the **Vrang-foss,** a beautiful fall of 120 feet caused by a dam constructed to maintain the level of the upper lakes. Here five locks raise the steamer to a higher level. Travellers need not wait on board while this admirable but rather monotonous feat is being accomplished. At Eidsfoss a path to the left of the locks leads through the woods to the head of **Vrangfoss Locks,** a pleasant walk of about twenty minutes. From this point one can watch the steamer being slowly raised through the chain of locks, so often photographed and pictured. The steamer takes about half an hour to get from the lowest lock to the highest, and gives ample warnings before resuming the journey.

Above the locks the steamer passes through the river and the small Nome Lake to a lock at **Lunde,** where the Sörland railway crosses the waterway and steamers connect with the trains.

From Lunde the railway, opened in 1927, goes southward through woods to **Drangedal** (28 km.), prettily situated near the Tokevatn (lake), and thence through a mountainous country and large forest tracts to **Neslandsvatn,** a junction on the South Coast main line (under construction), from which a branch line goes southward to **Kragerö** (70 km. from Lunde). Kragerö, on the coast, and surrounded by hundreds of skerries, is a favourite watering place for families from Oslo, many spending the summer months here in villas and fishermen's cottages (*Victoria Hotel* and others).

We come to another lock at **Kjeldal,** and the last at **Hogga,** where there are two. There is also a massive dam to maintain the level above Hogga. Thence we steam up the river to **Strengen,** where we enter the **Flåvann.** Dark forests fringe its sides, and the slopes run down to the water's edge in a succession of bluffs, with views of the distant Lifjell, Granafjell and Kollingerne. Close under the steep walls of the last-named the steamer threads her way through the narrow reach known as the *Fjågesund* into the **Kviteseid Lake,** lying beneath the precipitous side of the Brokefjell. At the far end of the lake is the narrow inlet of **Sundkilen,** and at the head of this arm is **Kirkebö** (*Kviteseid Hotel*), where the road from Hitterdal *viâ* Lövheim joins the steamer route. Kirkebö is described in E. J. Goodman's *New Ground in Norway,* and though the ground is no longer new, his keen appreciation of this delightful district will be shared by all who explore it. Returning along the Sundkilen, the steamer rounds the promontory and calls at **Smedodden,** neaı Kviteseid old church on the opposite shore.

Motor service between *Smedodden* and *Treungen* (p. 167), connection with the train from Arendal and the boat from Skien. The road runs alongside the Nisser Vann, a large lake south of the Kviteseid Lake.

Bandak Lake is entered by a narrow sound known as the *Skarperudström* ; the lakeside is almost uninhabited, so wild is it, and in places the jagged rocks lie in fantastic shapes, as in the case of *St. Olav's Ship,* on the north shore. The boat calls at Sandodd (Apalstå) and then at **Bandaksli,** about the middle of the south shore, from which it crosses to **Lardal,** almost opposite.

From Bandaksli a road (motor service) climbs in zigzags over the mountain and leads southward to the **Fyresdalsvann.**

From **Lardal** a road leads to **Mogen,** in Hordalsmö, on the main road between Kongsberg and Haukeli.

The remaining scenery is among the best on the route. Upon a lofty cliff on the north side is a rocky mass called *Munken* (the monk), from its fancied resemblance to a monk giving his blessing to a woman kneeling at his feet.

During the last part of the journey the head of the lake is visible, and lying in the little plain between the mountains is—

Wilse,] [*Oslo.*

VRANGFOSS LOCKS, BANDAK CANAL.

Wilse,] [*Oslo.*

THE AUSTMANNLI ROAD, RÖLDAL.

Dalen.

Hotels.—*Dalen*, on the lake, with large garden; *Bandak*, in the village.

Motor Services from Dalen to **Haukeliseter, Breifonn** and **Odda**; to **Rauland,** 45 km., on the Totak Lake, from which one can walk to the Mösvann and Mösdammen, and to **Vinje,** 33 km., at the western end of the Totak Lake.

Most travellers know Dalen only as a convenient halting-place between the Bandak Canal and the road to Röldal, but the village is worth a more prolonged stay. It lies at the mouth of the *Rokke-elv*, and, as though space were of little importance, scatters itself inconsequently among the pine-woods. Dalen is less stuffy than most valley resorts similarly situated; it seems to derive a constant breeze from the river gorge or the lake, and is rather invigorating.

DALEN TO BREIFONN.

Motors leave Dalen at 8 a.m. and reach Breifonn at 16.30, where connection is made with services for Odda and Nesflaten. (But see current time tables.)

The road, on leaving Dalen, runs straight into the forest, and after crossing the river by an iron bridge climbs by frequent windings up the hillside, with occasional glimpses of the rocky gorge through which the noisy waters of the Rokke-elv find their way to the lake. At Liåsving, 8 km., the road to **Nesland**, Sandåk and Rauland leads away to the right; we follow that to the left, climbing still higher through Rokkejuvet to **Mo,** at the southern end of the **Börte Lake.** Here we get a view of the **Rautefjell,** the steeps of which tower above the road; then, by a level road along the bank of the lake we come to **Börte** (*Börte Hotel*), 1,460 feet above the sea. The opposite shore of the lake, covered with trees that find a precarious hold on its slopes, rises to steep and rocky heights without a single path.

From the hotel a footpath leads through the Börtedal over the mountains to **Hovdenbro** Tourist Hut, in the Setesdal (10 hours).

The road follows the lake to its northernmost end, and continues northward by undulations through well-wooded country to **Svingen** in Vinje (where the road branches off to **Vinje** church, Amot and Rauland). From Svingen the route is over a plain alongside the river to **Grungebro,** 43 km. (*Grungedal Hotel*).

Now the road turns west, and skirts the narrow **Grungedal Lake** along its northern shore, the switchback road passing beneath boulder-strewn slopes, crowned with a jagged ridge of rotten rock. A couple of kilometres bring us to the simple hotel of **Rui,** where the view, which includes the massive Flåtnebunut, opens a little, and becomes grander as we go on to **Edland** village, where begins the fine Haukeli road which took thirty years to construct and replaced a bridle path, previously the only means of communication. It ascends steadily to **Flåthyl,** where there is a bridge over the river and from which a path goes to Bjåen and Hovdenbro in Setesdal (*see* p. 157). The rise in height becomes noticeable in the vegetation, and hardly less in the atmosphere. First the fir-trees disappear from the landscape, which becomes more and more rocky; then the birches grow more and more stunted till they become mere scrub, as at **Botn** (*Hotel Botn*) and **Vågsli** (*Hotel Vågsli*), between 1 and 2 km. farther, beside a chain of desolate lakes 2,500 feet above sea-level and abounding in fish. Both places are favourite summer resorts. Hard by the hotel at Botn is an elaborate stabbur. As we proceed the rugged heights of the mountain chain come into closer view, the Sessnut, the Vasdalsegg and the Bortedalsegg, with many others. At last even the scrub disappears, and the road rises higher as it follows the long ridge above the **Kjela Lake,** disappearing over the summit, with its perspective of gaunt telegraph poles.

A short run down brings us to **Haukeliseter,** 90 km. from Dalen, where Seter huts have been replaced by a fine hotel erected by the State. Opposite is a building constructed like a *stabbur*. The lower story mainly consists of a large dining-room, as here travellers from Dalen and other places take their midday meal. In the upper story are bedrooms. There are others in a neighbouring pavilion, but the greater part of the sleeping accommodation is in the main building. The hospice stands at a height of over 3,000 feet amid the utter loneliness of mountain peaks and gloomy tarns well seen from the plateau behind the hotel. It can be reached in half an hour.

From Haukeliseter may be ascended the Kistenut, 4,000 feet; the Store Nup, 5,800 feet, the Lille Nup, 4,160 feet, and other peaks.

Haukeliseter is also the starting-point of several pedestrian routes, all marked but only recommended to experienced mountain walkers.

To the south-east it is a day's walk to **Bjåen.**

Southward it is a day's walk through the Kvandal Valley to **Roaldkvam.** Midway is the Kvandal Hut.

Towards the north-west it is a day's journey to **Valdals Seter,** from which it is a short walk down to **Röldal** and a day's walk to **Litlos** Tourist Station on the Hårdangervidde, a vast alpine plateau some 4,000 feet above the sea.

The journey is continued alongside the Ståvann and the Ulevann, often ice-covered in the middle of July, and the road is sometimes not sufficiently free from snow to admit of the passage of motor-cars before July 1. Between the points which they can reach on either side, sledges are used for the conveyance of travellers. The road continues to rise to the **Pass of Dyrskar**; here the highest point of the road (3,679 feet) is reached. The view is splendid; the height itself is seldom free from snow, and all around it are snow-covered peaks surmounting the rough and rugged sides of black, forbidding walls. After a short run on the plateau the road begins to descend and at 18 km. from Haukeliseter reaches **Svandalsflona,** where it enters upon the steep part of the descent through the Austmannli into the Röldal Valley. As we swing round the sharp elbows in the winding road we get a view of the **Röldalssåta,** beyond the Röldal Lake. In the Röldal valley a gently-sloping road brings us into **Röldal** and to **Horda,** 5 km. farther, where stands the *Hotel Breifonn,* 35 km. from Haukeliseter and 125 km. from Dalen.

Tourists who stay here should not fail to visit Röldal Church, which stands a little to the south of the road. The exterior is modern. Interest centres in the interior, where is preserved a crucifix which was believed to work miraculous cures and to which pilgrimages were made until they were forbidden in 1835. There are also a mediæval censer and vestments 200 years old.

Here the road forks: (1) left to Sand and Stavanger, (2) right to Odda and the Hardanger.

1. BREIFONN TO STAVANGER.

Route.—Daily motor service from Breifonn *viá* the Bratland Valley to Nesflaten, about 24 km. By steamer from Nesflaten to Osen (Suldalosen) in about 2½ hours, starting Monday, Tuesday, Wednesday, Thursday at 8 a.m., Friday 10 p.m., Saturday 10.30 p.m. (times liable to variation: see current announcements). From Osen to Sand, 19 km., by motors awaiting arrival of steamer. By steamer from Sand to Stavanger, once (sometimes twice) daily in 3½ to 4½ hours; good boats with restaurant on board.

From Breifonn we proceed along the shore of the pretty **Röldal Lake,** at the end of which we pass the village of **Röldalsbotten,** and then follow the course of the short river connecting the Röldal Lake and the Lonevann. This we skirt and enter the famous **Bratland Valley,** renowned through all Norway as one of the most beautiful stretches of picturesque scenery in the country. The road, built on the face of precipices, lies above the deep ravine through which the river, falling in many cascades, makes its turbulent way. In some places the mountains overhang the road, and near Nesflaten it runs through a short tunnel. On the perpendicular walls immediately above the torrent vegetation finds scarcely a hold, but on the higher slopes, falling at a gentler angle, trees thrive and the valley is bright with the silver speckle of birch stems.

From **Nesflaten** (*Hotel Bratlandsdal*), with a fine view of mountain, glacier and lake, we cross the **Suldal Lake** (28 km.), the rocky terraces of the mountains, thinly clothed with trees, descending sheer to the water's edge. The steamers call at the village of **Våge,** and then proceed through the **Suldalsport** (Suldal's Gate), where the rocky cliffs approach so closely that between the frowning precipices the water is only about 100 feet wide for the passage of the steamer.

Soon **Osen** (*Hotel Suldal*), the terminus of the steamer journey, is reached, and we follow the road once more. For the first few miles it is fairly level; then, as we enter the Ryfylke country, it begins to fall very steeply, till, passing the Sandsfoss, we are once more on the level road and reach **Sand** (Sand in Ryfylke) (*Kårhus Hotel*).

Here several fjords, arms of the Bokn, unite and penetrate deep into the beautiful Ryfylke country. **Saudasjöen** (*Sauda Tourist Hotel*), in particular, is worth a visit by steamer, if only for the walk through the woods to Sönde. This district is one of the finest hill countries in western Norway, and is famous for its salmon, sea-trout and brown trout fishing.

The village is much visited both summer and winter by the inhabitants of Stavanger. From it a road (motor service) goes *viâ* Sauda village (chemical factories) through beautiful scenery to Hellandsbygda, reached in ¾ hour.

From Sand to Stavanger the steamer descends the **Sandsfjord,** and, threading the narrows above Marvik, passes between the point of **Jelsa** and the island of **Foldöen.** Next it crosses the broad **Nedstrands Fjord,** which, in a westerly or south-westerly wind, is liable to become very rough. Then, steering between the intricate channels among countless islands, we reach **Stavanger** (*see* p. 177).

2. BREIFONN TO ODDA (for Bergen).

Daily motor service from about June 20 to August 31. Distance 40 km.

From the Breifonn Hotel at **Horda** the road climbs the dip between the mountains (it can hardly be called a valley) by a series of some twenty terraces on the side of the Horda Heia, with a mountain torrent falling in cascades, separating it from the Elgers Heia. The view back as each successive terrace is attained repays the journey. Gradually the Röldal Lake disappears in the valley and the heights above it come into view, the long blue-white ridge of the **Breifonn Glacier** crowning them. Wilder and more desolate becomes the road as we ascend. Soon we pass the last trees, and only heather and moss find a hold among the débris of the shattered ridges. The road straightens as it nears the summit, and passes massive boulders scattered among the tarns beneath precipitous walls to Seljestadjuv, the summit of the **Selje Pass** (3,393 feet). Nothing grows in this waste of broken stone, where the snow lies throughout the year. A halt is generally made at **Seljestad** (*Hotel Folgefonn*), 17 km. from Breifonn. Having crossed the watershed we descend to the **Selje Gorge,** where the waters, fed by the mountain snow, fall into the valley, the road descending with many windings. The distant view is one of singular beauty, stretching over the green slopes of the valley to the blue mountains of the Hardanger and the white ridge of the great **Folgefonn Glacier.**

At 4 km. from Seljestad the road reaches **Utsigten** ("the view"), and 3 km. farther is **Skare.**

From Skare a good road leads to **Fjære,** on the **Åkre Fjord,** 18 km., which has steamer connection with Bergen.

The road winds steeply down after we have left Utsigten, and proceeds through the valley past the **Låtefoss** and the **Espelandsfoss** (*Hotel Låtefoss*). The valley becomes more pastoral as we approach the Sandven Lake; then, turning sharply, we begin to descend once more, with a view of the Sör Fjord (p. 86), and so reach **Odda** (p. 86), from which **Bergen** can be reached by way of the Hardanger Fjord (pp. 82–6).

OSLO TO KONGSBERG, THE NUMEDAL, HITTERDAL, ETC.

THIS is a favourite route among those who wish to see something of Telemarken without penetrating too deeply into the remoter districts of the country. If time is an object one may go to Rjukanfoss and back in two days; even the round trip, returning by the Norsjö and Skien, can be made in that time, but this involves leaving Rjukan about 7 o'clock in the morning and travelling until nearly midnight. As the excursion passes through some of the best scenery of South Norway, more leisurely travelling is desirable, and, as will be seen, other interesting excursions can be taken *en route.*

The tour begins with a train journey of less than three hours from Oslo's Vestbane station to Kongsberg. The line at first runs along the fjord and the best views are on that (the left) side. As far as Drammen, it is described on pp. 152–3. From **Hokksund,** 70 km., the train climbs steadily to **Vestfossen,** with fine views across **Lake Eikeren** and the Fiskumvatn. As we proceed the country becomes more open and mountainous. We pass **Darbu, Krekling** and **Skollenborg,** the station for the **Labrofoss** (about 15 minutes distant), now used for power, and then reach **Kongsberg,** 99 km. (*Hotels Grand* and *Victoria*).

The town stands high among the mountains on both banks of the Numedal river. The place owes its existence to the discovery of silver in the neighbourhood, in 1623, by a young peasant while herding cattle. The exploitation of the precious metal was at once begun by Christian IV.

The mines are State property. They are about 6 km. from the town. The principal mine is called **Kongens Grube.** An order for admission can be obtained in Kongsberg, and at the mine a guide and a miner's dress. The route lies along the road to the village of Saggrenda. A visit to the Labrofoss can be combined with that to the mine.

From Kongsberg **Jonsknuten,** 3,000 feet, can be ascended. Up and down, 6 hours. From the summit there is a splendid view of the Telemarken district.

From Kongsberg there is a road (motor service) to **Larvik,** on the coast, 99 km. The road lies along the valley of the Lågen.

In addition to that and the route to the Rjukanfoss, Kongsberg is the starting-point of (1) The route through the Numedal. (2) The route *viâ* Bolkesjö to Tinnoset and Hovin on the Tinnsjö Lake.

1. THROUGH THE NUMEDAL.

The Numedal is a long valley in a direction almost northwest from Kongsberg. Through it flows the Lågen. Although the upper part contains some fine scenery, the valley has not been much visited as it formerly ended in a cul-de-sac at Brösterud, leaving the traveller the choice of returning by the same route or of making his way by a bridle-path over the mountains to Geilo, on the Bergen Railway; but the road has been completed to Geilo and a railway was opened in 1927. The greater part of the line lies along the valley of the broad *Lågen.* The river makes several small falls of which the principal are the Pikefoss and the Trollerudfoss. After *Lampeland* (21 km.), the route lies through flat country and pine woods past *Flesberg Church* and through *Fekjan* to *Roilag* (48 km.). Thence through the steep Fekjankleiv to *Veggli,* from which a mountain path goes to Tinn, reached in about 8 hours. Now along the Norefjord or Kravikfjord to **Rödberg** (93 km.) (*Nore Hotel*), the terminus of the Numedal railway, where great electric works have been erected. Thence a road goes westward through *Liverud,* near which is **Opdal Stave Church,** especially noted for the fine carving of the doors. After having turned to the north-west the road reaches **Brosterud** (2,625 feet), 31 km. Thence the route is across a plateau to **Dagali,** 48 km., and onward through Skuradalen, 57 km. to **Geilo,** 73 km. (*see* p. 71).

2. KONGSBERG *viâ* BOLKESJÖ TO TINNOSET AND HOVIN.

(*Motor service to Bolkesjö and Hovin.*)

The road from Kongsberg lies first along the **Numedal to Stengelsrud,** where it turns left along the Jondals river and through the wooded valley between the Jondalsknut and the Dronningkollen and climbs to the Bolkesjö Plateau, with a fine view of mountain, lake, hill, river and dale away into Telemarken. Soon after passing the small **Buvatn** we reach **Bolkesjö,** 1,150 feet above the sea (*Hotels Bolkesjö* and *Gran*). It is a pretty village, 25 km. from Kongsberg.

In the neighbourhood of the village is the **Folsjö Lake,** in which is good fishing. About 15 km. northward is the

Blefjell, 4,500 feet. A path leads from Bolkesjö to Hitterdal by Lisleherad, reached in 6 or 7 hours.

From Bolkesjö an excellent road ascends in a north-westerly direction, affording magnificent views. Presently it takes a more westerly course.

Midway between Bolkesjö and Gransherad Church, a road goes off to the right to **Hovin,** on the Tinnsjö Lake, about 30 km. from Bolkesjö.

Continuing from the point where the Hovin road leaves it, the main road goes down to **Gransherad Church** and the River Tinn, where it meets the road from Heddal to **Tinnoset,** 27 km. from Bolkesjö (*see* p. 165).

KONGSBERG TO TINNOSET BY RAIL *viâ* HJUKSEBÖ.

Tunnels and forests characterize the opening portion of this route. At 14 km. from Kongsberg is **Meheia,** at an altitude of 1,050 feet. Not far beyond it we enter a tunnel rather more than a mile in length (1,745 metres). In the middle of it the line reaches its highest point, 1,320 feet above sea-level. Now southward, following the Elgsjö Lake and the Lövås valley, to **Öysteinstul,** in lovely scenery. A short distance farther on the line crosses the Nybu River, and then the Kolset River. After affording a lovely view over the Heddalsvann, and passing through another tunnel, it reaches **Hjuksebö** (*Buffet*), 37 km., the junction with the Skien-Tinnoset line.

From Hjuksebö one can go by rail to **Skien,** 44 km. to the south, and thence to Oslo by rail or by steamer (*see* pp. 150–153) or from Hjuksebö to Nordagutu junction (*buffet*), 10 km. south, and thence to **Lunde,** 32 km. farther, where the canal steamer can be taken to Skien (p. 155). A steamer to Skien can also be joined at Notodden.

Lunde is one of the principal stations on the Sörlandsbane (South-land Railway) under construction (opened to Kragerö, 1927).

For Notodden, Tinnoset and Rjukan the line takes us northward from Hjuksebö, along the Hitterdalsvann on the shore of which is **Notodden** (*Buffet*), 9 km. from the junction (*Hotels Grand, Bondeheimen*). In a few years Notodden has grown from a small village into a thriving town by reason of the erection of factories utilizing the electric power brought from the triple **Tinnfoss,** five minutes' walk from the bridge, and the *Svelgfoss* and *Lienfoss.*

On the **Hitterdalsvann,** steamers ply *viâ* Ulefoss direct to Skien.

Wilse,] *[Oslo.*

GAUSTA MOUNTAIN.

Mittet & Co.,] **[Oslo.**

TINNOSET.

Wilse,] [*Oslo.*

KRISTIANSAND S.

About 5 km. from Notodden, along a good road with a motor-car service, is the famous **Hitterdal Stave Church,** the largest in Norway. It was erected in the thirteenth century, and although to some extent spoiled by "restorers," is still a very fine specimen. The *Svalgang*, or cloister, is practically complete, and the exterior of the building is altogether more interesting than the interior, in which the principal objects worthy of attention are an altar-piece in the vestry and an ancient chair. (To enter, apply at the neighbouring parsonage).

The motor service through Hitterdal goes on to **Kviteseid,** 81 km. (p. 156), from which steamers go to Skien. The route, along the old Telemarken road to Kirkebö, encircles the spurs of the Lifjell. It is a pretty route, but since the construction of the Bandak Canal is less traversed by tourists. Beyond Hitterdal it passes through **Örvella** and then soon reaches **Sauland,** 20 km. (*Lövheim Hotel*).

Continuing from Sauland the route lies through **Skogheim** and Hjartdal (*Skogheim Hotel*), where the scenery becomes very mountainous and wild. The road ascends a rocky ravine to **Åsebrekke,** which commands one of the finest views in this part of Norway. By zigzags the road descends to **Flatdal** and thence continues along gentler levels to **Seljord,** 62 km. (*Fjellheim* and *Seljord Hotels*).

The valley from Seljord to **Kirkebö** in Kviteseid (*Kviteseid Hotel*) lies through a more evenly populated country. At Kirkebö the Bandak steamer can be joined, or if it does not call one can motor to Sandodd (Apalstå), 4 km.

From Notodden to Tinnoset is a short journey of 31 km., accomplished by an electric railway which runs along the northern shore of the Hitterdalsvann and through the valley of the *Tinn*. In the neighbourhood of all the small stations—Lisleherad, Grönvollfoss, Gransherad and Tinnoset—pleasant excursions may be made.

Tinnoset (*Tinnoset Hotel*) lies at the southern end of the **Tinnsjö,** a singularly beautiful lake upon which a steamer plies in connection with trains between **Mæl** (Rollag) and **Rjukan.** The steamer also plies between Mæl and Sigurdsrud, near the head of the lake. It takes 2¼ hours to go from Tinnoset to Mæl, and to Sigurdsrud an additional 70 minutes.

The route of the electric railway from Mæl is along a well-cultivated valley through which flows the *River Måne*. The distance is 16 km., the time occupied 40 minutes. On the way may be seen, south of the line, the **Gausta Mountain,** 6,300 feet, the highest mountain in South Norway.

Rjukan (*Hotels Grand, Rjukan*), 221 km. from Oslo, is a modern manufacturing town of some 11,000 inhabitants, dependent upon saltpetre factories which in their turn are dependent on the power obtainable from the Rjukanfoss, 8 km. distant. The height of the fall is 350 feet, but the volume of the water, once most imposing, has been greatly diminished through the harnessing of the fall by industry. Immense quantities of the water are carried through enormous pipes to power stations, whence its force, converted into electricity, is conveyed by wires to the factories. The water captured develops more than 300,000 H.P., but there is still enough water left to make the fall worth visiting.

The Rjukan railway station, the *Krokan Hotel* not far from the fall, and Överland Station are good starting-points for the ascent of the **Gausta,** not so difficult as it looks. From the Gausdal a path is staked to the summit, within half an hour of which is a hut where accommodation for the night can be had.

The more usual route is to return to Mæl and Tinnoset; but from **Överland,** in the Vestfjorddal, *Tuddal Mountain Hotel* can be reached. It lies 3,000 feet above sea-level, at the foot of the Gausta, and is connected with Hitterdal by the Lövheim-Tuddal road.

SKIEN (Langesund) TO KRISTIANSAND S.

The Oslo-Bergen coasting steamer leaves Langesund at 8 a.m. and arrives at Kristiansand S. at 8.15 p.m. A boat carrying the mails leaves Langesund 5.30 a.m. and arrives at Kristiansand S. at 4 p.m. (But see current time-tables.) A motor-boat plies between Skien and Langesund.

The sea journey can be shortened by making use of the Lunde-Kragerö railway (p. 155). The Oslo-Bergen steamer leaves Kragerö at 10 a.m.

From Stathelle near Langesund there is a motor-car service through beautiful scenery to Kristiansand S.

From **Langesund** the smaller boats thread their way through **Langö Sound** and the narrow passage at Langesundskreppen; the larger vessels enter, between the islands of **Skåtöy** and **Jomfruland,** the harbour of **Kragerö** (p. 155).

The steamer next calls at **Risör,** 30 km. from Langesund (*Hotel Risör*), a small trading town, and then proceeds to the neighbouring port of **Lyngör,** from which it goes between wooded islands to **Boröy,** at the mouth of a small inlet. Here passengers and goods for **Tvedestrand,** at the head of the inlet, are transferred to a small steamer.

Then through shallow water and pretty scenery the steamer goes to **Arendal,** lying behind a sheltering island (*Grand, Phönix* and others). The view of the town from the sea is delightful; the town rises in a sort of amphitheatre of terraces, and looks down upon the fjord, the river Nid and the sound between Tromöy and the mainland. There is usually a brief halt here; if there is time visitors should walk up to the terrace known as the *Övre Batteri,* a charming place with a good view over the busy life of the harbour and the calm waters of the fjord.

Arendal is a pleasant place for a brief sojourn. There are good walks, drives and steamer excursions; a railway connects it with **Treungen** (p. 156). It is on the route of the motor service along the coast, and a motor service connects it with **Bygland** in Setesdal (p. 171), 123 km. N.N.W.

The next port of call is **Grimstad** (*Hotels Central, Möllers*), of little interest, a small old-fashioned town with unusually beautiful surroundings, and a sandy beach. At the *Ibsen House,* before which stands a bust of the poet, Henrik Ibsen was apprenticed to an apothecary and in his leisure hours wrote *Catalina.*

From Grimstad the course of the steamer is along a bleak coast to **Lillesand** (*Hotel Norge*), a small trading town, once a place of some importance, but now dwindling, owing to the superior advantages of Arendal and Kristiansand.

For **Kristiansand S.,** about 157 km. from Langesund and 306 km. from Oslo by sea, see pp. 168–9.

KRISTIANSAND S.

Approaches by Sea.—From Hull direct in about 30 hours by the Ellerman's Wilson Line, leaving every Saturday (*see* p. 12). From London or Harwich to Frederikshavn (p. 14) and thence by steamer daily. From Oslo daily in 21¼ hours; from Bergen in 36 hours.

Hotels.—*Ernst, Missions.*

Inquiries.—Bennett's Travel Bureau, 16 Vestre Strand Gate.

Post Office.—Rådhus Gate.

Quays.—The passenger and commercial steamers lie alongside the piers in the Western Harbour, near the Custom House.

Railway Station for the Setesdal Valley: from the quay turn left into the Vestre Strand Gate; the station is in the square on the left.

KRISTIANSAND was built in 1641 by King Christian IV. It lies on a flat square of alluvial land (the "sand" from which the town derived its name), at the mouth of the river Otra, on the west side of Kristiansand Fjord, up which the approach is easy, and as the harbour is spacious and capable of accommodating the largest vessels, the port is a central point for coast and foreign shipping. Among the Norwegian ports it holds fifth place. The town and its environs form also an important industrial centre, with engineering works, foundries, shipbuilding yards, a nickel refinery, steam saw-mills, flour mills and other works. Like the old part of the capital, its ground plan, said to have been designed by the King with his own hand, is laid out in rectangular blocks with broad streets. Owing to the spacious lines on which it is built the town, although the population approaches 20,000, always gives the impression of being somewhat deserted. It has been burnt out repeatedly, the last time in 1892, and has been rebuilt in stone. It is the capital of the province, and the seat of a bishopric; its **Cathedral** stands in the centre of the town. Tourists are mainly drawn to it by its altar-piece, by Eilif Petersen, representing "Christ at Emmaus."

There are many pleasant walks in the neighbourhood. For a good view of the Harbour, climb the **Vestrevei,** on the Mandal road, cut in the rock; or cross the river and ascend the **Hamreheia** for a good view of the Fjord. At the mouth of the harbour is the beautiful island of **Odderöy,** joined to the town by a bridge at the junction of the *Vestre Strand Gate* with the *Östre Strand Gate.* On the west side are the *Sölyst Baths.* The half of the island nearest the town is laid out in gardens and promenades; the other part is fortified and is closed to the public.

The **Ravnedal** should be visited on foot or by motor-bus service. It is reached by the Setesdal road, turning to the right after crossing the railway. The road winds up the rocky valley to the lower slopes of the Ravnefjell, whence there are many paths and fine views. From the **Ravnehei,** a rocky height to which steps lead from the refreshment house on the shore of a lake, there is a particularly splendid prospect.

It is a round of 1½ hours to the **Folk Museum** (old houses, etc., from Setesdalen), on the Möllevann and back *viâ* Dueknipen.

Excursions from Kristiansand.

By steamer to **Lillesand** (p. 167) through the "Blind leads," a series of narrow sounds among the wooded islands, and return by motor. *Or* by motor along the coast through **Hövåg** and return by the inland route (*Flaksvatn, Birkenes*).

Steamer up the **Topdal Fjord,** to the east of Kristiansand.

Visit the **Vigelandsfoss** on the Otra River; train to Vennesla, 18 km., and walk to the fall. It is not a fall of the imposing kind seen in Telemarken, but is set in some pretty country. Walk to the **Helvedsfoss** on the same river, and return by train from Kvarstein, 13 km., or on foot.

By public motor to **Mandal** (p. 173), returning by boat or by public motor.

To **Ytre Flekkeröy**, an island with sea baths and the *Flekkeröy Skjærgårds* Hotel. Motor boat several times a day.

From Kristiansand one can pass—

THROUGH THE SETESDAL.

Route.—The railway goes from Kristiansand to the southern end of the Byglands Fjord, a distance of about 49 miles. After the arrival of the train, soon after midday, a steamer goes up the lake to **Osa,** if the depth of water permits, after calling at Bygland. On weekdays a motor runs from Byglands Fjord to Bygland in connection with the train arriving in the evening, and about midday it leaves Bygland in connection with the train to Kristiansand. This motor service is between Bygland and Arendal, 123 km. distant.

The **Setesdal** is a mountain valley running north and south northward of Kristiansand, remarkable for its fine and varied scenery. It is surrounded by mountain chains and lofty peaks, among which picturesque valleys cross from west to east. In some spots the mountains are forest-clad, in others almost bare, while at Bykle in the north they are never free from snow. In some parts the valley is so narrow that from the side of the mountain it is not noticed. Through the valley flows the **Otra River,** roaring and foaming and descending in huge cascades where most confined, and where the mountains are farther apart spreading out into a lake, the Byglands Fjord occupying nearly a fourth of the total length of the valley, about 96 miles.

All the streams and lakes teem with mountain trout. Hares, grouse and ptarmigan abound, and on the western heights reindeer are sometimes seen.

The Setesdal, more than any other district, has preserved its manners, customs, language and dress, but since the opening of the Setesdal Railway, the traveller is obliged to go far up the valley to find the native unchanged by contact with the world outside.

It is said by some that the people of the dale are descendants of Scottish settlers in Norway; by others that they owe their origin to a Dutch settlement. Their dress, still worn to a great extent in the upper part of the valley, is curious; the men wear trousers with a leather patch behind, the size of the patch being supposed to denote the social status of the wearer. The trousers come up to the armpits, and are braced over the shoulders by short leather braces. On that part which covers the chest are silver buttons and embroidery. The women wear a heavily pleated skirt, reaching only a little below the knee, with long stockings on which are sometimes silver garters. Around the waist is a leather belt with a silver buckle, and the bodice is fastened at the neck with silver studs.

The line runs through very pretty country with the Otra River almost always in view, with many glimpses of rapids and waterfalls, and on each side a forest. **Mosby** is a pleasure resort of the people of Kristiansand; **Vennesla,** near the Hundsfoss and Vigelandsfoss, is the site of large mills. Now the train passes along the shore of the **Langvatn.** At **Hageland** (*Höivoll Hotel*), the train makes a détour round the **Kilefjord** and follows the wide Otra to **Hornnes** (*Hornnes Hotel*), on the Breiflå Vann.

At Hornnes passengers for Åseral alight, and proceed by road through the valley to the left, past the Dåsvann and along the Fiskå Valley into **Åseral** (*Åseral Hotel*) (p. 174), at the head of the Mandal Valley.

The train to Byglands Fjord continues within sight of the pretty *Fennefoss* past **Evje** (*Dōlen Hotel*), a large village with nickel works, the fumes of which have destroyed the trees in the neighbourhood. Then the line runs beside the swift river through pine forests, past **Vassenden,** the southern boundary of the Setesdal, to **Byglandsfjord** (*Buffet*). The train arrives shortly after midday, and travellers bound for **Bygland** or for the Upper Setesdal usually travel straight on by boat or by motor. The scenery in this part of the fjord is very fine; the mountains are covered with pine and birch, sloping steeply from the rocky ridges. On the right bank, just beyond Byglandsfjord, is the **Årdalsnut.**

A road follows the eastern margin of the lake, and villages occur along the whole route; the opposite bank, which falls more steeply to the water, has no road, and is only sparsely inhabited. **Bygland** is reached in two hours by steamer; in three-quarters of an hour by motor. The hotel, *Setesdalens Sommerhjem*, is situated some fifteen minutes' walk from the quay: the motors go to and start from the hotel. It is a favourite place for a long stay, the lake and mountains offering an endless variety of excursions, and the fishing s excellent in the Byglands Fjord and the Sandnes Fjord.

The hotel has a fishing hut with sheds at **Hovatn,** about 2,800 feet above sea level. Upon the lake are boats. By car or steamer one goes to Åraksbö and thence climbs for a couple of hours.

The road crosses the river above Bygland, and proceeds along the west bank to **Osa** (*Osa Tourist Hotel*), prettily situated at the head of the lake, whither the steamer and the public motor also go.

In the village are an ancient house with the fireplace in the centre of the room, and two ancient stabburs in which are kept a few antiquities.

At Osa the motor service corresponds with the service to Vallarheim and Bykle.

From Osa a mountain path passes *Hovatn* and other lakes abounding in fish to Kvipt farm, where the night can be spent. Thence to **Breivik** on **Fyresdals Lake,** on which a steamer plies.

From Osa begins that part of the Valley in which the ancient ways are best observed. This upper part of the Setesdal is a fine country for walkers. It is accessible only by the single road from Osa, and by a few mountain paths leading over the lonely wastes into Telemarken, and amid such isolation it is not surprising that the inhabitants cling to their primitive ways. Accordingly, the traveller in these regions must expect only the simplest of accommodation.

Beyond Osa, the first place on the road (public motors on certain days), is **Granheim,** 8 km. (*Granheim Hotel*).

From *Langeid*, 2 km. from Granheim, a mountain path leads to **Hægstöl,** where the night can be spent, or one can go on to **Gaukhei,** 30 km. from Granheim. Thence by way of **Kvinem** or **Håhellerens Hut** to **Ådneram** in Upper Sirdalen and thence *viâ* **Lysebu Hut** or direct to Lysefjord.

Continuing from Granheim, the route lies through a well-wooded district, passing **Besteland** and **Helle,** with a very fine stabbur. Then follow **Hyllestad Church, Ryssestad, Nomeland** and **Upstad,** where the road crosses the river and then runs for about 7 km. to **Viken** or **Vallarheim,** 15 km. from Hyllestad, where is one of the finest old-fashioned houses in Norway. It has carved beds and a great beam from which the cooking pots are suspended over the fire. Another object of interest here is a fine stabbur transported from Rygnestad.

From Vallarheim there are two well-traversed roads across the mountain to Fyresdal. That to the north, called the Bishop's road, leads *viâ* Njusvik to **Metveit**; the other *viâ* Findalen to **Romsvatten,** where the night is spent, and thence to **Fardal** on Fyresdalsvann (p. 156).

Again continuing, we reach (12 km.) **Flateland,** a considerable village, immediately beyond which is the **Rygnestad** mentioned above and famous for its old buildings. About 8 km. farther is **Björnarå,** and some 3 km. beyond it is the *Byklesti*—steps cut in the rock—but the path is now avoided by following the road. About 13 km. farther is **Bykle** (*Solhaug Hotel*), from which the road is being continued to the Haukeli Road.

From Kristiansand one can take delightful journeys along the coast by public motor, eastward to Stathelle, within easy reach of Skien, and westward to Flekkefjord, from which the journey can be continued along the coast by rail to Stavanger.

OVERLAND FROM KRISTIANSAND TO FLEKKEFJORD.

This is one of the finest motor trips in the south of Norway. It passes through beautiful and varied scenery and is not long enough to be fatiguing, the distance between the

Mittet & Co.,] [Oslo.

THE RAILWAY AT FLEKKEFJORD.

Valentine & Sons, Ltd.,] [*Dundee.*

NORWEGIAN HAY-MAKERS.

Wilse,] [*Oslo.*

A STOLKJERRE.

termini being about 92 miles. The run is made in 5¼ or 5¾ hours, according to the time at which one starts. The charm of the route soon begins after the car is clear of Kristiansand. At **Rundinge** one has a very fine view of the town which has been left, and its environs, and also of the open sea. For about 5 km. the road is ascending the Groheia hill, and then it goes down to **Brennåsen,** beyond which it passes through a charming low-lying tract to **Holme.** Formerly those proceeding farther westward had to be ferried across the small fjord, and from the broad road, along which the motors roll, one sees the old road zigzagging down to the ferry far below.

The stranger may be puzzled by the two words Holme and Holum. The former is applied to the parish, the latter to an estate, upon which, on an elevated site in a wood, stands the one-time fishing house of the Hamiltons, an object of interest to the country-side through having been built, fitted up and furnished in the English style, and now of special interest to travellers as, after having been enlarged, it has become the *Hotel Elvehöi.*

Continuing, we draw nearer to the coast, which, after half an hour's run, we touch at **Mandal,** a pleasant place at which to stay (*Hotels Grand* and *Bondeheimen*). The town has a population of about 3,500 and is the most southerly town in Norway. It is irregularly built and mainly consists of small, low wooden houses. Surrounded by a beautiful park and gardens is the *Skrivergård,* a fine old private house belonging to the town. Mandal has sawmills and a few small industries, and, what is more remarkable on the south coast, a sandy beach affording good sea-bathing. The town park, *Furulunden,* offers beautiful walks among pine trees ; *Sjösanden* is a pleasant sea-shore walk, and another promenade is *Risöbank,* with a beautiful view seaward.

The river at the mouth of which Mandal stands abounds with salmon. The fishing rights are mostly in the hands of Englishmen.

The stream comes down **Mandalen,** the Mandal Valley, extending inland for some 60 miles. The southern portion is broad and open and contains many large farms. Farther north it is narrower, round about are hills and forests, and finally it has the character of a Highland district, and the visitor realizes, if he has not already done so, that if Southern Norway cannot boast the frowning precipices, snow-capped mountains, and roaring cataracts of the West, it has a beauty and grandeur of its own.

The valley is traversed by a good road with a gentle incline and has a service of motors as far as **Åseral,** 100 km. (*Hotel Åseral*), and 1,200 feet above sea-level. Åseral has long been known as an angler's paradise. The hotel has exclusive fishing rights over many lakes and streams. On the borders of the more distant waters are comfortable huts where anglers may spend a pleasant week or two. In the shooting season excellent bags of willow grouse can be made.

Motors run every weekday from Mandal to Åseral, which can also be approached by road from Hornnes station on the railway between Kristiansand and Byglands Fjord (p. 170).

From Åseral there is a path northward across the hills to the tourist hut *Gaukheihytten*, from which there are paths to *Granheim* in the Setesdal, to the *Sirdal* and to the *Lyse Fjord* (p. 180).

Continuing our journey from Mandal to Flekkefjord, we pass alongside the beautiful Skogs Fjord and the Fosselands lake, through woodlands and through mountain scenery ever changing, and after passing through Sör Audnedal, we reach **Vigeland.** Beyond it our road is hilly but good. After running through a charming valley in which are many farms and much woodland the route lies across higher ground, from which we have extensive views, the prospect being especially good from the **Lene Hills.** The Lyngdal Ridges follow, and from them the road descends to the parish of **Lyngdal,** 82 km. (*Grand Hotel*), attractively situated in a mountain valley.

From Lyngdal a road (motor service)leads south-westward to the little coast town **Farsund,** 18 km. (*Grand Hotel*), and a road (motor service) goes northward to Bryggesåk, 52 km.

Westward of Lyngdal we pass through a typically highland country by *Möskedalsveien*, a new road which lies through a delightful, wooded dale from which there is a long ascent, culminating in the wild and bare **Kvinas Ridge,** 1,000 feet above sea-level. From this high ground the descent is so charming that many consider it the prettiest part of the route. The road drops from the ridge to **Liknes** (*Höyer's Hotel*), a rather large place in the Kvinnesdal. Thence we go across the **Vestheiene** to **Feda,** from which the route lies over Sæluren to **Flekkefjord,** 147 km. (*Hotels Grand, Central*), a town of some 2,500 inhabitants prettily situated on the Stol's Fjord, a branch of the long Lister Fjord. Of its industries tanning is the most important. *Fjellpark* is a fine public tract belonging to the town, and a hill called *Trollebak* is a famous view-point. The district inland is very interesting with beautiful mountain walks from the Sirdal to the Setesdal or to Ryfylke Fjord.

FLEKKEFJORD TO STAVANGER BY RAIL.

The station at Flekkefjord (*Refreshment Room*) lies to the east of the town. The line climbs through grand scenery to **Flikkeid,** on the **Lunde Fjord,** and follows the east shore of the Lundevann, along which are fine views. At **Moi** (*Turist-hotellet*) it crosses the Sirdal river, and, crossing the Hove Vann, winds along the steep sides of the wild and narrow **Drangsdal,** the southern end of which is of singular beauty. The view is occasionally interrupted, the track being cut or tunnelled along the side of the valley, in places high above the waters. From **Heskestad** it passes through somewhat monotonous scenery, and continues to mount. Near Ualand is the highest point of the line, about 650 feet. It passes a number of small lakes, swings round the mountain tract about Helleland, 58 km., and runs into **Egersund** (Railway restaurant; *Hotels: Victoria, Grand,* in the market place). The town has a population of about 3,500, and makes pottery which is known over a great part of Norway. The train usually waits here ten minutes. It then shunts out, and crossing the river, enters the province of **Jæren,** a lonely district which differs in the character of the scenery and the people from the rest of Norway. It consists of flat, lonely wastes of lakes and moorland, exposed to the fury of the North Sea, which batters its defenceless, sandy coast-line, and to the sweeping winds from the Atlantic, which sweep across its exposed uplands. It has been treeless for centuries, but the population, energetic and industrious, is steadily converting the wastes into cornfields and forests, while the coast villages are engaging more and more in industry. The people of Jæren are a home-keeping race, but they count it to their credit that the expedition of Leif Eriksen, which discovered America centuries before the birth of Columbus, fitted out and sailed from Jæren. **Ogna** is frequented by artists. At **Varhaug** the line leaves the sea, and 5 km. farther reaches **Nærbö,** the site of a big wireless station. **Sandnes** stands at the head of an arm of the Bokn Fjord. Thence the line continues along the inlet to **Stavanger,** 150 km.

KRISTIANSAND S. TO STAVANGER BY SEA.

The direct Oslo-Bergen steamer leaves Kristiansand at 10.30 p.m., and passes some of the best scenery on the coast in the night hours; at arrives at Flekkefjord at 7 in the morning, and at Stavanger at 4 p.m. It does not call at many ports. There are numerous small steamers which stand in closer and call at many more coast towns; they are frequent, so the journey can be made in sections. The hotels are commercial, but fairly comfortable. This is the best way to see the coast. The direct steamer ticket is available from Flekkefjord to Stavanger by railway, but not by the smaller steamers.

The steamer cruises along the mountainous coast among the numerous small islands, and calls first at **Mandal** (p. 173), reached in about three hours. The town consists of three parts, Mandal, Malmöy and Kleven, the outer harbour. It is here that the mail boat stops. Timber, salmon, lobsters and mackerel are exported. English people who visit Mandal do so either for its salmon fishing, or *en route* for the Åseral Hotel (p. 174).

Beyond Mandal the course of the steamer is through open sea round **Cape Lindesnes,** the most southerly point in Norway, but its latitude is rather north of Banff in Scotland. The next port of call for the fast steamers is **Farsund** (p. 174), which is about 82 km. from Kristiansand and exports ice and fresh fish. It is a small town built on the side of a steep hill at the entrance to the beautiful Lyngdals Fjord, on which is situated one of Norway's largest agricultural schools. Next we round the sandy peninsula of **Lister,** a bad bit of coast in heavy weather, and having passed the Lister Lighthouse, we go through beautiful scenery up the Stols Fjord to **Flekkefjord.**

Few tourists pass by sea between Flekkefjord and Stavanger, as there are no sheltering islands, and the scenery is not of an interesting character. Leaving the **Lister Fjord,** we pass between the mainland and the island of **Hitteröy,** thence cross the mouth of the **Lunde Fjord,** and, passing the entrance to **Sogndal,** follow the coast to **Egersund** (p. 175), from which large numbers of salmon, mackerel and lobsters are exported. Thenceforward the course is similar to the route followed by the train as far as **Varhaug ;** but the coast becomes broken once more as we approach the headland of **Tungenes Fyr** and the islands of the **Bokn Fjord,** at the south-eastern end of which is **Stavanger,** about 120 km. by sea from Flekkefjord.

STAVANGER.

Approaches by Sea.—From Newcastle by the *Venus* of the *Bergenske-Nordenfjeldske* (B. & N.) Line, every Thursday* afternoon, arriving at Stavanger late on Friday evening. Fare, 1st, single, £6 2*s.* 6*d.* (including food on board). From Bergen by steamer in 10 hours; from Oslo by coasting steamer in about 42 hours.
Hotels.—*Victoria*, opposite the quay; *Grand* and others.
Inquiries.—Bennett's Travel Bureau, Valbergatten 2.
Population.—About 47,000.
Railway Station, beyond the Bredevann.

TRAVELLERS from England *viâ* Newcastle, who wish to spend a holiday in Southern Norway, usually get their first glimpse of the country at Stavanger, the steamer entering the **Bokn Fjord** from the North Sea. The town is prettily situated on the shores of the fjord, the fish-canning factories, the staple industry, coming down to the water's edge along the sides of the Western Harbour, giving the place an appearance somewhat reminiscent of a Dutch town. Above the clear waters of the fjord the town rises in steep streets, with the Cathedral and St. Peter's Church as prominent landmarks.

Stavanger is one of the oldest towns in Norway, and is the fourth of the Norwegian towns in point of population, those standing before it being Oslo, Bergen and Trondhjem. In 1814 the number of the inhabitants was only 2,500. The remarkable increase since that time is mainly due to the success of the fish-canning industry, which was established in 1873. There are now about 100 canneries, and for canned fish Stavanger is the emporium of the world.

The steamers usually wait in Stavanger for a few hours to discharge and take in cargo, and the visitor who does not wish to explore the environs usually finds the time allowed quite sufficient to get a good idea of the town.

At the head of the harbour is the Market Place (*torvet*), and here is the **Cathedral,** which, next to that at Trondhjem, is the finest Gothic church in Norway. (*Admission on applying at the Fire Station opposite the north side.*) In style it shows strong Anglo-Norman influence; it was, in fact, built by Bishop Reinald, a former monk of Winchester, at the end

* See footnote, p. 12.

of the twelfth century or the beginning of the thirteenth, and was dedicated to St. Swithun, some time Bishop of Winchester. In 1272 the greater part was burnt down. The nave, with massive Norman arches, supported by huge cylindrical pillars with crudely decorated capitals, is a portion of the original building. The choir was evidently added about a century later. It is pointed in style and more florid than the severe style of the nave. On each side of the choir are chapels used as vestries. They contain monuments of the seventeenth century. The communion table is the original stone altar. The Renaissance pulpit, an exuberant piece of work in wood and plaster, shows strongly-marked German influence. Stavanger became the seat of a bishop in 1125. In 1684 his stool was removed from the town, and was restored to it in 1925. In 1922 the Cathedral was furnished with a set of chimes, the first to be installed in Norway. They may be heard at seven o'clock each evening.

Opposite the south side of the Cathedral are the *Kongsgård Skole* and the interesting **Bispekapellet.** The former was the palace of the Bishop, the latter his private chapel. It has a beautiful stone roof. At the Reformation, the Bishop's residence was brought under the Crown, and was re-named Kongsgaard. It now houses the Latin School (grammar school). Behind the Cathedral is a small park which goes down to the **Bredevann,** a small lake bordered by a pleasant walk shaded by trees and leading, as do also Kongsgaten on the east and Jernbane veien on the west, to the railway station for the Flekkefjord line. Beyond this, a short distance along the *Musægate,* are the **Theatre** and the **Museum** (*free Sundays,* 11.30–2. *On other days there is a fee of* 25 *öre, and the doors are open from* 10 *to* 5, *except on Saturday, when they are closed at* 2). There is a good collection of northern antiquities, ethnological and natural-history objects. In St. Svithun's gate, on the opposite side of the hospital to the museum, is *Kunstforeningen* (The Art Union), *open Thursdays and Sundays in the forenoon, at other times on application at the Museum.* From the vicinity of the Museum we may cross above the railway line to the old Cemetery, and descend by the *Birkelandsgate* to **St. Peter's Church** and the **Nytorv,** the centre of the town.

There are several interesting **walks** in the neighbourhood of Stavanger for those who have more time than the brief call of the steamer allows.

The **Vålandshaug,** a hill at the back of the town, reached in about twenty minutes on foot by the Musægate and the Peder Klowsgate, running along the farther side of the hospital, affords a fine view of the town, the fjord, the islands, and towards the west over Ryfylke mountains. About a mile and a half farther is **Ullenhaug,** a mass of rock rising out of a swampy plain, and surmounted by a tower erected in 1896 to commemorate the victory of Harald Hårfagre over his last enemies (872 A.D.), whereby Norway was united under one ruler. Hafrsfjord, the scene of the combat, is almost at the foot of the hill. It may be visited on foot.

Half an hour's walk from the north side of the market place is **Bjergsted Park,** the town's prettiest and largest park. A little to the west of it is **Byhaugen,** a hill from which there are beautiful views over the town and the coast. The route to these points lies along either Nedre Strand or Övre Strand Gate, Rosenbergbakken, which cuts across them near the mouth of the harbour and is followed to the left, and Lökkeveien westward from Rosenbergbakken. The walking distance can be reduced by using the ferry across the harbour.

Pleasant excursions on a larger scale can be made among the many arms of the Bokn Fjord, or, as it is sometimes called, the **Ryfylke Fjord.**

The **Sandsfjord** has already been mentioned in connection with the route through Telemarken *viâ* the Bratlandsdal (p. 160). It is a very practicable route from Stavanger for long or short excursions. The steamers of the *Stavanger SS. Co.* leave Stavanger daily (twice on Fridays), arriving at Sand in 3½ to 5½ hours. This is a very picturesque route ; but the scenery of the Ryfylke district is seen to even greater advantage if the tour is continued to **Hylen** (steamers twice a week) or to **Sauda** (*Sauda Turisthotel,* Saudasjöen), on the Saudafjord (steamers as to Sand). On the way there are many picturesque stopping-places, but the district is very sparsely inhabited, and only the simplest quarters are to be had at all except the principal stations. There are good restaurants on the boats.

Steamers visit the Sandeid Fjord *viâ* the **Vinde Fjord,** which lies north of Jelsa. **Sandeid** (*Flögstads Pension*), at the head of the **Sandeid Fjord,** which is a northerly continuation of the Vinde Fjord, is reached, five days a week, by steamer from Stavanger in 4¾ to 6¾ hours. The steamers on this route call at the small ports on the east side of the main fjord, running into many lesser arms and touching some fine mountainous country. Sandeid is connected by public motors with **Haugesund,** on the coast (p. 181).

Twice a week steamers visit the **Hervik Fjord** and **Skjold Fjord,** calling at various places on the Tysvaer peninsula. **Skjold** (*Hotels Duelands, Nilsens*) lies on the road from Haugesund to Sandeid.

Lastly, though the possible steamer excursions from Stavanger are by no means exhausted by this list, there remains the **Lyse Fjord,** the most beautiful and mysterious of all the fjords in South-West Norway. From Stavanger we cross to the mouth of the **Högsfjord** (see below), whence the Lyse Fjord runs for 25 miles deep into the mainland, with an average width of about half a mile; the waters lie between steep precipices falling so sheer that there is hardly room for the small village to find a hold on its shores. Three times a week the steamer goes as far as **Lysebotn** at the head of the fjord at the foot of the **Kjerag Mountain** (2,790 feet). (Plain quarters are to be had at *Lysebotn Sommer Hotel* and at the farm Nedrebö.)

In this fjord, a little beyond Eidane (on the south side, about a fourth of the way up), is a curious rock known as the **Pulpit,** a flat-topped, overhanging crag, easily climbed. At the head of the fjord on the south side is a cavern "which occasionally emits a noise like thunder; this curious natural phenomenon, which has given rise to numerous legends, is only witnessed after strong westerly gales, and is supposed to be caused by compression of the atmosphere."

Högsfjord, the only other fjord worth noting, can be visited from Stavanger as far as Dirdal. Steamers call there six times a week. Dirdal may also be reached by motor from Stavanger, and from Dirdal may be taken an interesting motor trip by **Ween,** passing through one of the largest rock-falls in Norway, *via* Vikeså and Ålgård back to Stavanger.

A land excursion from Stavanger is to **Sola,** about 17 km. south-west of the town. It was the seat of Erling Skjalgson, the last of the great chiefs opposed to Harald Hårfagre, and is situated on a tongue of land on one side of which is the historic Hafrs Fjord. There are the ruins of an ancient stone church under the care of the Society for the Preservation of Ancient Buildings.

STAVANGER TO BERGEN.

The steamers from Newcastle proceed northward from Stavanger through the fjords and sounds among the islands of the Skjærgård. They do not call *en route.* The Oslo-Bergen mail steamers take 10 hours, calling at

Wilse,] STAVANGER. *[Oslo.*

Mittet & Co.,] *[Oslo.*

LOEN : NORD FJORD.

Kopervik and Haugesund and travelling at night. The express coastal mail service ("Hurtigruten") have a steamer leaving Stavanger on Sunday at 12 noon and reaching Bergen at 10 p.m. The Stavanger-Bergen mail steamers leave Stavanger every night at 8.30, and arrive in Bergen the next morning at 7.30. There are many local steamers; those belonging to the *Hardanger-Söndhordland Co.* are perhaps the best; they call at many small stations along the route, and for those who are not pressed for time this is the best way of seeing the country. These smaller boats follow the innermost lead, where the scenery is very fine, and the fjord views most varied and extensive. The *Rutebok for Norge*, published weekly, should be consulted.

Passengers from England to Bergen *viâ* Stavanger usually get their first experience of the delights of fjord travelling by this route. Except for two small openings, the passage is made in the smooth water behind the chain of islands that front the coast, known to mariners as the **Skjærgård.** After leaving Stavanger, we cross the **Bokn Fjord,** the first piece of unprotected water (it is rough only when a heavy westerly wind blows the rollers in from the North Sea) and steer north for **Skudeneshavn** (*Slåttebrœks Pension*), a small port at the south end of the island of **Karmöy.**

There is a good road from Skudenes to **Kopervik** and thence to **Salhus** at the north end of the island, just opposite Haugesund. Public motors go from end to end of the island three times a day in each direction and more frequently between Skudenes and Kopervik (*Tönjums Hotel*).

The boat threads its way through the Karm Sound, between the islands of Karmöy and **Bokn.** The latter has given its name to the great fjord in which Stavanger lies; but **Karmöy** is the more important and interesting. It lies due north and south, and is some 16 miles long by about 5 at its widest, a rugged, hilly, inhospitable-looking island. We pass, on the left, the rising town of **Kopervik**; perhaps this harbour is as old as any in Norway, for Karmöy was known in the days of the Sagas. Northward of Kopervik lies **Avaldsnes,** with a small church, beside which is the *Virgin Mary's Needle*, a leaning monolith. The legend runs that when it touches the church, the end of the world will come. A little farther, on the other side of the Sound, at the ferry, one sees five such stones in a circle; they are known as the five *dårlige Jomfruer*, or foolish virgins.

Opposite the north end of Karmöy, on the mainland, is the town of Haugesund—that is to say, it is partly on the mainland and partly on the islands of Risöy and Hasselöy. **Haugesund** (*Hotels Victoria, Norge, Metropol*) has a population approaching 17,000, owing to its fisheries and general trade;

but its connection with the outer world is almost solely by steamer, though roads (with motor services) run from it till they are interrupted either by fjord or by mountain. Standing north of the town and visible from the steamer, is an obelisk erected in 1872 on the traditional burial-place of Harald Hårfagre (Harold the Fair), who a thousand years earlier had welded the petty kingdoms in the country into the Kingdom of Norway.

The larger steamers now cross the short piece of open water called **Sletten,** and enter the broad **Bömmel Fjord,** where we get a first view of the Hardanger mountains. On the left is the small harbour of **Bömmel,** with a church, and farther along, on the left, is the island of Moster with the little port of **Mosterhavn,** where some of the local boats call. Here landed Olav Trygvasön, when he came from Dublin in 995 to claim the Crown of Norway, and here he built what was probably the first Christian church in the country. Upon its site is a stone church erected in the middle of the twelfth century. Some boats steer northward through the **Stoksund** from this point, passing beneath the **Sigga** (1,500 feet), a small mountain with a round top, a mark for mariners. The more usual route is to the eastward of the island of **Stord** (*Hotels, Furuly Helseheim, Leirviks*). At the south end of this island is **Leirvik,** where passengers change boats for the Åkre Fjord and for the island of **Halsnöy,** where there are the remains of a Benedictine convent. The larger steamers now steer through the **Langnuen,** between the islands of Stord and Tysnes; the local boats call at **Sunde** and **Heröysund** in Söndhordland. (Passengers from Stavanger to Hardanger, and *vice versâ,* have sometimes to change into the Bergen-Hardanger boat.) Here the scenery of the outer Hardanger begins. The boat crosses the **Kvinnherad Fjord,** and proceeds through the **Löksund,** a narrow sound between **Tysnes** and the mainland. On the north of Tysnes is **Godöysund** (*Godösund Hotel*; *see* p. 83), and the route thenceforward is the same for both large and small boats. They cross the wide **Björne Fjord,** and enter the Krossfjord, between the mainland and island of Sotra. Here the Bergen mountains, Lyderhorn and Lövstakken, come into view, and the steamer, rounding the point of **Skålevik,** between the mainland and the island of **Asköy,** comes within sight of **Bergen.** This first view of Bergen should not be lost. When the weather is fine it is one of the prettiest views in all Norway.

BERGEN TO TRONDHJEM BY SEA.

The express mail service (*Hurtigruten*) have excellent steamers running from Bergen five times a week at * 7 p.m. to Trondhjem, calling at Ålesund, Molde and Kristiansund N. the next day and reaching Trondhjem the day after at 6 a.m.

THE route has been described as far as the **Sogne Fjord** on page 91; thence to the **Nord Fjord** on page 99, and thence to **Ålesund** and **Molde** on pages 103–4. Here follows note on the final section.

The sea-route from Molde to Kristiansund is less protected by islands than any other part of the coast, with the sole exception of the Stat. It is, moreover, more remote from the mountain ranges, and the scenery is tamer. Only here and there do the mountains rise to any great height—as the **Stemshest,** on the right, some 2,500 feet high. But in places, where the fjords run inland from the coast, one gets a glimpse of the mountains of the Romsdal and Nordmöre.

Passing the island of **Averö,** we round the point of Kirkland beacon, and reach—

KRISTIANSUND N.

Hotels.—*Grand* and others.
Bennett's Travel Bureau.—7 Vågeveien.

A picturesque and important town of 15,500 inhabitants. It is built on four hilly islands, enclosing the harbour; is the centre for the North Sea cod-fishery, exporting large quantities of dried cod to Spain and Portugal; and it has a large trading fleet of steam and sail. There are many pretty walks in the town, and several well-laid-out promenades, especially in the neighbourhood of the Church. Artists who are fond of marine subjects find good material here, but the port is not much visited by tourists except as a junction for the Sunndal and Halse (or Surnadal) steamers (*see* p. 184).

As the steamer proceeds from Kristiansund N. in the direction of Trondhjem, the scenery again becomes grander. At first the route, particularly that of the liners, lies through open water, but soon we are under the shelter of the great island of **Smöla,** with the **Tusterö,** a mountainous island that has long been visible, rising to the right. The small steamers

* *See* footnote, p. 12.

keep closer in, and call at numerous more or less interesting ports; this is a pleasant route to the traveller to whom time is of little importance. **Hitra,** the great island beyond Smöla, is famous among sportsmen for the fact that it still has wild red deer, smaller game and good fishing. Opposite the centre of the south-east coast of the island is Hellandsjöen, between which and Kirkeseteröra, on the Hevne Fjord, is a motor-car service three times a week. On the other three days the cars run between Kirkeseteröra and Vinjeöra, whence there is an overland route to Vinje on the Vinje Fjord, connected by steamer with Kristiansund. The steamer continues past **Beian** on the left, and **Agdenes** on the right, at the entrance of the great Trondhjem Fjord. Passing along this, we have on a hill on the left the remains of the Reins Closter, founded in 1237 and secularized about 1550. Beyond it the fjord expands and both northward and eastward there is much water in sight. Having crossed the entrance of the Orkedals Fjord on the south, we are soon in the harbour of **Trondhjem** (p. 186).

THE SUNNDALS FJORD.

During the tourist season there is a steamer every day except Tuesday from Kristiansund to the **Sunndals Fjord,** 68 km. in length, which in its upper reaches is one of the grandest of the western inlets. The scenery does not differ from that of the coast until the boat is well in the Tingvoll Fjord. Then we call at Batnfjord (p. 109), where the direct road comes in from Molde. **Eidsöra** (p. 110) has been mentioned as the terminus of the road from Molde *viâ* Eidsvåg; after passing this place the steamer enters into the grander reaches of the Sunndals Fjord.

From **Opdöl** (*Skyss station*), at which steamers call, a path leads northward to **Rökkem,** on the Stangvik Fjord, an inner arm of the Surendals Fjord. This is part of a fine circular trip to be made from Trondhjem *viâ* Stören, Sunndalsöra and Surnadalsöra.

From Opdöl also one can drive to **Nerdal,** 14 km., and thence walk to **Inderdal** (1½ hours) where there is a tourist hut. Inderdal is a mountain valley at the southern end of the **Trollheim,** a district somewhat similar to the Jotunheim. Guides are available for the ascent of many fine peaks, including Skarfjell and Tårnet, both over 6,000 feet, and the neighbouring lakes are full of trout.

By walking for 5 hours northward from Inderdal one reaches **Kåvatn** at the upper end of the pretty **Todal Valley.** A path leads westward in an hour to the mouth of the valley, at the extremity of an arm of the Halse Fjord. Going eastward from Kåvatn is a steep path leading in about 8 hours through the narrow Neådal to **Trollheimshytten** (Trollheims Hut), 1,650 feet above sea level, the centre of excursions in Trollheim.

The last stretch of the Sunndals Fjord, as it turns south to Sunndalsöra, is particularly fine. **Sunndal** or **Sunndalsöra** (*Hages Hotel*) is much frequented by fishermen, but is also a favourite place with other tourists, the mountainous surroundings being particularly attractive as a playground for small excursions, and it is the best place from which to visit the Inderdal, for which the steamer is taken to Opdöl.

The principal excursions are to the small **Kaldfonn Glacier,** and to **Tredal,** whence a road leads through the picturesque **Lilledal.**

From Sunndalsöra there runs a good road with a motor service to **Opdal** on the Dovre railway. The road is described on p. 143.

The **Halse Fjord** and its branches, of which the **Surnadals Fjord** and the **Stangviks Fjord** are the principal, lie just to the north-east of the Sunndals Fjord. They have not the grandeur of the fjords to the south, and are not much frequented by ordinary tourists. From **Surnadal,** at the head of the Surnadals Fjord, there is a motor service to **Svorkmo,** on a route between the fjord and Trondhjem. It is described on page 193. The road and the motor service start from **Stangvik,** on the **Stangviks Fjord.** Higher up, the Stangvik Fjord becomes the **Todals Fjord,** terminating at **Todal** or **Todalsöra,** whence a rough road leads up the valley to **Kårvatn.**

TRONDHJEM.

Approaches.—The express mail service (" Hurtigruten ") have excellent steamers running from Bergen* five times a week at 7 p.m. to Trondhjem, calling at Ålesund, Molde and Kristiansund N., which are left at 12.30 noon, 4 p.m. and 9.30 p.m. respectively, and Trondhjem is reached at 6 a.m. From Oslo by train in 15½ hours by day, 13½ hours by night.
Baths.—Dronningens Gate 1a. Sea-baths near the Station.
Consuls.—*British*, Olav Trygvåsöns Gate 15.
Hotels.—*Britannia*, in the Dronningens Gate; *Angleterre*, in the Nordre Gate; *Grand*, Kongens Gate; *Phœnix*, Torvet.
Information Office.—The Railway Station.
Population.—About 57,000.
Porters (*bybud*) meet the steamers and quay trains.
Post Office.—Dronningens Gate.
Railway Station.—Across the Meraker Bridge, at the south end of the Söndre Gate.
Tourist Agencies.—Bennett's, Dronningens Gate; Cook's, Nordre Gate.

FLOWING down from Lake Selbu to the Trondhjem Fjord, the river *Nid* describes a sharp serpentine bend, and the town of Trondhjem stands on the peninsula thus formed. With the sea on its northern side, and the river on the other two, the town has in modern times begun to feel the need of expansion, and has consequently spread in trim suburbs to the opposite banks. But the old city, which traces its foundation back to the days of pagan Norway, is built on quite spacious lines, and has resolutely and rightly refused to suffer itself to be cramped. The result is in every way excellent; it is now a fine and spacious city, with wide streets and stately promenades shaded by trees. It contains some very fine modern buildings, and one or two ancient ones—in particular the Cathedral—which are the pride of Norway and the wonder of visitors.

Trondhjem is said to owe its foundation to King Olav Trygvåsön, who established it on its present site in 997. Quite possibly, however, there was a considerable settlement before; but Trondhjem is quite content to reckon its origin from that date, and in 1897 celebrated its 900th anniversary. Olav called his city *Nidaros*—the mouth of the Nid—but we know little of it beyond the fact that it had risen to some importance twenty years later.

The romance of the town is usually connected with Olav Haraldsön, the King of Norway who, with fire and sword, forced the Christian faith upon his rather unwilling subjects, and was slain by them in the Battle of Stikklestad (1030)

* See footnote, p. 12.

after a great fight (*see* p. 41). The faith triumphed, though the king was killed. His body was brought to Trondhjem, which had become the capital of Norway, and was buried beside a medicinal spring which still exists, and is now inside the wall of the high altar of the Cathedral. Over the spot where the king was interred a wooden church was built. In the year 1070 Olav Haraldsön's nephew, King Olav Kyrre, established a bishop's see in Trondhjem and built a cathedral church to the glory of the Holy Trinity and as a memorial to the martyr king. The site included the spot where his uncle had been buried, and who had in the meantime been canonized. To the Cathedral was brought St. Olav's shrine, which had been lodged in other churches in the town. It was placed over the high altar, and to it pilgrims flocked, as miracles wrought by the saint were reported. So rich were the offerings that it became possible to make the Cathedral an immense building of great architectural beauty.

In the history of the see are certain facts which invest the Cathedral with special interest for visitors from Great Britain.

In 1152 the Pope's legate visited Norway and readjusted the ecclesiastical situation of the country. That legate was an Englishman, Nicholas Breakspear, at that time Cardinal Archbishop of Albano, and later Pope, with the title of Adrian IV. He raised the see of Trondhjem to archiepiscopal dignity, and advanced the Cathedral to the rank of metropolitan church in the Norwegian province of Catholic Christianity. The province consisted of eleven bishoprics, among which were the Hebrides, the Isle of Man and the Orkneys.

If the stay to be made in Trondhjem is short, the visitor should go straight to the Cathedral, which, of all sights in Norway, should not be missed. From the station or quay, follow the Söndre Gate to the Kongens Gate, turn right to the Market Square, and continue left along the Munke Gate. The spire of the Cathedral is itself the best guide.

The Cathedral.

Open 12 to 1.30 and 6 to 7 daily.

Before entering, walk round the exterior, both to get some idea of the size of the building and to notice the various styles. Like all mediæval churches of these stupendous dimensions, Trondhjem's Cathedral was long building, and in it may be traced the successive developments of Romanesque and Gothic architecture. (Most of the historical facts which follow are taken by permission from *Trondhjem Cathedral* (20 views), published by F. Bruns, Bokhandel, Trondhjem.)

The oldest parts of the building standing to-day are the great Romanesque transepts, built in the twelfth century on to the Church of St. Olav. One of the side chapels, according to contemporary inscription, was consecrated by Archbishop Eystein in 1161, and the robing-house or Chapter, where Eystein was buried, was consecrated in 1188. After a three years' residence in England, during the fight with King Sverre, Eystein came back, no doubt with new ideas of what a cathedral might be. In 1183 he began to re-form and enlarge the chancel and high chancel. He built in the massive Romanesque of his period—it was, however, a period that was beginning to discard this style for the early Gothic. Eystein's work was finished and several times improved by his successors. The builder of the last portion, the octagon chancel, was Erik Valkendorf (died 1522), whose coat of arms may be seen in several places upon it. The proportions of Eystein's crossing seem to suggest that he intended the church to be built with a nave as large as that at present existing, but with a much smaller choir, probably terminating in a triple apse. When the building of the great choir, with its apsidal termination in the form of an octagon, was begun, the Gothic style had already taken hold of the cathedral builders of Europe, and the scheme of Eystein underwent a considerable modification. The result was the present choir, a gem of Middle Gothic in the refinement of its treatment and the delicacy of its detail. In 1230 Archbishop Sigurd began to enlarge and rebuild the unfinished Roman nave. It belongs to the order we in England sometimes refer to as the Decorated period, and it is in this period that Gothic architecture was at its summit. The west front was erected in 1248. It was decorated with gilded sculptures of the apostles and other saints in several rows. Of these only the lowest, and they only in an incomplete condition, have remained until the present time as witnesses of the high state of ecclesiastical sculptural art in Norway in the Middle Ages.

The Cathedral was approaching completion when it was destroyed by fire in 1328. The "Black Death" ravaged the country and brought lean years, so that it was impossible to maintain the great building in repair. In 1424 the nave stood without a roof. A few years later the church was again burnt, and in 1531 it was once more a prey to flames. After that only the transepts and chancel were kept in repair.

When Norway was placed under Danish rule and the evangelical Lutheran faith introduced, the king, Christian III, abolished the archbishopric and confiscated the archiepiscopal and cathedral properties. That was in 1537. A few years later an evangelical superintendent or bishop was appointed. The archbishop's palace was converted into barracks for the

Wilse,] [*Oslo.*

TRONDHJEM CATHEDRAL.

Wilse,] [*Oslo.*

IN THE TROLLHEIM.

king's soldiers, and it is still in military occupation. In 1540 St. Olav's shrine was taken to Denmark, and in 1568 the saint's earthly remains were buried in the church. In 1584 the Cathedral became a parish church. In the last year of that century the Chapter was dissolved and the daily church services were discontinued. In 1708 and again in 1719, the church took fire, but was put in some order and kept in a certain state of repair by the congregation. At the beginnng of the nineteenth century, however, it was in sad condition. But the national revival, which culminated in the great Thing at Eidsvoll, as briefly noted on p. 138, awakened the Norwegians to their duty towards their national monuments, and the rebuilding of Trondhjem Cathedral, in its original form and splendour, became a matter of national concern. Fragments from the ruined portions were sufficiently complete and numerous to render possible the solution of the archæological part of the task, with pious care. But the artistic completion of the Cathedral called for no less care from the master-builder, the sculptor and the artist in charge of the windows.

Not until 1869 was the actual restoration begun. It was then hoped that it would be finished in 1914, on the anniversary of the declaration of Norwegian independence. That hope proved impossible of realization, and then 1930, the nine-hundredth anniversary of the death of St. Olav, became the date on which all hearts were fixed for the completion of the great work.

The Cathedral is entered by the **Chapter House.** This leads by a small stairway into the exquisite **Octagon Choir ;** this is encircled by an **Ambulatory,** the altar being screened off by an arcade of eight arches, delicately cusped and crocketed. In the outer wall of this octagon, immediately to the left of the central recess, is a small door concealing a recess from which one can look into **St. Olav's Well.** The outer choir, of perfect proportions, consists of six bays, with arcades of pointed arches, supported on clustered shafts, surmounted by delicately carved capitals. Note also the work in the clerestory, the side choir aisles and the sedilia.

A colossal arch divides the Choir from the transepts. The visitor receives something of a shock in proceeding so abruptly from the soft and graceful outlines of the Choir, with its wealth of foliage and its quaint conceits of carving, into the work produced under the earlier school of the Anglo-Norman builders, bare, rugged, massive and almost terrible in its gloomy severity. Immense recesses on the east walls do duty for chapels ; here and there are traces of rude carvings, but in the main, and especially about the centre under the tower, the work is devoid of fancy in ornament or design.

But in the great **Nave** we come once more upon the more pleasing aspects of the Gothic, though here they have become rather more formalized, and we begin to feel the foreshadowings of the movement that reawakened in the Renaissance.

In returning to the Chapter House, pause a moment on re-entering the nave to observe the simple beauty of the Octagon Choir, and the delicacy of the slender white marble shafts, which, springing free of the main supports, do but show off the soft and graceful lines of the soapstone columns beside which they stand.

Many Norwegian kings have been crowned in the Cathedral, the last being Håkon VII, in 1906.

If time does not press, the town can be seen to advantage by the following itinerary :—

On leaving the railway station follow the tram lines over the bridge spanning the **Östre Kanalhavn** (East Canal Harbour), and along the **Söndre Gate.** Turn with them to the right into the **Olav Trygvåsöns Gate,** the principal shopping street of the town. It crosses the Nordre Gate, the promenade street. In sight at the upper end of this broad avenue is the **Vor Frue Kirke** (Our Lady's Church, see below). Continue along the Olav Trygvåsöns Gate, following the tram lines into the **Munke Gate,** the broadest thoroughfare in the city and the site of some of the finest buildings. On reaching it turn to the left. Then having passed two openings on the left, you come to **Dronningens Gate,** in which are Bennett's Office, a little higher up the **Post Office,** and beyond that the **Kunstindustri Museum** (Museum of Industrial Art. *Free daily,* 12.30–2.30; *at other times kr.* 1). Having crossed this long thoroughfare, you have, on the left, the **Stiftsgård**, probably the largest and most ornate wooden building in Europe. It was erected in 1770, and is used as the royal residence when the King comes to Trondhjem. (*Admission on application to caretaker.*) A little farther is an open square, where the Kongens Gate crosses. This is the **Market Place,** where in July and August fruit is abundant. The column standing here, and so long in sight, supports the figure of Olav Trygvåsön. The Cathedral, already described, is straight ahead at the end of Munke Gate.

In the left-hand portion of the Kongens Gate is **Vor Frue Kirke** (Church of our Lady), the oldest of Trondhjem's churches (other than the Cathedral). It dates from the 13th century. The church officer is in attendance at 10, 12, 5 and 7.

(*Gratuity.*) Opposite it are the *Telegraph Office* and (just in Nordre Gate) Cook's Office. Farther along, on the left, is a **Picture Gallery.** (*Admission daily, except Saturday, 12 to* 2.30. *Sundays, free ; other days, small fee.*)

As one faces towards the Cathedral, the extensive white building on the left contains various public offices, of which one, bearing the word *Politikammer*, is the police office. The large building on the right, with the date 1770, contains Assembly Rooms and Club Rooms. Its local name is the equivalent of Harmony Building. Farther along, Munke Gate crosses Erling Skakkes Gate. At the junction of the right-hand portion of this with Prinsens Gate, along which trams run, is the *Theatre*, and beyond that is the **Museum of the Scientific Society** (Videnskabernes Selskab), which contains some zoological, mineral and archæological collections. In the grounds of this Society is a small wooden stave church, brought hither from Holtålen in 1884. (*Open daily, except Saturday,* 12–2.)

Then in Munke Gate, the very large, red-brick building attracting attention on the right is the **Cathedral School** (Grammar School), at which King Håkonsön was a pupil. The present structure is one of the oldest in Trondhjem. On the same side of the thoroughfare are military premises ending with the General's Quarters.

The thoroughfare going right and left at the end of Munke Gate is Bispegaten. Much of the eastern portion borders the Cathedral grounds and passes before **Thomas Angell's House,** a very large grey building, now a home for elderly ladies without means. Thomas Angell was a rich merchant who bequeathed all his possessions to charitable institutions. A statue of him stands before his house.

Behind the Cathedral is the **Archbishop's Palace,** which since the Reformation has been in military occupation. It is reached from the Bispe Gate by the narrow thoroughfare Kongsgårdsgaten, just west of the Cathedral. (*Open Sundays,* 12–1.30. *Other days,* 9–12.)

Arkitekt Christies Gate, going westward from the palace, leads in a few yards to Prinsens Gate. To the right this leads through the town ; to the left to the Elgeseter Bridge. From the farther end of the bridge is a road to the great **Technical College** (Norges Tekniske Höiskole) (*apply to custodian,* 9–2 *and* 4–7, *except Saturday and Sunday*), one of the finest in Northern Europe. The return may be made by the same bridge, or by way of the fortress at Kristiansten (turn to the right just before reaching the bridge) and so over the **Bakke Bridge** in the industrial and shipping quarter; or by turning to the left through the suburb of **Öen,** and crossing by the footbridge.

On the west side of the town is the suburb of **Ilen.** The tramway along Kongens Gate leads to its church, and thence it is a pleasant walk either, in half an hour, to Stenbjerget and Åsveien for a view of the surrounding country, or, in three-quarters of an hour, to Elster Park and Strandlinien for a charming view of the fjord.

On the east side of the town the walks are less interesting. The best is that to the dismantled fortress of **Kristiansten,** built in 1680. From it there is a fine view of the city and its surroundings.

EXCURSIONS FROM TRONDHJEM.

The more distant excursions from Trondhjem are many and full of interest. The most popular are:—

To the **Island of Munkholm,** in the fjord directly north of the town (10 minutes by motor-boat from Ravnkloa (fish market), opposite Munkegaten, every hour). On the island stood in the eleventh century a Benedictine Monastery; all that remains of it is enshrined in the name. The island became a fortress, and is now covered with dismantled earth-works and redoubts. In the seventeenth century it became a state prison. As such it held the patriotic but misunderstood Peter Schumacher, Count Griffenfeldt, who spent eighteen years (1680 to 1698) pacing his cell. The flagstones are shown as they were worn by his footsteps.

To the **Lerfoss,** two falls of the Nid, about 6 km. south of the town. Motors run to them several times a day from Dronningens Gate, in the neighbourhood of Stiftsgården. Although the lower fall is utilized for industrial purposes the volume of water is considerable. The height of the lower fall is about 80 feet, of the upper fall about 100 feet. Against the lower fall, at which the cars stop, is a restaurant. It is a pleasant walk alongside the river to the upper fall.

To **Fjellseter on Gråkallen,** by public motor, starting as above. The route affords very fine views. At Fjellseter, about 8 km. from the town and 1,300 feet above the sea, was a large tourist hotel which was burnt down in 1916. A small hotel has since been erected close by. From it the way to the summit of Gråkallen is easy to find. At the end of 1 km. it passes the *Skistue*, the headquarters of the Ski Club of Trondhjem, where refreshments may be had. Thence it is only a fifteen minutes' walk to the top of the mountain, the highest point in the immediate neighbourhood of Trondhjem, although only 1,800 feet above sea-level. The prospect is extensive, while the view of the fjord is superb.

To **Steinviksholmen,** the much besieged stronghold of the last Roman Catholic Archbishop of Norway. The castle was erected in 1530 and destroyed in 1564. The ruins are very interesting. By rail *viâ* Hell to **Langstein,** and thence half hour's walk.

To **Molde** (overland)—

1. By rail *viâ* **Dombås** to **Åndalsnes** and thence by steamer.

2. By rail to Opdal, thence by public motor to **Sunndal,** steamer to **Eidsöra,** and public motor to Molde.

3. Steamer from Trondhjem to **Thamshamn,** 2 hours. Thence by electric train through a picturesque valley to **Svorkmo,** 19 km., a small village (*Svorkmo Hotel*). Thence by public motor to **Surna,** 71 km., and thence by steamer *viâ* **Kristiansund N.** This route is the least used.

The electric railway continues from Svorkmo to *Lökken*, 7 km. farther, and is the most picturesque portion.

Near Lökken (*Orkla Hotel*) are the celebrated Orkla copper mines, the largest in Scandinavia.

From Lökken motors run to **Berkåk,** on the Dovre Railway.

To **Namsos** and **Mosjöen.** The route lies through much charming and grand scenery. As far as Steinkjer one has a choice of rail or steamer. There is a steamer four times a week, and it takes from 7½ to 12 hours. The railway passes through **Hell** (*buffet*) and **Levanger** (*buffet*) and reaches **Steinkjer,** 126 km., in about 4½ hours (*Hotels: Grand, Bondeheimen*). From Steinkjer direct to **Namsos,** 80 km., by public motor, 3½ hours (*Hotels: Grand, Hospitset*), or by rail alongside Lake Snåsa to the village of the same name, 182 km. from Trondhjem, a journey of 6¼ hours and then by public motor car to Namsos, 91 km. (p. 195), or to **Mosjöen,** 255 km. farther, a town of some 2,000 inhabitants at the mouth of the Vefsen River. From it several pretty tours can be made. Local steamers call (*Fru Haugans Hotel*).

THE NORTH CAPE CRUISE.

The Bergenske Nordenfjeldske, Vesterålske, and other steamship companies arrange for a visit to the Lofoten Isles, to certain northern ports on the west coast of Norway, and to the North Cape. From Newcastle to Newcastle the cruise, which includes certain fjords and the northern points just mentioned, occupies 13 days. From Bergen to Bergen 10 days. Full particulars of dates, fees and general conditions are prepared annually and can be obtained on application to the Companies' Offices or to the principal Tourist Agencies.

The Norwegian Express steamers provide a service from Stavanger to Kirkenes once a week, from Bergen and Trondhjem to Kirkenes six times a week, from Trondhjem to Narvik once a week. A call is made at the prineipal ports *en route*, but not at the North Cape. For comfort and good food the boats can be recommended. The trip from Bergen to Bergen occupies a few hours less than 14 days, and from Trondhjem to Trondhjem 9 days.

The Midnight Sun.—The following table shows the dates between which the sun is partly or wholly above the horizon at midnight, but disappointment will be avoided by recognition of the fact that clouds or fog may hide the sun all the time it might be visible.

	Upper Edge.	Whole Disc.	Whole Disc.	Upper Edge.
Svolvær	May 25	May 28	July 16	July 19
Tromsö	,, 18	,, 20	,, 23	,, 25
Hammerfest	,, 14	,, 16	,, 27	,, 30
North Cape	,, 12	,, 14	,, 30	Aug. 1

THAT part of Norway which lies between Trondhjem and the North Cape is nearly twice as long as the portion which extends between Trondhjem and the most southerly point. The tourists who know most about it are those who go to the North Cape and beyond, and their acquaintance with it is necessarily very limited.

The country immediately north of Trondhjem is not much visited by tourists, and most steamers carrying passengers to the North Cape do not make any call at all before reaching the Svartisen Glacier, through which the Arctic Circle runs. A railway is being constructed from Trondhjem to Bodö, the most southerly point at which the midnight sun can be seen. A portion of it has been opened, and public motors carry passengers farther northward, but, speaking generally, the traveller who wishes to visit this district is dependent upon the mail coasting steamers, which call at numerous out-of-the-way ports, where he is usually surprised to see a busy life going on. A thriving population inhabits the fjords and islands of the coast, and though the towns are not large, they are prosperous in their way. Along the fjords and in the valleys between the mountains there is arable land, and in the interior of the country are large forests. During the herring and cod-fishing seasons, the fishing stations present a scene of great activity, and a considerable income is derived from the eider-down collected on the cliffs and rocks. The most southern part of this section of Norway is called **Nordland**; and north and east of it is **Finmark,** where the Lapps are chiefly found. The country is rugged and wild, as in the districts to the south of the Trondhjem Fjord; but as far north as Tromsö, over 500 miles by sea from Trondhjem, the climate in summer is quite mild.

Namsos (p. 193) is the first place of any importance reached after we leave Trondhjem, but it is not a calling-place of the Midnight Sun steamers. If they leave Trondhjem in the afternoon, the fjord up which Namsos is situated will be passed during the night, and the following afternoon all who feel interested in what can be seen will be on the look-out for the curiously-shaped island of **Torghatten,** so named because the hill of which it consists has the outline of a tall-crowned, battered "wide-awake" hat, an additional curious feature is a hole right through the middle, which can be seen clearly from the steamer. The rocky island is 827 feet high; the hole through it is 407 feet from the ground. The tunnel, caused probably by erosion, varies in height from 60 to 250 feet, and in width from 36 to 88 feet.

After passing through Brönnöy Sound, the next point of interest is the large island of **Alsten,** with seven peaks from 2,600 to 3,400 feet high, called the **Seven Sisters of Alstahaug,** said to be witches turned into stone by the Fates of ancient Norway. A monument, seen from the vessel, commemorates Petter Dass, the poet of the Nordland, who as priest here lived in the old parsonage of Alstahaug, where he died in 1708.

The tourist steamers continue to follow the coast, but the local steamers run in the **Ranen Fjord** to **Mo** (*Mo Hotel*), where iron ore is shipped from the Dunderland Valley mines, owned by an English company.

Not far from the town is a fine waterfall. A public motor runs through the **Dunderlandsdal,** a charming valley containing many caves, and excursions can be made to branches of the Svartisen Glacier. The nearest is about 6 km. from Mo.

A brief journey onward brings us to another curiously-shaped rocky island known as the **Hestmann,** or horseman, said to be no other than the All-Father Odin. The similarity of the outline of the rock to the figure of a cloaked and seated horseman will be seen immediately if the ship is at the right angle. As the vessel passes him, the report of the ship's gun marks the crossing of the **Arctic Circle** (66° 32′ 30″.)

Beyond the Horseman and the **Red Lion Island,** the steamer turns into a narrow fjord, with green water telling of the near presence of a glacier. It is the **Svartisen Glacier,** seen clearly from the sea as a long white ridge extending along the coast. A few peaks, running up to nearly 4,000 feet in height, rise through the great icefield, which measures 35 miles by 10 miles. It is the only glacier in Europe descending almost to the sea. At the head of the fjord is a rustic landing-place, from which a path, called Prins Olavs Vei, goes right up to the ice.

Continuing northward, **Grönöy,** an island green with birch trees, is passed, and just beyond it **Melöy,** in the neighbourhood of lofty mountains. Then for a short time the vessel is in the open sea. On a tongue of land on the north side of the Salt Fjord is **Bodö** (*Grand Hotel*), a town of some 5,000 inhabitants. It is, as mentioned on p. 194, the southernmost town at which the Midnight Sun is seen. The Midnight Sun steamers, however, pass it, but the mail steamers and many other vessels call, as it is an important coaling station.

In the neighbourhood of the town is the **Rönvik Mountain,** which although only 530 feet high commands a magnificent view. A road leads to the foot and it can be ascended in 15 minutes. (*Restaurant.*) About a mile from the town is the old church containing a curious monument to a priest who died in 1596. Bodö is a good centre for excursions, as the Salten's Steamship Co. has regular services to the neighbouring fjords and to the Lofoten Islands. Readers of Harriet Martineau's *Feats on the Fjords* will recall that the scene is laid on the Salt Fjord and its branches.

From Bodö the view of—

The Lofoten Islands

is very fine. At their south-west end, beside the island of **Moskenes,** is the famous **Maelström,** the magic and dreaded whirlpool that was supposed to overwhelm all who ventured upon it. Like the Lorelei and other such marvels, its terrors have no existence outside the imagination of poets. The first reference to it is in the writings of Bishop Arrebo, who died in 1637. The steamer steers through the **Vestfjord,** between the mainland and the Lofotens, of which the magnificent panorama fills all the northern and western horizon. Like blue saw-teeth rises a long line of jagged peaks upon islands innumerable. The tourist steamers call at one or two of the islands, but those who are travelling by the local steamers should do more than that, as the islands are well worth visiting for the scenery and for the kindly, unspoilt people. Steamers ply in and out among the islands, and since the extensive introduction of the telephone, life has been shorn to some extent of its loneliness in this outpost.

The capital, **Svolvær** (*Hotel Lofoten*), quite a thriving little town, is the natural centre for excursions to the Troll Fjord, Raftsund and the Lofotens. It is situated on several islands in a small bay at the foot of rugged mountains, of which one, the **Svolværsjure,** is worth ascending for the prospect from its summit. Svolvær is one of the most important centres for the Norwegian deep-sea fisheries.

Most of the tourist steamers call (either on the outward or on the return journey) at **Raftevoll,** on the **Raftsund,** an extremely narrow fjord with great mountains on each side, but the principal attraction is the visit to the **Troll Fjord,** a branch of the Raftsund, which presents the finest piece of scenery in the whole range of the islands, though many other places are little inferior to it. So narrow is the entrance of the Troll Fjord that the yacht seems to be heading for a wall of rock, until at the last moment an opening appears, and the vessel glides through into a small lake bordered by perpendicular cliffs.

Steering by the **Vesterålen,** the islands north of the Lofotens, we pass **Narvik** (only the local and mail steamers call here), a town of about 5,000 inhabitants (*Hotels : Phœnix, Royal*), an essentially modern town. It had no existence before 1902, when it sprang up in connection with the Swedish iron mines.

Narvik is connected by railway with Stockholm, 1,581 km., *viâ* Lapland. The line extends for 24 miles from the coast to the frontier, through wild, uninhabited country, beside sheer precipices and through many tunnels.

The next place of importance on the journey is **Tromsö**

(*Grand*), a thriving town of about 10,000 inhabitants, delightfully situated on the forest-covered island of Troms, surrounded by snow-capped peaks. It has a busy harbour, where ships of all nations may be seen. It is the headquarters of the seal and walrus hunters, and is of note as the starting-place of several Arctic expeditions. It is also an important agricultural centre, for, in spite of the value of its mines and the importance of its fisheries, the chief industry of the district is the raising of crops and cattle. And the fact that Tromsö is the seat of a bishopric must not pass unnoticed. The Cathedral is a bare-looking church in the centre of the town. Southward of the town is the only *Museum* in North Norway. Its collection from the Arctic regions is probably unrivalled, while the Lapp articles and the interior decorations from churches alone would well repay a visit.

Tromsö merits a longer stay than the hour or two that the tourist steamers can allow their passengers to remain. The district of which it is the centre is extremely interesting and of a character surprisingly different from what one would expect. " Who would believe," asks a local writer, " that here in 70° North latitude (far within the Arctic Circle) are found in warm summers regular bathing resorts, where life is amazingly active." As the enthusiastic scribe quaintly says, " the district of Troms is a God-favoured part of the country, in spite of its location so far north." Steamship lines with their short and long runs take one to all parts of the coast. At most stopping-places motors meet the boats, and both by boat and by car it is possible to go direct to Narvik, where connection is made with the continental railway system. Tromsö is so up to date that it has its Tourist Society, which arranges trips across the Tromsösund and to the **Lapp Encampment** in the Tromsdal, where herds of reindeer may be seen. The Society, through its Secretary, gives advice about excursions and accommodation.

The scenery between Tromsö and Hammerfest, about 120 miles farther north, is perhaps as fine as any on the whole coast. The jagged mountains of the promontories and islands rise to a height of about 6,000 feet, falling steeply to the water; they are nearly always snow-covered. Between them is the **Lyngen Fjord,** a majestic inlet surrounded by mountain and glacier scenery. Indeed, in some respects it is the finest fjord in Norway. The tourist steamers go up it to **Lyngseidet,** a lovely spot, where a fertile tract and

Wilse,] [*Oslo.*

THE HORN AT NORTH CAPE.

Valentine & Sons, Ltd.,] *[Dundee.*

THE HESTMANN, OR HORSEMAN.

Valentine & Sons, Ltd.,] *[Dundee.*

TORGHATTEN.

birch-clad hills are in striking contrast to the wild grandeur passed on the way to it. Passengers go ashore and walk or drive to a Lapp encampment situated but a short distance from the landing-stage. The curious earthen huts, the herds of reindeer, and the people in their native dress, combine to make a memorable scene. Lyngseidet is the best centre for climbers in these parts.

Hammerfest (*Hotels: Jansens, Grand* and *Andersens*) is situated in lat. 70° 40′ 11″, on the island of Kvalöy. It has about 3,500 inhabitants. Its position amid bare rocky hills is in keeping with the fact that it is the most northerly town in the world. It is, however, as abreast of the times as any southward place in regard to its own needs, and it boasts a very efficient telephone service and electric light. It is not an ideal place for a long stay, as it is the chief market of the train oil trade and consequently rather malodorous. It is also the home port for the cod-fishery of these cold latitudes, and in former days carried on a large trade with Russians from the White Sea. About a twenty minutes' walk from the west side of the harbour is the Meridianstötte, a column recording the completion of the Swedish, Norwegian and Russian measurement of degrees between 1816 and 1852.

An agreeable excursion is to the summit of the **Tyven,** a mountain 1,350 feet high southward of the town. The ascent is easy. One can go and return in 4 hours.

Along the coast north of Hammerfest the only inhabitants appear to be sea-birds. These make their homes in vast numbers on and in the ledges and crevices of the rocky shore. Adventurous cragsmen get some sort of a living by plundering the nests. The most densely populated of these bird colonies is that on Hjelmsöystauren—the Bird Rock—a cliff at the northern end of the island **Hjelmsöy.** The steamers usually sound a syren or fire a gun to scare the birds into flight, and for some minutes the sky seems to be literally clouded with birds; yet the rock appears as densely inhabited as ever.

Fifty-eight miles from Hammerfest is—

The North Cape,

"that huge and haggard shape," as Longfellow's lines have it, "whose form is like a wedge." It is on the island of **Mageröy,** on lat. 71° 10′ 40″, and was for a long time supposed to be the most northerly point in Europe, but it has been discovered that the point of **Knivskjerodden,** on the same island, stretches nearly a mile farther north ; while **Nordkyn** (Kinnarodden), to the eastward, is of course the most northerly point of the mainland, being 71° 8′ 1″. The tourist steamers land their passengers in the little bay of **Hornviken** for the ascent of the rock, which rises perpendicularly from the Arctic Ocean. The climb to the summit, which is rather under a thousand feet, is facilitated by a zigzag path, and has been made easier still by ropes placed against the walls of the path by the steamship companies. Alongside the paths are beautiful wild flowers. At the summit, which is a plateau, are a small obelisk and one or two cairns, and in 1928 a restaurant was licensed—the most northerly in Europe. The view is very grand, but the surroundings are dreary and desolate in the extreme.

When the ship's gun announces the hour of midnight, those standing here "on the threshold of a continent and on the edge of this immeasurable sea, watch, without one moment's interval of darkness, the past transform itself into the present and yesterday become to-day."

The tourist steamers turn here, and return south. The local steamers go on to **Vardö,** a town with 3,500 inhabitants on the east coast of Finmark, and to **Vadsö,** 2,000 inhabitants, on the shore of the **Varanger Fjord.** Two miles beyond Vadsö is **Kirkenes,** the turning point of the mail steamers. It has extensive works for the extraction of iron ore. The population is about 4,000.

From Vardö Nansen started in 1893 in the *Fram* for the North Pole, and returned to it in 1896 in the *Windward.*

"FARTHEST NORTH."

To Spitzbergen and the Polar Ice Wall.

At the end of July or the beginning of August, to the cruise to Norway's Fjords and North Cape of the Bergenske S.S. Company's *Stella Polaris* and the Nordenfjeldske S.S. Company's *Prince Olav*, there is added a cruise to Spitzbergen and to the most northerly point which the ice allows the vessel to reach. From Newcastle to Newcastle the time is 22 days, from Bergen to Bergen two days less. One vessel calls at Trondhjem on the outward voyage, and the other when homeward bound.

Spitzbergen (or Svalbard as the Norwegian Government has re-named it) is an archipelago lying 400 miles north of Norway. It embraces half a dozen large islands and numerous smaller ones. Its familiar name, given by the Dutch explorer Baerents, who discovered the archipelago in 1596, has reference to the pointed peaks of the mountains.

In 1607 Henry Hudson, after whom the Canadian Hudson Bay is named, visited Spitzbergen and having reported an abundance of whales, seals and walruses, the hunting of them began, and during a long series of years it was continued by hundreds of ships from England, Holland, Norway, France and Russia. King Christian IV professed to have rights over the islands, and from the companies sending the ships demanded contributions which were sometimes paid and sometimes not. No effective sovereignty was established over the Archipelago, and it remained a No-man's-land until after the conclusion of the Great War when, by the Treaty of Versailles, a mandate for Spitzbergen was conferred on Norway, as Norwegian interests were already strong there, in connection with the mineral wealth which had been discovered. The wealth drawn from the sea has dwindled to a small fraction of what it was, while the newer found wealth of the land has been increasingly exploited. The soil of the Archipelago is frozen to a depth of 700 feet, and, with the exception of a few dwarf birches, confined to an area of a few square feet, there is not a single tree on the 25,000 square miles made by the surface of the islands. Yet they were once covered by a tropical jungle whose carbonized remains are now being dug up for coaling steamers and to supply the needs of towns in Norway. In West Spitzbergen, the largest of the islands, several mining companies are working. The ocean on the west side of that island is kept open by the warm currents which come to it; the water on the eastern side is not navigable.

The steamers for Spitzbergen, on leaving the North Cape, steer for **Bear Island,** a whaling station, which is reached the next day. **Advent Bay,** Spitzbergen, is reached on the day following. Here is a population of 4,000 persons employed in working the rich coal mines. On succeeding days, the steamers visit **Sassen Bay, Green Harbour, Cross Bay** and **Magdalene Bay,** with marvellous scenery of glaciers and peaks. Passengers have the opportunity of going ashore at the various ports, of visiting the coal mines and the fossil-strewn valley, in which tropical fossils may be picked up at the foot of a glacier. In spite of the ice and snow, botanists may find over six score plants.

Certain spots are interesting by reason of their association with notable deeds. From **Dane Island** the explorer André set out with two companions, on July 11, 1897, on his ill-fated balloon expedition to discover the North Pole, and was never again heard of. From **King's Bay,** in 1926, Amundsen's airship, the *Norge*, carried an international expedition across the Pole and landed them in Alaska. In the same year and from the same bases, Lieut. Byrd, an American airman, flew to the Pole and back. In April, 1928, Captain G. H. Wilkins, an Australian, landed on Spitzbergen after a flight from Alaska and across the Pole. In May, 1928, the Italian General Nobile set out from King's Bay, Spitzbergen, to fly over the North Pole in the airship *Italia*.

Of the adventurers of all nations, who in olden days braved the terrors of climate and scurvy in pursuit of the whale and the seal, and who sometimes lived on the archipelago, the only memorials are ruins and burial-places. On a rocky peninsula there are hundreds of open graves of the seventeenth century.

On the third day the prow of the vessel is again turned towards the Pole, and the voyage in that direction is continued until floating pack-ice puts a stop to northward progress. The point reached varies a little from year to year. It has been as far north as lat. 81° 1′ 11″, that is to say, only about 525 miles from the Pole.

When the Farthest North has been reached, the vessel swings round and begins its return journey, and when it once more comes to rest alongside Newcastle quay, it will have carried its passengers some 4,380 miles.

Wilse,] *[Oslo.*

THE MIDNIGHT SUN ON LYNGEN FJORD.

Wilse,] [*Oslo.*

LYNGEN FJORD.

INDEX

NOTE.—For convenience of reference, words beginning with Å and Ö are placed immediately before those beginning with A and O.

Where more than one reference is given, the first is the principal.